Design Thinking

Design Thinking is a set of strategic and creative processes and principles used in the planning and creation of products and solutions to human-centered design problems.

With design and innovation being two key driving principles, this series focuses on, but not limited to, the following areas and topics:

- User Interface (UI) and User Experience (UX) Design

- Psychology of Design

- Human-Computer Interaction (HCI)

- Ergonomic Design

- Product Development and Management

- Virtual and Mixed Reality (VR/XR)

- User-Centered Built Environments and Smart Homes

- Accessibility, Sustainability and Environmental Design

- Learning and Instructional Design

- Strategy and best practices

This series publishes books aimed at designers, developers, storytellers and problem-solvers in industry to help them understand current developments and best practices at the cutting edge of creativity, to invent new paradigms and solutions, and challenge Creatives to push boundaries to design bigger and better than before.

More information about this series at https://link.springer.com/bookseries/15933.

Mindful Design

A Survival Guide for Responsible
Product Designers

Second Edition

Scott Riley

Apress®

Mindful Design: A Survival Guide for Responsible Product Designers, Second Edition

Scott Riley
Liverpool, UK

ISBN-13 (pbk): 979-8-8688-0142-6   ISBN-13 (electronic): 979-8-8688-0143-3
https://doi.org/10.1007/979-8-8688-0143-3

Managing Director, Apress Media LLC: Welmoed Spahr
Acquisitions Editor: James Robinson-Prior
Development Editor: James Markham
Editorial Assistant: Gryffin Winkler
Copy Editor: Mary Behr

Cover designed by eStudioCalamar

Cover image designed by Vic Bell

Distributed to the book trade worldwide by Springer Science+Business Media New York, 1 New York Plaza, Suite 4600, New York, NY 10004-1562, USA. Phone 1-800-SPRINGER, fax (201) 348-4505, e-mail orders-ny@springer-sbm.com, or visit www.springeronline.com. Apress Media, LLC is a California LLC and the sole member (owner) is Springer Science + Business Media Finance Inc (SSBM Finance Inc). SSBM Finance Inc is a **Delaware** corporation.

For information on translations, please e-mail booktranslations@springernature.com; for reprint, paperback, or audio rights, please e-mail bookpermissions@springernature.com.

Apress titles may be purchased in bulk for academic, corporate, or promotional use. eBook versions and licenses are also available for most titles. For more information, reference our Print and eBook Bulk Sales web page at www.apress.com/bulk-sales.

Any source code or other supplementary material referenced by the author in this book is available to readers on GitHub. For more detailed information, please visit www.apress.com/gp/services/source-code.

Paper in this product is recyclable

Table of Contents

About the Author

Scott Riley is an independent designer specializing in interface and interaction design. He has written extensively and spoken at conferences around the world on the intersection of cognitive science and design. You can find details of his work on his website, `scott.is`.

About the Technical Reviewer

 **Daniel Kolodziej** collaborates with the C-Suite of the world's biggest brands to create tangible business impact via strategic innovation and venture building. For 15 years, he's been leading multi-disciplinary teams through Lean, Agile, JTBD, and human-centered design processes.

He's founded his own startups with VC backing, worked in startup studios funded by well-known investors, and designed and built innovative digital products, services, and ventures, creating millions of pounds worth of value.

He is also a regular speaker on product, design, and innovation in both practitioner and academic settings.

Acknowledgments

First and foremost, a huge thank you to everyone at Apress who has helped make this second edition a reality. James, James, Shobana, Gryffin, and everyone else who has worked behind the scenes to help bring these often-obtuse, always-messy ideas to life.

To Dan Kolodziej, for his tireless work as a technical reviewer, but also for being an absolute gem of a human being and a truly treasured friend. Last time I told everyone about your Cream tattoo and it's not escaping this second edition either.

To Zach Inglis, for the technical editing work on the first edition of this book, but far more importantly for the unique blend of compassion, kindness, and unwavering proclivity to stand up for others you put into this world.

To my amazing wife Roxie. Thanks for putting up with my shit, and for having faith in me even when I don't. You are resilient and inspiring in infinite ways. I love you more than life and I am beyond fortunate to share this journey with you.

To Lorna, my best little pal, even though you can't read this. You'll always be my fav.

To my wonderful family; Mum, Molly, Lili, Astrid, Nan and Gags. You keep me going, and I hope I've done you proud.

To Nikki, who won't read this book, or will stop here, shrug, and put it down. I love you. Thanks for keeping me humble and sticking with me for decades.

To Chad, the light of my life. You're everything that is good with this world and I adore you.

To Vic Bell, the lushest human being on this whole entire planet. You mean the world to me and I'll never not be in awe of the things you make.

To Laura Bee: pure, undiluted loveliness made manifest.

To Luke Murphy, a kindred spirit who somehow made it from the other side of the planet and into my life. What a treasure you are. Get the pub quiz on lad.

To Adriana, Tilly, and Emily. Thanks for trusting me and always having my back. Managing a design team is hard. You made it easy. Most of the time.

To Meg Lewis, for teaching me how to be myself, and remaining unequivocally themselves. The joy you bring to this world is endless.

To my Simple as Milk family, without whom I'd have quit design a decade ago. Glen, James, Vic, Spadge and Greg: you're all smashing.

ACKNOWLEDGMENTS

To Spadge (again) for kicking my arse into gear and encouraging me to write the very first abstract of this book many years ago. Run yourself a bath mate.

To Owen and Dan, in the hopes that by the time this book is published you can get a squat to depth and a deadlift past your knees, respectively. Love you lads.

To the incredible scientists, authors, designers, engineers, and even the odd CEO whose work far surpasses my own and fills the pages of this book as examples and aspirations. The world is full of good things; thank you for putting them out there.

To the Paper team, for their fabulous Wireframing Kit that's used throughout the projects in this book.

Finally, to everyone who fights the good fight in the face of the growing apathy, centrism and outright fascism that percolates within and without this industry of ours. To the anti-racist tech activists, the queer and trans tech community, the eco-conscious makers, and every individual who is willing to speak truth to power through their work, words, and actions. Y'all are the best of us.

Introduction

Well shit, here we go again. How are we? To say a lot has happened in the five (yes, five!) years since the writing of the first edition of this book would be something of an understatement, would it not?

From a personal perspective, I've been married, adopted the cheekiest little street dog you'll ever meet, became an uncle, started (and left) two jobs, bought a house, lost friends and loved ones, gained friends and loved ones, and have regenerated somewhere between 50 and 60% of the cells which made me up at the time. A different person in almost every conceivable way.

In the wider world, we've had a years-long pandemic to contend with, robbing us of friends and family, quality of life, time with our loved ones, and any semblance of truth to the idea that politicians have our best interests at heart. We've stood in horror to a backdrop of genocide, war, and invasions, and endured the ever-churning machinations of propaganda that strives to paint these as normal or acceptable. Politicians have hoarded more power, the ultra-rich have hoarded more wealth, landlords have hoarded more property, and our social platforms have hoarded a user list of apologists and sock puppets for them all.

And what of our beloved tech industry? Augmented and virtual reality were the next big thing, until they weren't. Then Web3 and Crypto were the next big thing, until they weren't. Now, AI is the next big thing, and I can't help but wonder where that one's going to wind up. Elon Musk bought Twitter for $44bn to show the world how well he was coping with a divorce. 140 Twitter clones were built in the weeks and months after. None of them were good. Adobe was acquiring Figma, until they weren't. Facebook rebranded to Meta to try and launder their reputation (that went well). An entire bank went bust and VCs lost the actual plot, wreaking havoc on an industry whilst simultaneously revealing the rather suspiciously sandy-looking foundations on top of which it is built. Is that everything? Probably not.

And finally, what of Mindful Design? I've had the privilege of being able to roll out many of the practices and methods touted in the first edition, across many products in many verticals. As such, the concepts have evolved, the process has been optimized, and the cream has risen to the top, so to speak. Furthermore, the attitudes and approaches to which Mindful Design—as a *thing,* not just a book—strives to be antithetical or antidotal are still as pervasive in our industry. We still have cult-of-personality leaders spending money earned nepotistically in terrifyingly irresponsible ways. Technology still outpaces regulation. Untempered growth, inaccessible products, systems of self-perpetuation and grossly non-diverse teams still pervade. Designers are encouraged to design for predictability and coercion, still relying on outdated and disproven behaviorist approaches, and 'persuasive design' is still a thing.

While I'm loath to add to the arrogant noise that lives in the dusty corners of the idea that being a designer somehow makes us special, it remains impossible to ignore the fact that design decisions, even—perhaps especially—in their absence, impact the world. As such, us designers find ourselves in a position where our decisions, ideas, failings, and oversights will, invariably, affect other humans—they're *supposed* to.

When we consider that any interface is a product of thousands of these decisions, ideas, failings, and oversights, we are faced with little choice but to accept the responsibility that comes with that.

Design, in its most abstract sense, is emotional manipulation. It is a mechanism for eliciting changes in the brain. This doesn't, however, make design unique, or evil, or inherently problematic. Music, art, video games, food, literature, film, photography, and myriad other indulgences to the senses all instigate their own, visceral reactions— lighting up neurons, exciting receptors, uncovering buried memories, and exploring the pathways that form new ones. Whether knowingly or unknowingly to their creator, they are odes to the plasticity of our brain, to the malleability of our mind.

Design's quirk—what makes it something of an outlier among the arts—lies in the perverse desire to knowingly and measurably manipulate. We want people to tap the right buttons, we want them to share links, to use our interfaces in certain ways. And, usually, we want people to do these things in the ways which make our products the most profitable.

While so-called "real" art encourages emotional exploration and ambiguity, basking in the in-betweens, design strives for surety, for absolution. This is evident in the buzzword-laden landscape of how we talk about our work. We might *funnel* people into our product, then *convert* them to users, and subsequently *activate* them into paying customers.

We often fall into the trap of treating our work as linear, constraining our design thinking into a neat little one-lane road of successful micro-interactions with various milestones along the way. We even create nice little user flow diagrams, like an electronics engineer planning the nodes their signal will pass through between origin and destination. We sort people into personas and categories and deal with them in averages and denominations, often blighted and constrained by our own biases and assumptions.

The question here is, bluntly, where does real humanity fit into this equation? When "empathy" is our buzzword, our yardstick for abstract adeptness as a designer, why are we diluting our understanding and appreciation of humans down into decision trees and reductive personas? Why can your average designer write an atomic user journey, but tell you little to nothing about the workings and the wonders of the mind?

Through the reading of this book, however deep you delve, I'd like to propose we flip conventional design vocabulary, in relation to people, on its head. Rather than thinking about how we can manipulate people to buy into our products—using product-centric verbs like activation and conversion—I'd like to explore what products and interfaces can *give back* to the people who use them. Not necessarily in a broad, feature-level sense of addressing needs and solving problems, but in a more empowering, emotional one. I want to introduce new questions to our decision workflow, mainly, "How could this make people feel?"

We all have the ability to knowingly add to the world, yet we often refuse to acknowledge just how much we can potentially take from it. Design *can* solve problems, but we rarely accept that it can create them as well. It can empower millions, but we rarely accept that it can equally, aggressively oppress. Design is a responsibility.

I feel, passionately, that an understanding of the mind—however basic—is increasingly essential to anyone who wishes to design. If you champion design's ability to empower, if you fetishize its capacity to "change the world"—consequently, I feel you have no choice but to accept its potential to damage, to accede to the fact that your decisions can alienate, that your negligence can marginalize.

Now, this is no attempt to denigrate the pursuit of design, nor is it a doom-and-gloom psycho-novella about the impact of poor design. Both of those exist already, written by people far more capable of such than myself. My intention with this book is to provide a *spark*. To distill the often-saturated worlds of cognitive psychology and neuroscience down to concepts and knowledge that I feel can best inform a pursuit of empowering and positively impacting real humans. To pass on a sense that has grown and been shaped by the study of these fields. A sense of togetherness, of a self-imposed obligation to be diligent and cognizant of our design decisions' impact on others.

INTRODUCTION

Writing a second edition of this book is unequivocally a privilege that I'm delighted to have been afforded. I'm a better designer, a better manager, and (hopefully, let's find out!) a better writer than I was when the first edition was published. If you're on board with understanding the human mind, if you're open-minded to different ways of thinking about and approaching design, and if you're willing to try things that fly in the face of conventional industry wisdom, then let's not waste any time.

PART I

The Theory

CHAPTER 1

Attention and Distraction

Attention is a precious mental resource. Every day we are bombarded with information, decisions, distractions, and things we need to remember. *What should I wear today? What should I make for breakfast? Did I lock the door? Can I just hide under the duvet and play Pokémon until June?* Even though we can often instinctively—and seemingly instantly—answer these questions, there's a real cost incurred when doing so.

Examining attention lets us see just how much heavy lifting our brain does for us. Through a process of selective attention, it's constantly analyzing our environmental stimuli and deciding where our focused attention needs to be applied. We can think of this as a kind of filtration—the process of analyzing a huge range of inputs and deciding which might be salient or imperative based on myriad factors. Or, to frame it differently, which incidental stimuli are *allowed* to become distractions.

This process of attentional filtration is one of the most interesting and enlightening facets of human cognitive evolution, and, as designers, we must endeavor to hold ourselves accountable for the degree to which—and methods with which—we impact this. We must understand that there is invariably and demonstrably a mental cost to distraction and interruption, and likewise to any period of held attention. We must therefore acknowledge that part of our job is to consider, preempt, and analyze these costs when making design decisions.

In this chapter, you'll explore just how fallible and vulnerable human attention can be. You'll explore the idea that most people—through merely existing, thinking, and working—find themselves placed under a notable cognitive load. You'll also explore technology's strange and often damaging fetishization of attention, the human brain's need for rest and daydreaming, and the price of ignoring or avoiding restful mental states.

To do all this, though, you need to first understand the various concepts and connections that make up our attentional system.

© Scott Riley 2024
S. Riley, *Mindful Design*, Design Thinking, https://doi.org/10.1007/979-8-8688-0143-3_1

Our Attentional System

Ever worked from a busy coffee shop? Let's go back to that moment. You've packed your stuff up; walked, wheeled, scooted, cycled, or otherwise propelled yourself from home to your favorite caffeinated haunt; found a seat amidst the bustle; grabbed the trendiest drink on the menu (you've earned that Cortado, yes you have); and set yourself up for a productive few hours of drawing rectangles and ignoring PMs on Slack.

Let's take a breath here, though. Think of all the stimuli you encounter buzzing around you. The blitz and whir of a hopper full of coffee beans grinding away. The clang and clatter of espressos being pulled and tables being set. The smell of fresh ground coffee beans and overpriced sourdough dancing through the air. The almost rhythmic coming and going of customers and staff. How much of this do you actually pay attention to? You know it's there. Maybe you can even recall a few details, like what song was playing, or the outfit of a person that piqued your interest. But it's probable that the vast majority of this is relegated to "background noise."

In fact, it's imperative that we're able to tolerate this kind of cacophony—and we should consider ourselves privileged if we can, as the inability to regulate or tolerate stimuli like this can be extraordinarily overwhelming and debilitating—given that it's what allows us to attain that ever-more-elusive state known as *focus*.

If you've found yourself somewhat impervious to this aforementioned assault on the senses, then you've seen selective attention at work. When you need to focus your attention on a specific, important task, your brain adeptly shuts out low-priority environmental stimuli, banishing them to your subconscious and allowing you to affix your attention to the task at hand.

This is an amazing function of the brain. Think of all that's going on around us in that kind of environment—every stimulus within it is a potential focus of our attention. Even so, we're able to primarily direct our attention and mental resources to our work. When we're focused, we pay very little attention to the everyday buzz of our environment. Auditory stimuli blend together to form a blanket of sweeping background noise and visual stimuli are ghosted into our periphery. Everything that isn't related to our task can feel worlds apart from our current self in that current moment.

Sensory Distraction

Let's go back to the coffee shop (Figure 1-1).

Figure 1-1. *A bustling coffee shop full of potential distractions*

Again, let's quickly set the scene. You've sipped away at your beverage of choice. You've drawn some of the best rectangles ever to be gazed upon. Virtual post-its are flying. PMs on Slack are nothing to you. Everything is Zen, you're in flow, nothing can stop yo—**BANG! CRASH!**—there goes a whole tray of $5 lattes.

It's highly likely, unless your hearing is impaired, that your focus is snapped immediately away from your current work and you've whipped yourself around to focus on the source of the crash.

Your brain has just alerted you to an environmental stimulus that it deemed irrepressible from your conscious attention. It has, quite actively and quite instantly, distracted you from the task at hand and diverted your attention toward something deemed an attentional focal point. The crash was visceral and unexpected, and it contrasted with the humdrum background noise of the coffee shop. This kind of interruption—part of a phenomenon known as a startle response—is innate and defensive, and it triggers one of the most instantaneous reactions that the brain is capable of performing.

Our startle response is low-level, innate, and deeply rooted in our survival throughout prehistory. It provides a rather crude example of how our attention can be ripped from a task-positive mindset. *Thing go bang, brain alert to bang, body prepare for bad stuff.* Science.

Other, subtler environmental distractions are what we more often find ourselves facing in our daily lives, though. The buzzing and pinging notifications on our devices. A colorful outfit in a sea of cheap suits. The appetizing smell of good food. All have the ability to distract us when they are processed by our brain, and they all have an inclination to interrupt our current object of focus.

Other Distractions

So far, we've really only explored sensory and environmental distractions. Things like loud noises, eye-catching outfits, cluttered environments, and similar all tend to work *mostly* at a sensory level.

There are many other types and categories of distractions, and many attempts have been made to produce a definitive taxonomy of distractions, to little avail (social sciences and definitive lists don't really pair well together). You might come across the idea of *social* distractions—distractions that relate to people, social cues, and conformity. Similarly, you'll likely read about *technological* distractions—a growing category that includes things like phone alerts and social media notifications. There's also *physiological* distractions like hunger or fatigue; *mental* distractions such as being anxious, stressed, or depressed; and many more.

While the categorization of distraction types is quite fluid, the general idea of how they work is not: our brain processes something and it is seen as important or salient enough to take our attention away from a given task at hand.

It's important to note that distractions are not ostensibly good nor bad. They just … are. Distraction is an unavoidable and imperative cognitive function. Being overly prone to distractions, however—especially in the modern age of capitalistic, output-driven overworking and obsequious, hustle-porn subservience—can leave us in some desperately difficult situations. Further to this, just look at the physiological and mental states that can lead to distraction: hunger, worry, stress, anxiety, depression, pain, and fatigue are all undeniably shitty things to feel, but—in a tragic case of exponential shittiness—they're also outright distractions themselves. Just one of these physiological or mental states can make it impossible to focus or make well-informed decisions, and far too many people in society suffer with several of them at once. It sounds sensationalist to say, but *being able to focus is a privilege.* These are the times we live in. Go us.

Attention in Action

Let's explore attention as it applies to focus and task performance. This is one of the most accessible contexts for explaining attention, and it encapsulates quite a lot of what we need to explore when discussing distractions. However, it's important to remember that I'm not just talking about "getting a bit of work done" when I talk about task-positive modes or task completion. I'm also talking about the ability to make decisions, to properly assess a situation, and to remember the things encountered along the way.

Task-Positive Mode

Behind the scenes, what is actually happening between a task and an interruption?

While our mind is focusing on a task, we're in what is known as "task-positive mode"—a state of mind exemplified by concerted focus on a single task. In this mode, our conscious attention is directed towards the work we must do to complete a task at hand.

However, buzzing away in our subconscious, environmental stimuli are still constantly being analyzed, with our attentional system deciding what to hide from our conscious attention and what should be presented up front as important and critical. When something occurs that is deemed worthy of our focus, mental resources are shifted and a new object of attention emerges in the foreground.

This is evolutionary, bottom-up human behavior and has long been integral to our survival as a species. This innate function of our attentional system dates back to prehistory, honed over tens of thousands of years during which failure to react to a clear environmental hazard was less likely to result in getting coffee on your shoes and more likely to result in getting your face eaten off by an actual bear.

I'll discuss top-down and bottom-up processing in more detail on occasion throughout this book, but for now, they can be loosely defined as the following:

- *Bottom-up*: Fast, instinctive, intuitive, subconscious

- *Top-down*: Slower, more reflective, conscious

In his excellent book, *Thinking Fast And Slow*, Nobel Prize winner Daniel Kahneman discusses a two-system model of human thought. System 1, he suggests, works heavily on heuristics and cognitive biases. It is "intuitive thinking." System 2, on the other hand, is "rational," working at measured, more meticulous levels.

Kahneman presents a compelling case for the notion that we're still impulsive by nature, preferring heuristic to contemplation and instinct to pontification (whether that's good or bad for us or what the ideal balance between instinctual and purposeful might be is a source of endless debate). While we like to think of ourselves as attuned and intellectual animals, we're far more instinctive and irrational than most of us wish to imagine. Our mind still hasn't shaken off the cobwebs of our reliance on survival instinct.

In our modern lives, with our modern comforts, we're much less likely to be in situations where actual bears are trying to eat our face and are much more likely to be in situations where we need to apply critical and empathetic thought to succeed in life. Still, millennia of surviving bear-face-eating have our brains wired a certain way.

Back to the coffee shop one last time. If you've ever experienced the kind of unavoidable distractions discussed earlier, you perhaps would have spent a few post-distraction minutes more aware of those background stimuli. Perhaps you'd have listened in on a conversation, or actively paused and listened to whatever song is playing.

Or something previously meaningless caught your attention and maybe you found yourself lost in thought for some untold moments. Your mind, previously dedicated to a specific task, now drifted from thought to thought, idea to idea. Whatever the resulting focal point (or lack thereof), it almost felt as if the initial distraction "ripped" you out of your focused mode and—depending on your discipline, context, and mindset—you faced a potentially uphill battle to get back on track and achieve your previous, task-focused state.

These scenarios provide examples of just a few of an infinite number of daily life's attentional undulations. Perhaps on some days we never achieve that focused state and spend our time, for better or worse, daydreaming and mentally meandering. Maybe on other days we get into a true state of flow and work for hours on end, cocooned from environmental stimuli and life's incessant distractions. More likely, however, we modulate between the two states.

The Default Mode Network

Beyond an evolutionary, focus/interrupt imperative, our attentional system also allows for switching between an intrinsically task-focused mode to a more reflective one—one that incubates and allows moments of introspection, creativity, empathy, and nonlinearity.

In foregoing our surroundings and perceptions when nothing requires our direct focus or attention, we're placating an innate desire to pontificate on ourselves, putting ourselves in a mindset to philosophize and internalize, or simply allowing our minds to wander and our thoughts to drift. This state of daydreaming occurs within what is known as the default mode network.

The default mode network was a landmark discovery for neuroscience and cognitive psychology, sparking a wave of new thinking and new questions about how the brain operates in a conscious resting state. This network, comprising discrete neural networks in various areas of the brain, becomes active when we have no specific task at hand, or when we're not having to immediately react to environmental stimuli or situations.

This mode of thinking—of being—is widely seen as our brain's psychological baseline. In a nutshell: our minds default to wandering, and we daydream until we need to actually do something. Once we've accomplished what we set out to do, we no longer need intense focus, and we're back to meandering. It sounds counterintuitive given the always-on nature of modern life, but work and tasks are supposed to be interludes between resting mental states, not the other way around.

While many individuals are often able to focus single-handedly on a task, "zone in" on problems, and generally get things done, we more often find ourselves in a state of mental wandering, self-narrating, future-planning, reflecting, and just outright daydreaming. Neuroscientists call this type of thinking *stimulus-independent thought*; it's essentially a category of thoughts that are outside of—and unrelated to—our immediate environmental stimuli.

In their 2007 study, W*andering Minds: The Default Network and Stimulus-Independent Thought*, Malia F. Mason and colleagues showed a correlation between subjects' moments of stimulus-independent thought and activity in the various brain regions that form the default mode network. When our mind is "at rest," our thoughts are drifting, amorphous blobs of introspection. Freed from the need to react to the environment or focus on an intensive task, our minds produce unique images, create melodies, and transport us through mental time and space—allowing us to imagine ourselves in the future and to reflect upon our past.

While there is evidence that our default mode network is responsible for this stimulus-independent thought, the reason *why* still remains elusive. In concluding their study, Mason and colleagues offer a philosophical and erudite set of possible explanations for the mind's propensity to wander and deviate from assigned or assumed goals. Perhaps our brain is providing us with a baseline state of arousal to get us through remedial tasks. Or engaging in "spontaneous mental time travel" in order to bring coherence to experiences we've had, are having, and are yet to have. Or maybe we're all just overthinking this shit and the mind wanders *"simply because it can."*

The nature of the default mode network remains a debated subject and is as much a source of philosophical debate as it is one of neuroscience and cognitive psychology. While there remains no direct evidence of the network's association with creativity (the cognition of creativity is unto itself a field of immense complexity), there is growing research and burgeoning theories that link the mind's resting state with divergent thought—a simplification of what goes on in our mind when we're being creative.

Further, the phenomenon of insights occurring when we remove ourselves from a problem is widely reported and commonly observed. Think of how many times you attempted to solve a tricky problem, focusing for hours on end, and gave up for the day only to solve it that night via a seemingly spontaneous *eureka* moment 40 seconds into a relaxing bath.

Given that this daydreaming network is likely invoked during spontaneous thought, improvisation, self-projection, and empathetic response, it's hard to not imagine it having a net impact on creativity and self-actualization. In their excellent *Ode to Positive Psychology*, Scott Barry Kaufman and Rebecca L. McMillan posit that these feelings are the *intrinsic rewards* of stimulus-independent thought. While the mind may not be actively engaging with a task—or on the path to achieving a specific, known goal— daydreaming opens us up to highly gratifying personal realizations; potential creative insights; and self-rewarding, top-down introspection.

While to some observing neuroscientists and psychologists, this "task negative" mode of thought is seen as inefficient and counterproductive, to their subjects—the ones actually experiencing the phenomena—it presents a complex web of intrinsic, highly personal rewarding moments and introspections. Kaufman and McMillan suggest that "we need a new focus and new metrics" when studying and measuring personal psychology. Viewing these intrinsic discoveries and moments of self- projection and unbridled imagination as just as important—if not more so—than goal-focused tasks is a compelling notion, one rooted in humanism, which embraces the complexity and contradiction of human nature rather than attempting to distill it into the closed-box, functional and predictable paradigm behaviorism so desperately seeks.

We know that our brains are essentially wired for distraction. We also know that task-intensive processing is a temporary diversion from a world of stimulus-independent thinking. In an ideal society, with an ideal brain, we'd have a very simple approach to tasks: get in, get focused, get it done, get out—as quickly as we possibly can. This is utopian to the point of obsoletion, though, for myriad reasons.

Most of us have daily tasks to perform. Many of us need to work to stay alive. If we weren't lucky enough to inherit an Apartheid blood emerald enterprise or be born into a family of bankers and bureaucrats, then we probably even have to face god and walk backwards into the hell of *doing chores*. Productivity is now a meme. There's an entire industry of products and books and grift-filled podcasts focused around *getting things done*. We're constantly being conned into seeing ourselves as nothing more than the sum of our outputs, eschewing the undulating nature of attention, focus, rest, and recuperation in favor of a dystopian, ham-fisted brand of burnout–inducing, influencer–peddled min–maxing of our time and efforts.

As if that wasn't enough, for many of us with mental health issues or neurodevelopmental disorders, our default, resting, daydreaming state isn't exactly a happy place.

Danger in the Default Mode

Our daydreaming, default mode is not all positive reflection and creativity. For clinically depressed individuals, the daydreaming, projection, and self-analysis of this mental mode can instead be taken over by feelings of guilt and shame. This creates a horrendous situation where an unoccupied, depressed mind defaults to what is known as depressive rumination—a constant and churning negative association with one's self, one's past experiences, and one's future prospects.

In their meta-analysis of studies on the default mode network's association with depression, Dr. J. Paul Hamilton and colleagues portrayed that depressive ruminations were essentially "hijacking" our self-reflection and introspection processes.

Hamilton and his colleagues suggest that an overactive default mode network unto itself is not an indicator or predictor of major depressive disorder, but that a "functionally united" subgenual prefrontal cortex (the area of our brains that handles emotional regulation, among other things) and default mode network "often predicts levels of depressive rumination." Our default mode network is as apparently responsible for insight and reflection as it is rumination.

The "mental time travel" the default mode network seemingly allows us to perform is, too, not always a fantastical window into an endless play of plays. For every exciting projection of ourselves into the future as the atomic "me" we strive to be, there's the shame-ridden journey to the past—where we accidentally called our teacher *Mum* or our sexual partner *Adrian*. In our daydreaming, we're just as capable of negativity and self-deprecation as we are positivity and self-indulgence.

Individuals with ADHD can find themselves trapped in the default mode network, making the switch to task-positive thinking extremely difficult, leaving seemingly basic tasks incredibly difficult to perform. The self-rewarding nature of the images and thoughts posited by Kaufman and McMillan is seemingly a double-edged sword. The ADHD brain might find itself so engrossed with the mental imagery and stimulation of the default mode that it doesn't want to budge. We also know that ADHD individuals often "bring along" this type of thinking during task-focused mindsets, with the default mode network rarely being fully disengaged as it often would in a neurotypical individual.

While these may seem to be extreme examples and notably low on the subtlety scale, there is, for every individual, a range on a spectrum between hyper-focus and perpetual mind-wandering that constitutes as "balanced" for them. A disruption in either direction to that balance is something we must be wary of and at least be able to empathize with.

The Cost of Distractions

The Internet is a hotbed of distraction. Social media actively profits from "eyes on pixels" and news outlets rely on revenue from increasingly obnoxious advertisements or through pay walls—often presented in their own unique brand of obtrusiveness—that block content from non-paying readers. Products and tools strive for "stickiness," where "habit-forming" is a lucrative goal. Human attention is the golden goose of the tech industry.

Our phones are vibrating—or when they're not, we might just treat ourselves to some phantom vibrations to let us believe they are—to alert us to any and all possible bits of information or occurrences that might be of note to us. In modern times, attention is a powerful currency. There are many apps, advertisers, and products out there that will snatch it from us without deliberation or morals. Tech companies are almost invariably attention vampires.

It's important to note that our attentional system, like a muscle, has a finite and depleting amount of energy available to it. Neurons are organic parts of a living ecosystem and, just as our muscles require and consume more glucose when put under stress, so too do the neurons in our brain. By asking our brains to switch focus throughout our daily life, we're actively depleting these energy stores. The constant depletion of this energy without the requisite replenishment from a good, old-fashioned rest can result in damaging levels of mental fatigue, irritability, and—ultimately—burnout.

While all mental tasks require some degree of energy—often regulated by how familiar we are with the task, how well our brain can predict the outcome, or the level of processing required to successfully perform it—distraction costs double. This is due to a mechanism known as "neural competition." Essentially, our task at hand is making use of a neural network, and any distraction away from it requires a new neural network to activate. That costs glucose, which powers our brain, and when depleted leaves us—if you'll allow me a local colloquialism—absolutely cabbaged, lads.

Learning this was hugely eye opening and a cause for genuine pause and reflection for me. How often had a mistake or poor design decision in a product I'd designed been the one tiny but critical bit of cognitive effort that caused someone's burnout? Quite melodramatic, right? But the point remains that small but frequent acts of attentional switching and cognitive load slowly sap us of mental energy. We're faced with more information in our day-to-day lives than ever before and, as our technology evolves far faster than our brains, we've entered a point of incessant information overload, arriving hand-in-hand with perpetual decision overload.

Decision-Making

It seems, too, as though every bit of content we see online is an entanglement of decisions. Content is no longer viewed as *just* content. It is social currency. It exists, at least in part, to be shared. By attaching actions beyond simply consuming the content, we're raising myriad questions and decisions. *Do I read this? Do I trust it? Do I like it? Should I respond? Report it? Should I ever, ever read the comments?* By simply asking our brain to make these decisions, alongside the continual attentional-hopping from one distraction to the next, we're slowly sapping ourselves of mental energy.

If that sounds somewhat exhausting, consider how many individual "chunks" of such content you might see on one platform in, let's say, 15 minutes of browsing. Now, extrapolate that over however many social networks you use. Now further extrapolate that over how long you spend browsing social media during an average day. That's a potentially huge amount of attentional switching and decision-making for something so seemingly trivial, and that's before we even take into consideration the cognitive load of notifications.

While we're shifting our attention like this, we're depleting our brain's nutrients. By asking our brain to focus on different things and to make a slew of decisions, we're forcing our prefrontal cortex to consume glucose, an energy source of limited supply. Once this is depleted, our ability to focus drastically lowers and we make irrational and impulsive decisions. Deprived of its cognitive fuel, our unfocused brain releases adrenaline and cortisol, hormones that are inherently tied to stress and anxiety.

Once we enter this state of depletion, we're cognitively hamstrung, unavoidably bottom-up thinkers, and we make more mistakes more often. The cure for this is proper rest and replenishment. Allowing the mind to wander, taking a break to eat, and getting a good night's sleep are all remedies for a nutrient-starved mind and, somewhat ironically, are all things that distractions, interruptions, and notifications often keep us from indulging in.

And what of notifications? Glenn Wilson has shown that simply through knowing you have an unread email in your inbox, your effective IQ during task-positive focus can be lowered by as much as 10 points. This reduction (almost double that attributed to casual marijuana use) is attributed to a compelling need to respond, as noted by Dr. Wilson and colleagues' subjects. Further on this subject, Gloria Mark and colleagues conclude in *The Cost of Interrupted Work: More Speed and Stress* that constant attentional switching and interruptions cause people to exhibit "more stress, higher frustration, time pressure, and effort." IQ is a hugely problematic concept, one rooted in supremacy and untold layers of bias, but effective IQ during task-positive focus does go some way to showing how capable we are in a given context. A 10-point drop for just *knowing* you have something unread on your device exemplifies a hefty cognitive burden.

There are parallels between the high-tech attentional exploitation we see in modern technology products and the labor exploitation that's been spiraling out of control since the western world went all-in on capitalism in all its perfidious forms. Companies, their cult-of-personality founders, and their often-insufferable shareholders profit from surplus wealth. The physical and mental energy of some actors in a system create wealth and opportunity, which is then sucked up disproportionally by other actors within that system.

While we're being spoon-fed adverts and information, others are profiting. We receive almost no compensation or reward (more on that later) for our energy, and enough people are left tired and impulsive enough to buy the crap that's beamed in front of their face. Products are sold, subscriptions are made, propaganda is pushed. Everyone profits but us, it seems.

Saving Mental Energy

Given how all these decisions and distractions costing all this energy seems so overbearing and overwhelming, you'd think we'd have ways of reducing the cost, right? Turns out we do.

There are two key concepts to lowering the cost of decision-making and cognitive processing in general. One of them is the fact that the brain works on a system of predictions that can be observed all the way to the neural level. This is *really fascinating*. And I'll get to that a little later in this book. The first key concept of mental energy conservation you'll explore is *heuristics*.

Heuristics

Heuristics are mental shortcuts. They allow us to abdicate much of the processing required in our decision-making, eschewing deep processing in favor of less-taxing abstractions. Essentially, in many cases of decision-making, we skip all the expensive, top-down processing and lean on our bottom-up instincts to lead our decisions.

Heuristics—as well as a number of concepts and theories that build from the understanding of them—show that, for many of life's mundane, day-to-day decision-making, we almost always prefer *good enough* to perfect. We work—in an instant—on levels of bias, availability, and bottom-up mental processes that many of us would be loath to admit to.

Heuristics are our biases manifest. It's incredibly important to understand commonly-observed decision-making heuristics, but it's also important to acknowledge that these are so often exploited, even by the well-intentioned among us.

The Cognitive Miser Theory

The concept of a *cognitive miser* constitutes a theory of social cognition that, ultimately, boils down to the notion that we're all cheapskates when it comes to our mental energy expenditure. This theory, introduced by Susan Fiske and Shelley Taylor—expanding on the work done by the likes of Daniel Kahneman, Amos Tversky, and their colleagues on the subject of heuristics and attentional biases—suggests that, at our core, we consistently default to easier, more-available methods to solve problems and understand our world.

Earlier, we explored the notion that the mind has two modes of processing: bottom-up, where we respond intuitively and instinctually, and top-down, where we are more analytical and sophisticated in our thought. The cognitive miser theory is rooted in the notion that the low-effort, bottom-up processes will generally win out in situations where they can be safely applied. The vast majority of our decisions and problem-solving involve some form of simplification, shortcut, or heuristic. If we have the opportunity to apply a simpler heuristic to a problem or a decision, then we almost always will. This defaulting to low-effort processing, like so many of the brain's complex processes, wildly varies in usefulness depending on the context and the individual.

As an example, imagine you're at a restaurant and you're trying to decide which meal to order. A top-down approach to this decision would likely be to slow down and think about your requirements, perhaps calculating how many calories you've consumed today and what a reasonable further number of calories would be; to consider whether you've eaten enough protein; to take each option that meets your nutritional needs and compare its price to the other options that fit your requirements and to maybe ask your server for some paper and a pen to work it all out, and oh look now everyone hates you. More likely than not, you've probably engaged in what Nobel Prize winner Herbert Simon coined as *satisficing*—the notion that, in most noncritical situations in life, we're inclined to select something that appears *good enough* rather than performing the rather effortful task of finding the absolute best candidate from a list or group.

Chances are—when choosing food from a menu—you'll engage in this act. The process of satisficing doesn't ignore critical information or result in random selections—if you're on a high-protein diet, or you're vegan, or you're on a strict budget, then you'll actively steer clear of the options that obviously defy your diet or budget—but beyond that, your choice is quite likely going to be *good enough*, but not ideal. We engage in this act all the time. We might not categorically know that we've picked the best tool for a specific job, but we're generally content to opt for something that checks enough boxes to be a decent option, favoring it over others because of its availability or through some other cognitive bias.

Satisficing is what allows us to settle on sufficient candidates for the mundane decisions in our life without wasting precious time and cognitive effort processing them beyond their most obvious characteristics. Did you wear the right socks today? Chances are you barely paid any attention to that decision. Perhaps if it was cold, you opted for the first pair you found that was thick enough to keep your toes warm. Or maybe you wanted a specific color, material, or length. What you probably didn't do is empty your drawer of socks, lay each one down individually on the floor, stand in the epicenter of your newly formed sock circle, and perform a deep CSI-style forensic examination of each sock's ability to stand up to the trials and tribulations of the upcoming day. Unless you did. In which case, you're my hero.

There's a real danger in assuming that people will perform an effortful cost/benefit analysis when using our products or interfaces. Even more so when they're choosing between them. Instead, we must embrace satisficing, along with the many other mental shortcuts our brains make when cognitive effort is at a premium. I believe that what we really mean when we say that good design simplifies is that good design strips away information to a density level that allows for optimal satisficing.

By managing the amount of content and features we present to someone at any one time, we're maximizing the possibility that a non-ideal process may still result in a positive decision.

Of course, the flip side to this is that by thoroughly obfuscating information that may be useful to a person, or overly highlighting information that isn't, our efficient-but-naive decision-making process can be exploited. Think of how many products add friction to their cancelation process through things like suggested downgrades, or, in an act of pure evil, forcing you to call and *speak to a person* to cancel. Creating an account was likely a breeze. Here's my name, here's all my data, here's my soul, get me in! But when making a decision that might benefit us, but harm the company, navigation to your goal suddenly becomes a drawn-out, grueling dirge for the ages.

Such nefarious behavior has led to myriad user-hostile patterns across digital products—little traps of malpractice that lay in wait to exploit our fast-paced decision-making. If you get far enough through this book, we'll have a proper little sit-down and talk about why these eventually pan out to benefit no one, but for now, just know that they exist, people hate them, and the people responsible for them should feel bad but probably don't.

Designing Around Attention

Right, let's start putting all of this together. We've tackled some pretty meaty topics and explored some hard-hitting truths about how we really make decisions and process the world around us. Just how do you take this theoretical understanding and apply it to your day-to-day work in design?

Design for Focus

Trace the lineage of a design decision far enough back and you will always hit a presupposed "need" for attention. Our errors are red because red is a *danger* color, and high contrast elements cause a distraction powerful enough to capture attention. We animate objects when their state changes because we believe that new state to be important, and change—especially when interpolated through motion—is a sure-fire path to grabbing attention. By acknowledging the fact that directing attention away from Thing A and toward Thing B has a very real cost attached to it, we're able to rationalize, and hopefully empathize with said switch—especially, for example, if Thing A is a compelling long-form article and Thing B is a bouncy red advertisement with an auto-playing video. (We actually want to double that distraction cost, at least, given that there's an inkling of hope that our reader would continue after that full-on sensory attack.)

One very simple—or at least simple-sounding—approach to incorporating pretty much any cognitive function into our design work is to copy what the brain already does. We shouldn't do this arbitrarily and think it's enough, or assume that doing so could never be problematic, but I bet you'd be surprised how far it gets you in terms of creating work that's accessible and considerate of cognitive burden. After all, given its propensity towards conserving cognitive energy, what better inspiration than the brain itself?

Nowhere in cognitive science does this show through as more plausible than in the realm of focus and attention. As you explored in the coffee shop example, the brain is often adept at relegating stimuli it deems irrelevant into background noise, giving us the opportunity to focus narrowly and uninterruptedly on a task at hand.

So what happens if we take the *"the brain does it, we should too"* approach to designing around focus and attention? We get iA Writer's focus mode (Figure 1-2).

Figure 1-2. *iA Writer's focus mode dims all content except for the currently-focused paragraph or sentence*

This aptly-titled mode takes the concepts we already know to be innate to our environmental processing and plays out some fine mimicry of attentional filtration on the screen.

The surrounding words fade into insignificance and your current focus is obvious. This simple, single feature allows for such in-the-moment consciousness and focus that it's actively more difficult to be distracted when using it. It's selective attention in microcosm. By actively fading out all but the most crucial aspect of the interface, iA uses design to (knowingly or not) mimic the spotlight of human attention. Design has already done some of the work for us, and we'll soon see that our brains really, really like that.

Mindful Design Principle: Design for Focus   *Mimic the spotlight of human attention when you're confident doing so makes sense. Bring the most relevant information to the forefront by muting less relevant information. Sometimes the best way to guide attention is to remove noise. Do this contextually and progressively, without sacrificing autonomy.*

Distraction by Design

It's important to keep in mind that our brains don't necessarily do things because they're *good* or *bad* for us. The cognitive processes that allow for distraction, or automaticity, or working memory weren't designed by a benevolent creator. They evolved, sure; but that doesn't mean we need them now as much as we needed them when becoming a meal for a saber-toothed tiger was a common concern. This is why we don't necessarily want to just aimlessly and haphazardly embrace the approach of mimicry touted above.

Automaticity is a great example of something that our brain does to conserve energy that can become problematic very quickly. I'll cover this in real detail in Chapters 3 and 4 when you explore learning and mental schemas, but right now, just know that the more we repeat something, the less costly it becomes to perform again in the near future. This plays a huge part in how habits get formed through repetition, or how things like sporting techniques or dance moves can be mastered through consistent practice. However, this is where we hit a *"just because the brain does it, doesn't mean we should too"* conundrum, flying in the face of the conventional wisdom of ... well ... this book. Seven paragraphs ago.

I'm sure many of us have one or several—or several *dozen*—bad habits. Maybe you bite your nails, smoke, grind your teeth, or even whistle in public like a complete degenerate. These habits will generally occur automatically, usually without us even noticing, and they don't really cost anything in terms of mental resources because performing these acts is ingrained at a neurological level.

Now think about *digital* bad habits. How often do you find yourself pulling to refresh on your phone? How many times a day do you check your email inbox, Instagram DMs, or TikTok feed? The sequence of picking your phone up, unlocking it, opening a specific application, and performing a string of interactions is somewhat complex, but many of us are so well-practiced at this that we don't even register doing it. We've automatized the whole process so much that it barely registers, and there might even be some reward in doing it! More on that later in the book.

When faced with the choice between "real" work, like performing or continuing with a task, and this nice, simple, low-cost habit, what do you think is going to be more appealing? Consider too that we're supposed to be in a default state of resting; not zapping our attention through habitual consumption, and the cost of digital mindlessness can be pretty staggering.

There's a somewhat counterintuitive approach that can be taken here, which essentially boils down to *distract from the distraction*. By requiring active engagement and deeper levels of processing, we can bring a sense of intentionality and rationality to a flow or environment. Not everything we do needs to be instinctual or low-cost all the time.

Clearspace is an example of this in action (Figure 1-3). It brands itself as an "intentionality layer" for iOS and simply asks you to take some breaths before you open certain apps—usually social media blackholes like Instagram, TikTok, and Twitter. This adds an unexpected and unpracticed step to a previously habituated sequence of actions, breaking us out of our usual path, and forcing us to be mindful, present, and intentional with our actions.

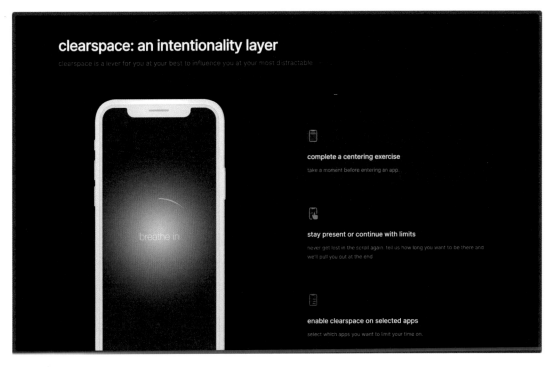

Figure 1-3. *Clearspace's prompt to take a breath forces us to take a few moments before opening an app in what might otherwise have been a habitual process*

More generally, we can see this as a form of intentional slowdown, or *friendly friction*. For many of our interactions, we'll be on autopilot, going through those bottom-up motions, and satisficing our way through our day. However, sometimes we'll do this to our own detriment—and a little reminder to be a bit more intentional, careful, and mindful is all we need.

A prime example of this is GitHub's repository deletion process. As the most prominent collection of free and open source software, GitHub makes it possible for millions of people around the world to use and reference your code. By deleting a repository, there's a very real chance that a project many people rely on will cease to exist. Naturally, GitHub wants to prevent such occurrences—hence, their rather obtrusive delete flow (Figure 1-4).

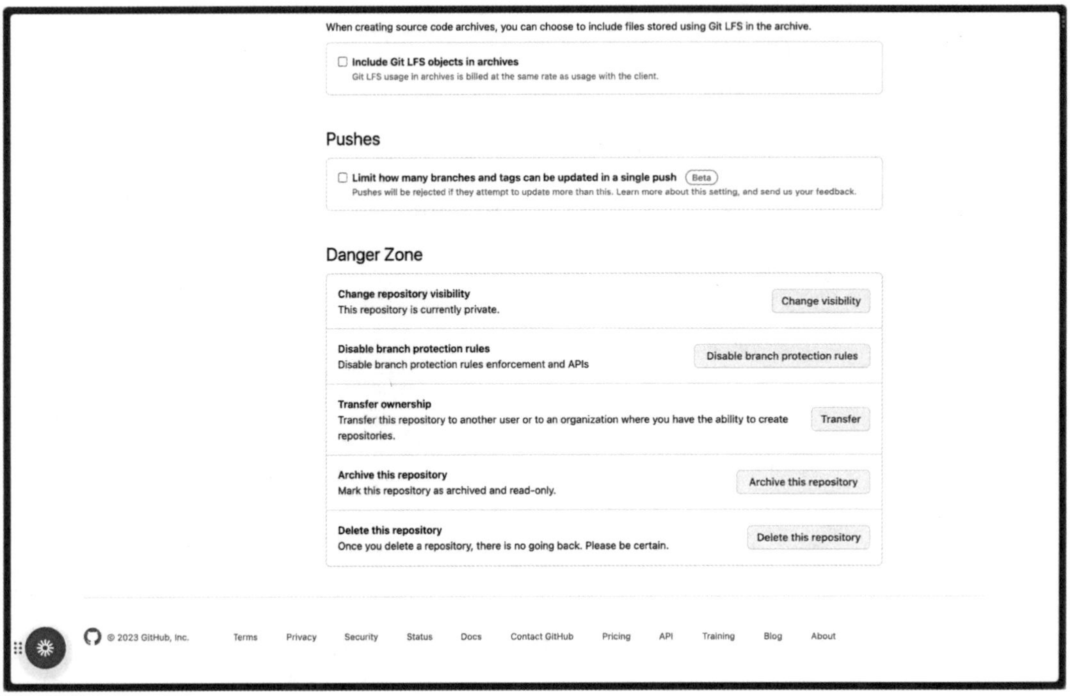

When creating source code archives, you can choose to include files stored using Git LFS in the archive.

☐ **Include Git LFS objects in archives**
Git LFS usage in archives is billed at the same rate as usage with the client.

Pushes

☐ **Limit how many branches and tags can be updated in a single push** (Beta)
Pushes will be rejected if they attempt to update more than this. Learn more about this setting, and send us your feedback.

Danger Zone

Change repository visibility This repository is currently private.	Change visibility
Disable branch protection rules Disable branch protection rules enforcement and APIs	Disable branch protection rules
Transfer ownership Transfer this repository to another user or to an organization where you have the ability to create repositories.	Transfer
Archive this repository Mark this repository as archived and read-only.	Archive this repository
Delete this repository Once you delete a repository, there is no going back. Please be certain.	Delete this repository

© 2023 GitHub, Inc.   Terms   Privacy   Security   Status   Docs   Contact GitHub   Pricing   API   Training   Blog   About

Figure 1-4. *GitHub's Danger Zone*

To delete a repository on GitHub, you follow some pretty standard steps—there's a settings screen that's split into useful categories and tabs. Some way down that page is a section, with a big red border, aptly titled Danger Zone. Just in case you were still wondering if they meant business, here they are throwing Kenny Loggins at us. The Danger Zone is home to destructive actions that GitHub really, really doesn't want you accidentally performing. Still, a decent smattering of red coupled with Kenny Loggins' greatest hit might not be enough, and GitHub has one final trick up its sleeve to make absolutely certain you want to delete your repository. You have to actively type the full name of the repository into a text input to confirm the deletion (Figure 1-5).

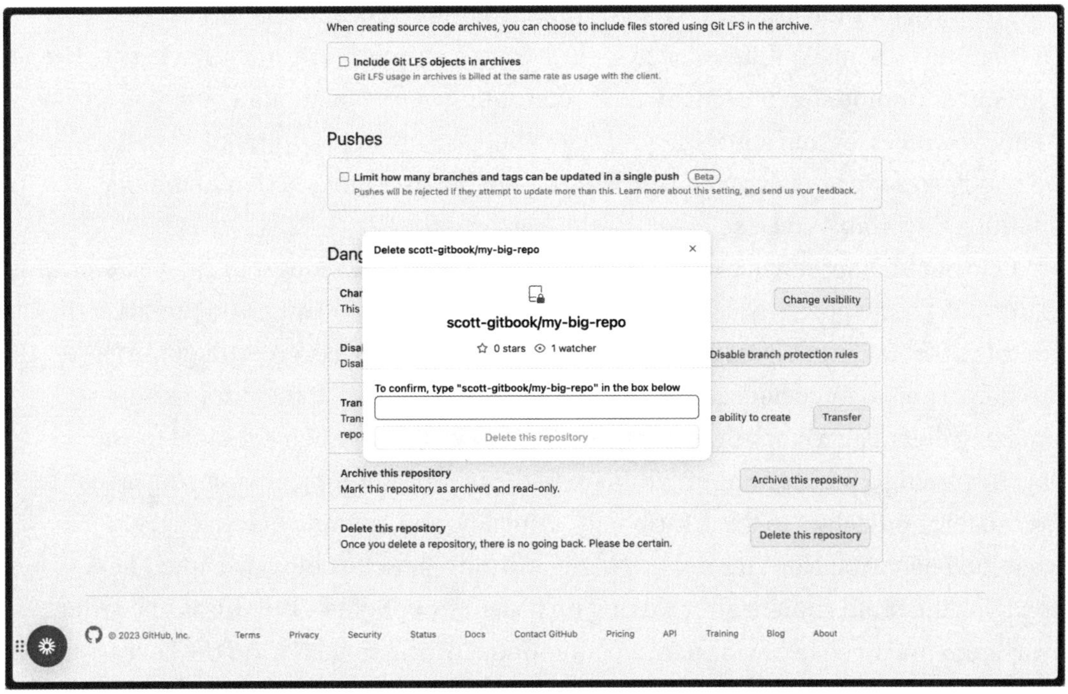

Figure 1-5. *GitHub forces you to type the full repository name in order to confirm deletion*

Attentional blindness means we can miss a lot in our environment, and this is amplified when using a device that is itself a cause of many distractions and interruptions. It's feasible and fair to assume that, in certain situations, we may be too distracted, tired, burned out, or stressed to notice the red, to notice the Danger Zone, and to remain on autopilot and accidentally hit the wrong button. I think we've all lost work due to similarly inattentive reasons before. GitHub looks to prevent this with a task that is extremely difficult to *not* focus on. It grabs your attention, with zero subtlety, through actively reducing simplicity. By forcing you to slow down (typing is hard, relatively speaking), the designers at GitHub are doing their best to make damn sure you actually want this codebase gone.

Think of this as intentional friction or positive disruption. It's the counterbalance to the whole *"make it really difficult to cancel so fewer people do it"* anti-pattern that so many companies adopt into their products. Sometimes we *need* a bit of intentionality—perhaps even difficulty—to protect us from ourselves.

The push for individual digital mindfulness has people using techniques like this on themselves in many different ways—providing seemingly arbitrary blockers between a person and some step of an activity. By disrupting neural facilitation and the various cognitive processes that allow for automatic, bottom-up, heavily-practiced behaviors, we're able to snap ourselves out of a sequence of habituation and demand more intentionality from ourselves.

One popular approach to this for the chronic snoozers amongst us (hi, yes, welcome to the club) is the puzzle alarm clock. There are a vast array of apps and products out there that fall into this category, but they're all aimed at a pretty straightforward problem: some people hate getting up in the morning so much that they're better at snoozing their alarm clock than they are at actually opening their eyes and facing the day. By placing a puzzle or math problem in the way of stopping or snoozing an alarm, we can force ourselves to think rationally, critically, and laterally before engaging in a habitual behavior. Now, it's not *just* habit and automaticity being disrupted here— engaging the brain straight after waking up has many benefits—but this initial switch away from practiced behavior to more intentional processing is key to the success of these kinds of approaches.

This creates a really interesting paradox where sometimes the healthiest way to present a feature (say, snoozing an alarm, or deleting all your data) is to actively make it more effortful to access. This might fly in the face of one of the main principles of this book and the approaches laid out within. In a chapter so bullish about the need to respect attention, limit distraction, and be wary of the cost of interaction, it might be strange to read recommendations for more complex interaction patterns. However, the key thing here is *intentionality*. Not everything should be done on auto-pilot, and many practiced behaviors can become harmful addictions.

Making it easy to place a bet in a betting app just makes sense, right? It's the main feature. The main CTA. The source of profit. Think, though, in a world where gambling addiction is ruining lives, where money gatekeeps almost all avenues of enjoyable existence, and where regulations are almost always decades behind reality, what impact does friction-free gambling really have? For the *happy path*—a phrase you more than likely will encounter in product design, referring to a successful sequence of interactions towards an assumed goal—of a betting app, you have the casual gambler, spending an affordable or negligible amount of disposable income on a quick *flutter*. They open the app, choose an event to bet on, see the odds, and seamlessly buy their entrance into the given lottery.

Happy paths tell an overly optimistic story, though. For every casual bet-placer there's a desperate person gambling their rent away, or an addicted gambler unable to resist the temptation of bigger, more exciting odds that *just might* pay out this time. For these people, lack of intentionality and impulsivity govern their lives. They do not make good decisions. Your *frictionless* interface enables mindless usage and bottom-up thinking.

Mindful Design Principle: Embrace Intentionality   *Understand the real-world impact of interactions, and always ask when or whether intentionality is required. Use positive disruption and friendly friction as intentionality layers in your work, to encourage mindful decision-making where required.*

Categorize and Group Appropriately

I'm going to go out on a limb and say that 90% of design is about creating and communicating hierarchy and interrelatedness. Hierarchy is pretty straightforward to explain—and I'll touch on it a lot in the next chapter—and essentially boils down to ensuring that information is effectively chunked, grouped, and weighted in any given context or scenario. Interrelatedness, though, is a fun one, and to understand why it's so important, let's look at how we approach categorization.

Categorization is part of our evolution and continued survival. Through sensible, culturally sensitive, and well-considered grouping, we can take even the most complex, monolithic masses of content and turn them into a guided tour of knowledge and progression.

While design's role in an interface is not static—that is to say, sometimes its purpose is to intentionally obfuscate, sometimes to alert, sometimes to be invisible—its need to effectively communicate structure, state, and hierarchy is almost omnipresent. For such a fluid, undulating concept, the core of almost any design decision lies in grouping and manipulating content based on its current importance in a given situation—to highlight the content that is relevant and to quieten the content that is not.

Good design reduces the cognitive burden of information processing by optimistically performing a lot of the tasks we'd ask of our attentional system in the first place. The power of good categorization in this process cannot be understated. It's also important for us to remove the somewhat narrow lens with which we view categories. Generally, when designers and developers think of categorization, we're thinking in terms of a literal taxonomy. Think news sites with categories such as *Sports* or *Politics*.

When we make trivial decisions, we almost always work based on categories. Certain objects have certain characteristics that cause us to mentally group them together. Sometimes these are based on physical characteristics. For example, we generally call all those weird flappy-feathered things with wings and hard noses "birds." Other times, we group things by function; for example, matches, lighters, and flint are physically dissimilar but can be categorized as "things that we use to make fire." This is known as *functional equivalence.*

How we assess the various properties—or affordances—of the objects and stimuli in our environment can form and reinforce mental schema—a kind of cognitive framework that builds up, through our experiences in life, expectations around how the world works. I'll talk a lot more about schemas later in this book, but they're inseparable from categorization, essentially forming a co-dependent suite of cognitive processes that allow for contextual grouping based on how we analyze or perceive things.

By grouping and categorizing items in the world around us, with the filter of our current needs and desires, we're able to very quickly make a decision about their application for a specific role. In the real world, we may be faced with the task of hammering a picture hook into a wall. The absolute best tool for this job is likely to be a hammer (probably a very specific kind of hammer, but let's not get carried away) but let's say we're not sure where our hammer is and, for whatever reason, next to us we have a book, a sandwich, a shoe, a brick, and our pet tortoise. Without schemas and satisficing, we'd just go look for our hammer, but that'd likely take longer to find than it would for us to just improvise. So let's satisfice: the book is paperback and a bit too flimsy to hammer a nail, and a sandwich is out of the question no matter how well-toasted it is. So we're left with shoe, brick, and tortoise in a very strange, situationally dependent category of "things I can hammer a hook into the wall with." Your shoe is expensive, and poor Frankie doesn't deserve to pay for your laziness by being bashed into a wall, so the brick it is.

Now, we know from earlier that satisficing—like most techniques the brain uses to conserve energy—is contextual. The threshold for good enough will depend on, amongst other things, how important we deem a certain task or goal to be. If the picture hook was going somewhere unimportant, like inside a utility cupboard or your middle child's bedroom, you might be fine using an inadequate tool. However, if the picture was going to be placed somewhere important, or you cared deeply about the placement, maybe you'd be less likely to satisfice and you'd actually go and find that elusive hammer.

While this is a rather crude example, it shows how we can very quickly use the affordances we expect objects to possess and group them into all kinds of functional categories. Without our ability to acknowledge that *bricks are hard* and *hard things can be used to bash other things*, we'd be stuck looking in every room for that hammer we haven't used for a year. Now, think about the ways those items are related outside of the lens of the task at hand. There's practically nothing that intuitively links a shoe to a brick, yet based on our needs we are able to recognize their suitability to a task.

Categories also go hand-in-hand with reduced cognitive effort. This is especially true for complex interfaces, where the need to individually process every action or item would be an incessant assault on our attention. Through the process of good categorization and a resulting interface that correctly communicates those categories, we allow the mind to disregard entire chunks of an interface at a time. If you're using a product that has a wide range of features, but you only care about a categorized subset of those features, being able to zone an entire group of information out at once is infinitely less taxing than asking your brain to individually process every tool you have available to you.

Many apps will use *modes* to allow for this context-specific navigation. Some documentation tools have discrete *reader* and *writer* modes, with the writer mode more focused on content creation and the reader mode more focused on consumption. Perhaps in the writer mode you have features such as text formatting, drag-and-drop restructuring, page renaming, and such. Maybe the reader mode eschews these and focuses more on features like highlighting, taking notes, and sharing chunks of content, of course all alongside the overall focused reading experience.

Now, depending on the application, people's behaviors and goals, and contexts in which the app is used, this might not always be the best approach. While discrete modes for writing and reading might chunk-away features and provide more focused experiences depending on goals, people whose goals lie somewhere between the two might have a worse time of things. Imagine a proofreader or copy editor in this situation. An editor might need a focused reading experience mixed with lighter editing features to make quick changes, such as rephrasing sentences or fixing grammatical errors. Switching between different modes like this might get tedious for them, and a more fluid environment might better serve them rather than two rigid, discrete modalities.

Another good example of different features and interaction patterns being chunked away behind interface modalities can be seen in Blackmagic Design's video editing tool, DaVinci Resolve (Figure 1-6).

Figure 1-6. *DaVinci Resolve splits its core feature setup into broad, contextual modes that provide their own, self-contained experience*

Modern video production is a hugely complex and broad topic, and DaVinci Resolve is an ambitious attempt to combine almost all of the major concerns of video production into a single tool. You can edit, trim, and combine clips from multiple sources; color grade and color correct your videos; apply visual effects and transitions; edit, mix, and master audio and much more.

DaVinci Resolve balances this through clear, self-contained modes of the application. While there is a degree of global chrome to the application, almost every tool and feature you see will depend on the mode you're currently in. Edit mode (seen above, in Figure 1-6), for example, provides all the expected tools for video editing—think trimming clips, combining, and transitioning between them, etc.—while Color mode (Figure 1-7) provides features for color editing and grading—things like setting color curves and HDR grading.

Figure 1-7. *Color mode feels substantially different to Edit mode, shown in Figure 1-6. While the overall visual language is the same, the interaction patterns and information hierarchy are notably different*

What we see here is structurally a million miles from the Zen-like harmony we saw in iA Writer's focus mode, yet they're both prime examples of good design mimicking the mind's innate proclivities. By preemptively categorizing and proactively juggling the visibility of whole suites of features in DaVinci Resolves's case or through selectively lowering the prominence of unimportant information in iA Writer's case, the interface is a precursor to the likely cognitive functions that would take place within the mind itself.

We're a species that thrives on making our internal manifest in the external. Just as we've evolved to annotate and distribute our brains' content to our external worlds, design is in a position to enrich this aspect by becoming a conduit for cognitive *function* itself.

This, to me, is the core premise of mindful design. And, yes, it sounds incredibly lofty, but through a concise understanding of the brain's attentional system, its ingrained desire to categorize, and its penchant for shortcuts and heuristics in decision-making, we can set ourselves the goal of mimicking these characteristics in our interfaces— where it makes sense to do so—to the best of our abilities. And we can start small! Your interfaces don't have to instantly become cognitive savants; you can do better than most by simply categorizing well, communicating system state, and being economical with attention. In fact, there's an inherent risk to trying any of this. It only takes a small overstep or a modicum of naivety to come out the other side and produce an interface that's too obtuse, hampered by a desire to obfuscate that results in key features being hidden too deep, or one that's too bottom-up, promoting mindless usage and eschewing intentionality. Like everything else, there's a balance to be found.

Mindful Design Principle: Create Interrelatedness   *Strive to create different layers of relatedness and cross-categorization between objects within your system. Think about how disparate system objects might be related beyond assumed or organizational categories. Understand how a specific task or goal might make seemingly discrete concepts contextually relevant to one another.*

Design Is Attention Manifest

You've seen that our mind's mental modes are never inherently positive or negative, and that daydreaming can be as much about rumination as it is about creativity. So, too, we must acknowledge that our brains' inclinations toward shortcuts and biases as a whole are both essential and wildly detrimental, depending on circumstance and application. If we're unscrupulous or careless in applying this knowledge, we can actively harm and alienate vulnerable people. Our responsibility as designers lies first and foremost in the facilitation, protection, and agency of the people who use the stuff we make. This is increasingly important as tech (and, by proxy, design) infiltrates more and more aspects of human life. The current climate of venture-capital-backed startups; fast-paced design and iteration; a grossly under-regulated industry; and a hyper-focus on growth, money, and attention can often come to blows with the notions of little things like ethics and responsibility.

In this chapter, you learned that the human mind is often found in a state of daydreaming, where thoughts often pass fleetingly from one to another. This is known as the default mode network, and it can be viewed alternatively as a "task negative" mode, where the mind is free to wander in the absence of mentally demanding tasks.

I discussed how apps such as iA Writer, with its "focus mode," can replicate the attentional filtering that the brain performs, fading unnecessary information into the background and highlighting the information we care about.

You also explored the cost of distractions—something that we should be especially aware of given the addictive and often over-reliant relationship we have with our devices. Switching attention from one task to another has a very real cost attached to it, and a mind that is neither left to wander nor allowed to partake in prolonged, focused flow is a mind rendered inefficient by the very tools that are supposed to allow for and accommodate increased efficiency. GitHub's repository deletion Danger Zone and subsequent warnings, as well as the requirement to actively type the repository name to fully confirm deletion, were used as examples of how attention-grabbing, or friendly friction, can be used as a preventative or protective measure to facilitate more mindful, intentional decision-making.

The *cognitive miser* theory offers an explanation for how we use things like heuristics—mental shortcuts that allow us to operate in a bottom-up, autopilot-like mode—to conserve mental energy, acting somewhat as economists of our own attention. *Satisficing*, you learned, is a means of shallowly analyzing the information in front of us to make a decision that we *believe* will do the job to a contextual threshold, rather than painstakingly performing a cost/benefit analysis of every option presented to us. We can see our role, at least in part, as designing an external layer to this equation, acting as facilitators of attention economics by preemptively shaping the information presented at any one time, in any one context.

You learned that we, by nature, categorize the world around us, building and reinforcing mental schemas and unique associations between objects. This is especially evident in our remarkable ability to functionally, or temporarily, categorize items that, when taken out of context, lack any kind of similarity. The example of deliberating between a brick, a shoe, and a tortoise as members of the functional category "things we can hammer a picture hook into a wall with" shows how categorization and schematic evaluation allows us to present novel and creative solutions to problems. By pursuing, creating, and communicating interrelatedness between system objects—such as intra-object interaction patterns, or application modalities—we can mimic the brain's approach to chunking information, objects, and stimuli to support more efficient decision-making. Don't fall into the trap of thinking categories are purely taxonomical or literal and broaden your perspective of categorization in design to include things like context-dependent categorization and functional equivalence.

What good, responsible design gives us is the luxury of cognitive headroom. By operating efficiently and simplifying complex tasks, an uncluttered interface puts itself in the best position to be impactful *when necessary or welcomed*. A seamless, streamlined baseline allows us to promote intentionality and deeper, top-down thinking for important interactions or when highlighting key changes in system state. This isn't restricted to destructive actions, either. Small degrees of friendly friction or slight difficulty bumps here and there can actively promote learning and memorization—it's part of why education apps are often so heavily gamified. Another friendly example of attention-grabbing is guiding someone's focus toward a success message after they complete their task. Positive feedback is another integral component of affect and education, so if you have the mental space to sprinkle in some cutely animated success message, then you absolutely should!

If you take one thing from this chapter to apply to your design process, make it the understanding that there is a real cost associated with attentional switching and that distractions and held attention do not come free. Be as objective as possible when balancing the attentional requirements of people against the business goals your product is attempting to achieve.

CHAPTER 2

Vision and Perception

In 1872, a painting was painted. Now, in the 1800s, lots of paintings were painted. But this particular one was an important one—and not just because it's my favorite painting of all time. This painting is Claude Monet's *Impression, Soleil Levant* (Figure 2-1) and I love it, in part, because it embodies the Impressionist movement, one of the most beautiful—and beautifully dysfunctional—marriages of art and science in history. I'm going to spare you the full meandering history of Impressionism and post- Impressionism, but I implore you to do some further reading if you're in any way interested in art, bohemia, or anarchy. What is important to understand is the insight Impressionism gives us into some of our brain's perceptual processes.

Figure 2-1. Claude Monet, Impression, Soleil Levant—1872, oil on canvas, Musée Marmottan Monet, Paris (public domain)

© Scott Riley 2024
S. Riley, *Mindful Design*, Design Thinking, https://doi.org/10.1007/979-8-8688-0143-3_2

Around the same time that Manet, Monet, Bazille, Renoir et al. were hunched in Cafe Guerbois, twizzling fancy mustaches, cursing the memory of Napoleon, and plotting the downfall of the bourgeoisie (the "Batignolles" were reportedly staunch anarchists and bohemians), science was making its first strides into understanding the separation between sensory input and perception. Namely, we were just coming to terms with the fact that what we see is not what we see. How cryptically enticing.

In the previous chapter, I touched on the idea that the brain is concerned with regulating—most importantly, saving—mental resources. It's also incredibly adept at pattern recognition, and we're able to perform a whole suite of perceptual shortcuts and acts of visual field organization to make sense of our environment.

While our understanding of the intricacies of perception has become more refined, more rounded, and deeper than these seminal discoveries and theories, the science *du jour* in the late 1800s still rings true: the eye and the retina are only half of the equation when it comes to visual perception. Without a form of organization and resolution in the mind, the things we "look at" would be perceived as little more than visual mush. Impressionism played to this reality and embodied, to its core, the true nature of human perception. Perception is how we organize our environment, how we take what we *sense* and transform it into something meaningful in what we *perceive*—and it is hugely impacted by our own experiences of the world. What we know, what we expect, and how we feel all influence what we perceive.

Vision is the *bottom-up* sensory process of transmitting light information from our environment to the brain. Light is captured, turned into neural signals, and then sent to the brain for processing. This is vision. The brain then applies some form of order to these signals—it catalogs, organizes, and contextualizes the discrete elements of what we see into objects with meaning and interrelatedness. This is perception, and everyone's perception is different. It's theorized that varying amounts of this sensory data are lost before they even reach the visual cortex of our brains; thus, what we actually perceive once visual information has done its eclectic round-trip to the brain is actually often informed by assumptions and hypothesizing—a kind of *best guess* combination between objective visual signals and assumptive fill-in-the-blank mental mystery solving.

When you look at *Impression, Soleil Levant*, what do you see? I see a river; I see a few scattered boats with people in each, some seated, some standing; I see birds in flight over the river; I see a bridge, a sunrise, and the reflection of that sunrise in the water. I see a living scene—a moment in time. Remove the romance, though, and look slightly closer; it's really a whole mess of visible brushstrokes and vaguely-rendered forms. Even now, Monet's work looks almost unfinished—form is hinted at and suggested rather than meticulously rendered, and there's a gritty, primal, textural nature to the work. At the time, this style was shunned, almost heretic in its brazenness.

Before Impressionism, fine art was on a crusade of realism. Brushstrokes were deft and unnoticeable; art was aspirational and hyper-realistic; important people were painted in important situations; and the mainstream audience at the time was— quite ironically—rooted in the avoidance of harsh reality through escapism. The Impressionists sought to bring their own form of realism to art; to bring it down to earth; to paint the peasants and the *bohemes*; to capture the purity of moments, not the glutton of fantasies. To paint these moments—to acquiesce to the ephemerality of natural light, to paint with an obsession for minimizing brushstrokes, to immerse oneself in a fluid, shifting environment— was to realize, on canvas, the nature of human perception. To me, Impressionism embodies a notable array of the modern quips and knowledge we have in design, through its striving for minimalism and its refusal to patronize.

There's certain magic to this work, along with the neo- and post-Impressionism and abstract art that followed it, and that magic lies in just how well it lays bare the workings of our mind's eye. When we observe a work like this, we're almost compelled to insert ourselves into it. The soul of an Impressionist painting cannot be found on the canvas; it's in the mind of everyone who's filled in its blanks. Impressionism and abstract art only truly occur in our minds. We use our past experiences and our knowledge of the world to extrapolate form into meaning. There is a visceral, individual component to experiencing a piece of art that, for me, has never quite been captured better than in the masterpieces of the Impressionist movement. Without this extrapolation, we would see art how we would see the world without perception—as a mess of lines and color and incoherence. Impression leaves room for our own affect, our own emotions—it is exploration on canvas, and it has changed art forever.

The Iconic Abstraction Scale

Creeping further toward modern day now, in his quite excellent book *Understanding Comics*, Scott McCloud theorizes that the more "iconic" an image is, without losing its meaning, the higher chance that we'll apply to it some of our self by attaching our own inferences. Similar to the act of observing Impressionist art, when we see simple illustrations, we're asked to fill in some blanks and to come to our own conclusions.

McCloud uses the term "iconic abstraction" to denote the level of deviation from real-world form—the premise being simpler, more cartoon-like forms represent higher levels of iconic abstraction from a real object than, for example, a photograph (see Figure 2-2).

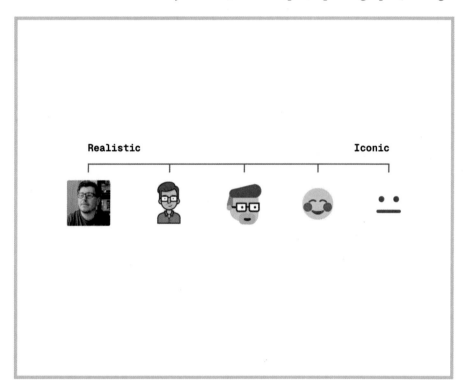

Figure 2-2. *An example of iconic abstraction: going from realistic (left) to iconic (right)*

While there's little in the way of empirical evidence for this theory, I do believe it's a wonderful meditation on just why we're so enamored with the abstract. Artworks that, without our ability to fill in blanks and create associations, would essentially be discarded as a cacophony of lines and brushstrokes become something more than the moment or object they seemingly nonchalantly represent. There exists enough conceptual space in these works for us to impart our own ideas and weave the threads of our own stories. I've long said (while acknowledging the inherent bias from the fact that some of my favorite humans are illustrators) that illustration is one of the most integral aspects of a modern brand, website, or interface, and I think McCloud's theory and our willing cultural embrace of impressionist and abstract art gives us a hint as to the real power of emotional illustration.

Furthermore, what we *see* when we look at these works actively changes based on our working mental models of the world. Ask yourself this: when looking at *Impression, Soleil Levant*, how—do you imagine—would your perception of this image change if you were familiar with the river on which it is based? If, as part of your daily routine, you spent every afternoon in the Le Havre port, saw endless sunsets like the one depicted, and attached endless memories and associations to those moments? Conversely, what if you'd lived a life in which you had never seen a boat or even a bridge? How would you make sense of Monet's work without the requisite mental model? This is the power of abstraction. It nods toward a form that cannot exist without the inferences of our mind's eye. It's why we can see the sunset and its reflection in Monet's masterpiece, or the seemingly bemused face in that doorknob we walk past every day, or Jesus Christ burned into our toast. When there is a form to be found, we will usually find it (see Figure 2-3). In fact, even when there is no explicit depiction of form, we can always convince ourselves there is.

Figure 2-3. *Can you unsee the "face?"*

Iconic Abstraction in Design

Presenting people with simple visual language is integral to usability. Modern product design especially makes heavy use of iconography, often at sizes as small as 16px squared. While it's possible to convey a surprising degree of complexity inside a seemingly minuscule canvas, great icon designers are experts at using *just enough* visual density to simultaneously communicate meaning and personality. Even larger, so-called *macro icons* and product illustrations make use of this willingness from humans to fill in the blanks when presented with visual information.

In websites and print material, we're far more likely to encounter photography and higher-fidelity illustrations, tapping into *mimetic desire*—the notion that we don't really desire something until we see another human doing or using it. We constantly compare ourselves to others, for better and for worse, and seeing powerful, happy, and competent people can really hit home emotionally—provided the subjects are relatable enough for your audience. Another huge factor, especially with aspirational photography, is that of diversity. If you're using photography in an attempt to uplift and empower, and you omit an underrepresented group, you're making a pretty plain and clear statement that you don't care about that group's members. The whole act of one's relating to a piece of media relies on the ability to find or place a manifestation of one's self within. If your imagery excludes, your potential impact diminishes. That's not to say that by simply adopting a more iconic approach that you magically have no commitment to representation—just that the effects are starkest with the representational nature of photography.

The level of abstraction we want to use in our work will vary greatly depending on context and content around which we're designing. It's *probably* unwise to replace detailed, meticulously-directed product photography on the Nike store with a rough sketch of a pair of shoes worn by a smiling stick person—although it would definitely be a brave brand decision. When we do have the luxury of choice, however, it can be greatly rewarding to simplify your illustrative forms to reach the levels of self-imposition that comics, cartoons, and even impressionist art allow for.

Simpler visual language is also often less cognitively taxing than its more realistic counterpart, allowing us to use fewer pieces of visual information to convey meaning and creating more recognizable, memorable signifiers. Now, this doesn't mean that we should necessarily simplify to the point of abstraction—go too far towards abstract and you exacerbate many of the problems you're trying to solve, with overly-simplified, vague, and confusing forms requiring a second or third *glance* to figure out just what the heck we're looking at. We must also consider personality and brand in this equation too. Having everything in its simplest possible form—whether we're talking about entire interfaces or smaller product illustrations—can easily become boring and insipid. Making decisions appropriate to our audience and subject matter is, of course, paramount; but more engaging, dynamic, colorful, or otherwise personality-laden illustrations and icons can really bring a simple interface to life.

The pursuit of simplicity will be a common theme throughout this book, but take it with a pinch of salt, and remember that this push for simplicity does not exist in a vacuum: the sites and apps we're most exposed to are often grossly dense, full of adverts, or embodiments of feature creep—almost universally tailored towards neurotypical audiences. Pushing too hard for simplicity can lead to insipid environments full of drab elements and monotonous interactions. People deserve fun things, especially when they're tastefully done. Don't skimp on whimsy or personality—most products are better for it. Context is, of course, key here. Adding playful interactions and a cute grim reaper mascot to a funeral home contact form is probably not the best approach; but even boring-sounding products like Enterprise User Management Solutions as a Service or some other random thing over caffeinated dudes in ties try to sell can be embellished with a bit of edge and fun. The key thing to remember is that simplicity is not a heuristic for mundanity. In fact, the better you get at designing simple baselines, the more freedom you have to sprinkle in some fun and personality. Do this with intent and with good reason and you're golden.

The Gestalt Principles of Visual Perception

To understand how you can arrive at the kind of simple, harmonious baseline I keep blabbering on about, you first need to understand how we perceive our environments in the first place. The Gestalt Principles of Perception are a set of guidelines that aim to explain some of the inherent biases and approaches humans apply as part of our environmental perception.

Gestalt is most effective at explaining how we look to *group* elements of our visual environment. As you progress through this book, you'll see time and again how important groups and categories are when it comes to navigating the world. You explored this a little in the previous chapter when you looked at how the mind uses affordances and mental schemas to contextually group objects and make decisions against whole groups. We do this in a more ambiguous visual sense *all the time*, and the easier our visual environment is to chunk away into groups, the more efficient we can be with our attention and decision-making.

Understanding Gestalt *will* make you a better designer. There are quite a few concepts in this book that I optimistically lay claim to being *designer improvers* but you're about to dive into something so fundamentally linked to design that you'd struggle *not* to do better work through developing a practical understanding of it. Practicing how to use visual organization and styles to infer groupings and interrelatedness is the nucleus of any good visual design. Learn Gestalt and how to use it well and you're well on your way to designing consummate visual interfaces.

Proximity

The Gestalt principle of proximity states that objects that are closer to each other are seen as grouped. This is probably the universal principle of visual design and goes a good way to informing why whitespace and layout are so integral to harmonious design. Figure 2-4 shows proximity in effect—chances are you've naturally grouped these objects based on proximity alone.

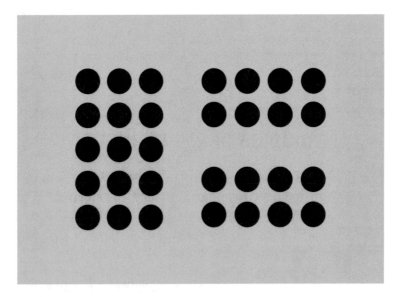

Figure 2-4. *Proximity in action*

In design, proximity informs some of our most basic guidelines. For example, when setting type, ensuring that a heading is closer to the paragraph it introduces than it is to the preceding paragraph (Figure 2-5) enforces the relationship between the two, detaching it from the less-relevant content.

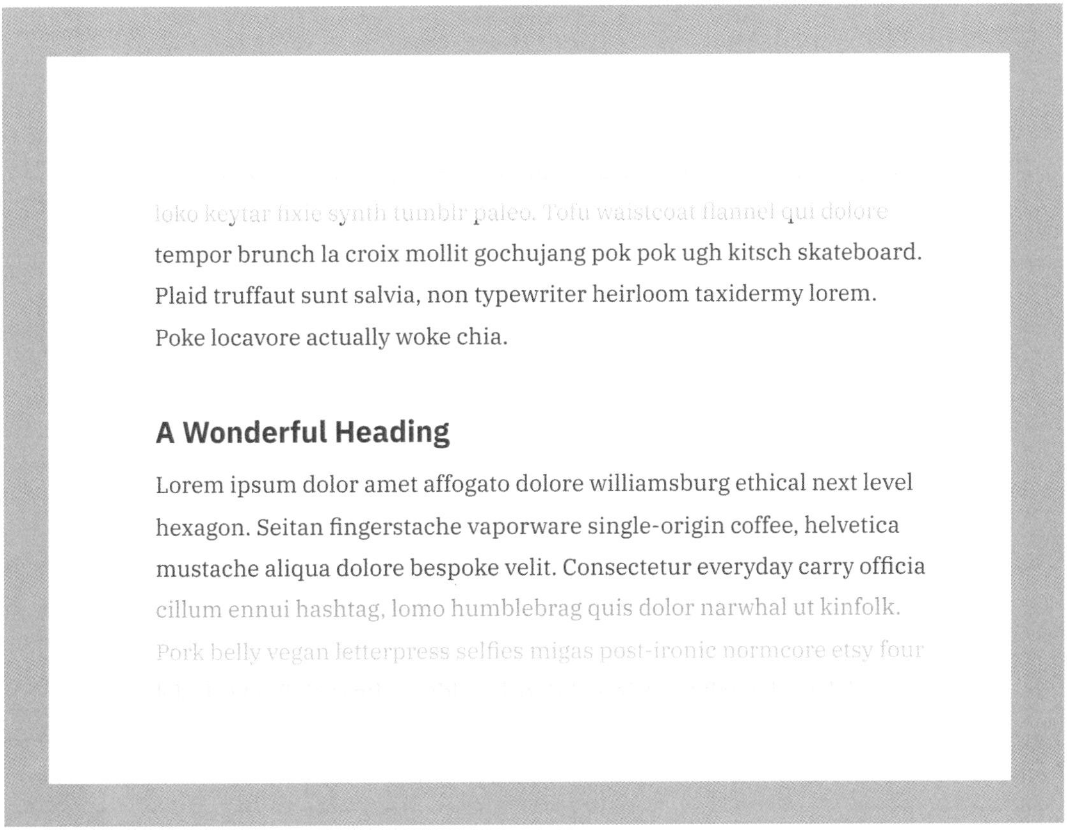

loko keytar fixie synth tumblr paleo. Tofu waistcoat flannel qui dolore tempor brunch la croix mollit gochujang pok pok ugh kitsch skateboard. Plaid truffaut sunt salvia, non typewriter heirloom taxidermy lorem. Poke locavore actually woke chia.

A Wonderful Heading

Lorem ipsum dolor amet affogato dolore williamsburg ethical next level hexagon. Seitan fingerstache vaporware single-origin coffee, helvetica mustache aliqua dolore bespoke velit. Consectetur everyday carry officia cillum ennui hashtag, lomo humblebrag quis dolor narwhal ut kinfolk. Pork belly vegan letterpress selfies migas post-ironic normcore etsy four

Figure 2-5. *The heading's proximity to the second paragraph indicates relatedness, as does its relative separation from the first paragraph*

The power of understanding this principle lies in the fact that it allows us to communicate grouping, structure, and hierarchy without adding any extra elements to our designs. Many simpler designs can communicate relationships and hierarchy through proximity alone.

Challenge: Proximity in Action   Build up a practical understanding of the proximity principle by taking a screenshot of an interface and marking out what you believe to be grouped based on proximity. Mark out and label each group. Find as many good— and bad!—examples as you like, taking into account how obvious the grouping is and whether it makes sense to visually group such elements. You'll be surprised how often proximity is used poorly to create confusing visual environments!

Similarity

The principle of similarity suggests that items with similar appearances and physical qualities will be grouped together. When you look at Figure 2-6, it's quite likely that you'll categorize the shapes into vertical columns of circles and triangles.

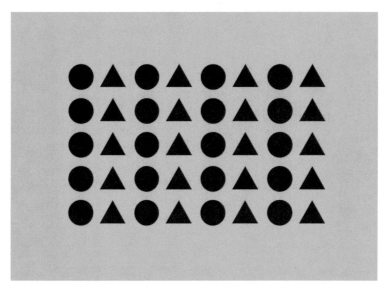

Figure 2-6. *Similarity in shape language enforcing the perception of columns*

Even though the shapes are spaced equally and are of roughly the same visual weight, your brain groups them together by their most obvious similarities. In Figure 2-7, however, it's much more likely you'll perceive horizontal rows of different shapes.

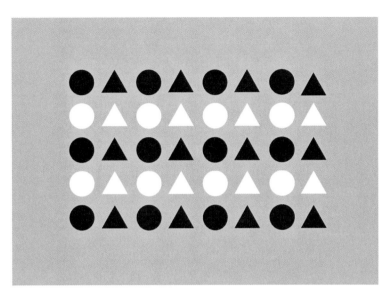

Figure 2-7. _Color similarity overriding the initial perception of columns and instead suggesting rows_

In this case, we observe something rather elemental to Gestalt: the _degree_ to which something adheres to a principal is often just as important as the principal itself. In Figure 2-7, while the objects could easily be read _vertically_ as alternating columns of circles and triangles, the inclusion of a _more obvious_ similarity across the horizontal axis—a stark contrast in color compared to a relatively subtle differentiation in shape language—promotes an entirely different observed structure. Things aren't just a binary of _similar_ or _not similar_, they're _more similar_ and _less similar_, or _closer together_ and _further apart._ Naive binaries make for great posters and great examples in a book, but they're not indicative of the complex visual environments we navigate every day, on and off screen.

Indeed, these examples are atomic, and you'll notice there's an element of proximity at play in making both of these examples still feel like self-contained _wholes_. Similarity doesn't usually play out like this in UI design and is far more often used to link certain visual qualities to semantics or action possibility. Let's take the humble button as an example. There's a touch of real-world metaphor going on (although modern buttons don't tend to rely so much on the verisimilitude of _skeumorphism_ to appear like photo-realistic examples of real-world buttons) and a boatload of convention—buttons are _everywhere_ in digital design—but similarity allows this meaning and convention to prosper in the first place.

While button style might differ subtly between applications based on things like brand identity, market standards, and user preference, most buttons will have similar traits that make them recognizable. They'll usually be a rectangle—perhaps rounded to some degree—with either a border or a background color to provide contrast and differentiate it from normal interface text or icons. Sometimes they'll have a shadow, or a gradient background, or any other visual flourish that felt *buttony* at the time of design. If they've been designed well, they'll also have clear hover, active, and focus states to correctly communicate various phases of interactivity. Most importantly, though, they're recognized and codified as interactive elements and share traits with every other button in an interface. While things like the background color (primary vs. secondary buttons, or a delete button being a "danger" color are good examples of this) or elevation might differ, they will all have many more similarities than differences.

This gives us a sense of cohesion, predictability, and balance when we design. Think how chaotic an interface would be if every button had a different shape and color treatment! Ensuring a degree of similarity between things like buttons, icons, and alerts makes our interfaces more cohesive and predictable. This is one of the primary forcing functions behind design systems—similarity and consistency at the most atomic level of a designed interface provides a platform from which we can create seamless, coherent environments.

It's this consistency and predictability that lets us codify different qualities of interface components and, in doing so, infer meaning or potential action based on the visual and aesthetic qualities of each component. Our brains are constantly making predictions based on qualities—visual or otherwise—of objects in our environment in order to chunk objects and conserve energy. Adhering to this with intelligent and appropriate use of similarity is the backbone of any well-made interface.

Challenge: Similarity in Action   Find or create examples of similarity being used in various contexts. Consider how things like button shape, border radius, padding, line width, and typographic consistency create harmony within an interface. Then do the opposite! Take or create a somewhat complex UI screen, and mess it up completely by making every element unique.

Continuity

While proximity and similarity encompass many of the basic concepts we use most commonly in design, they don't fully account for one of the most important: alignment. The Principle of Continuity suggests that elements that are aligned with each other are perceived as grouped due to our natural desire to visually "follow through" an element along a specific path or in a specific direction, as seen in Figure 2-8.

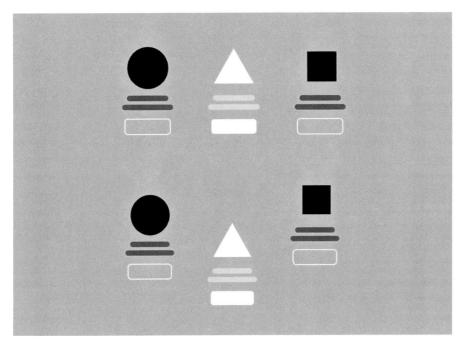

Figure 2-8. *Continuity helps us group the top row of elements together—the second row, not so much*

The first row in Figure 2-8 shows an extremely common row of elements and, while proximity and similarity have a say in their grouping, possibly the strongest indicator that they're a group is their alignment along the vertical axis. The second row shows a rather exaggerated misalignment between the elements, making it much more difficult to perceive them as a group.

Continuity can be enhanced with flowchart-style lines or arrows or hinted at with smaller design flourishes should you need to communicate a cohesive group that doesn't strictly align along an axis. Figure 2-9 shows an example of this; by drawing out a "path" that the eye can follow to connect each element to the next, their relatedness is communicated in spite of their misalignment.

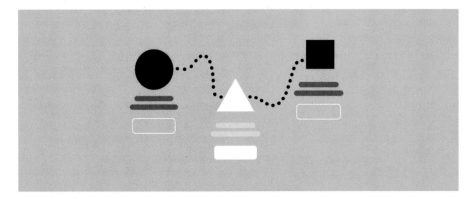

Figure 2-9. *Continuity inception—the line connecting the elements helps signify their grouping, and the line itself isn't a line at all. Continuity has us filling the gaps between the circles to perceive a line*

The path itself is also an example of continuity, with the brain perceiving the separate shapes of this path as a continuous line.

Common Fate

The Principle of Common Fate shows that items that move along a similar or shared path are seen as related—an insight that should heavily inform our animation design decisions. A remarkable example of common fate in nature can be observed in the flocking of birds, particularly that of starlings, turning and twisting in unison—appearing as a single unit. Common fate becomes exceptionally useful when we need to group nested items inside an already similar group. In situations like this, where similarity and proximity are important to maintain, we can use common fate to move one group of items along one path and another along a different path. This can be seen in Figure 2-10.

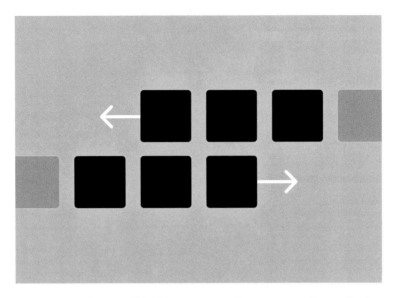

Figure 2-10. *Common fate will help separate the top row from the bottom, even though it's highly likely they'd be perceived as a cohesive group without their opposing movement directions*

In Figure 2-10, the first row of elements and the second row are visually similar and grouped close together in order to appear connected, yet the different movement of the rows—imagine the top row animating in from right to left, the bottom from left to right—communicates a further intergroup relationship. This approach works really well in indicating a subtle hierarchy among elements of the same type, for example, a row of featured posts and a row of suggested posts might benefit from similarity, continuity, and proximity but be differentiated slightly by having a different entrance animation.

You'll see that as you build up from more fundamental principles you will encounter more and more "mixed" examples, where things like proximity and similarity communicate the broad structural hierarchy, and subtler touches like common fate can communicate interrelatedness within these broad sections. This isn't necessarily a hard and fast rule—you can likely create a very well-made, simpler interface using just different degrees of proximity and a touch of similarity—but it does show that you can use varying degrees of all of these principles to lay out increasingly complex visual environments.

Challenge: Common Fate in Action   Common fate is, by nature, pretty difficult to show in action through the static pages of a book. For a quick challenge, why not take a UI you've already designed (or just recreate an interesting UI from an app you know quite well) and prototype a common fate animation to group items together. Some good examples of this are album covers in different sections of a music player app or icons in different sections of an app store or digital video game catalog.

Closure

Closure is an extremely interesting perceptual trait and is used extensively and cleverly in logo and icon design. The Principle of Closure shows that we'll "fill in" forms that don't actually exist—provided there's a "hint" to that form. In Figure 2-11, it's likely you're able to perceive the "S" in the word "closure" and the diamond, square, and triangles in the shapes beneath it, even though those shapes don't actually exist.

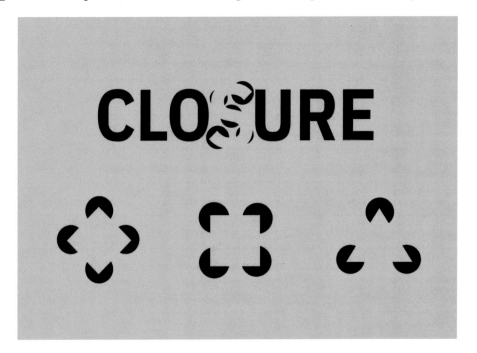

Figure 2-11. *Closure allows us to perceive forms that don't actually exist*

We have little use for closure in interface design, but it's extremely useful in illustration and iconography, allowing a form to be communicated using negative space and a much lower visual complexity.

Common Region

While the Principle of Common Region isn't part of the "classic" principles of Gestalt, it's a concept of perceptual grouping that is used extensively in visual design. Proposed by Stephen E. Palmer in 1992, the Principle of Common Region states that, quite simply, elements that are contained within the same region are seen as grouped. Figure 2-12 shows the same grid of shapes as you saw in Figures 2-6 and 2-7 when discussing similarity, but with alternating rows contained within white rectangles.

Figure 2-12. *A common region allows for very explicit groupings*

Just as you saw when the colors of the shapes in the rows were changed, the common region appears to overrule the subtler similarity in shape language and quite clearly communicates a row-based organization.

An obvious example of this is when we zebra-stripe a table—a visual treatment that involves differentiating alternating rows of a table to make it easier to read long rows of data, seen in Figure 2-13—or how we place our navigation links in a top bar on a website to separate them from page content.

🖼	Juanita Durgan	ⓘ Admin	hi@juani.ta	Active	⋮
🖼	Darrin Hahn	ⓘ Guest	darrin@ha.hn	Idle	⋮
🖼	Jeffery Hermann	ⓘ Admin	jeffery@mail.me	Pending	⋮
🖼	Susie McLaughlin	ⓘ Guest	susie@email.com	Active	⋮

Figure 2-13. *Zebra-striping a table*

Putting It All Together

These principles have fed into later theories and form the basis for a broader subject known as *visual field organization*, which basically spices Gestalt up with a few extra principles from modern observations of perceptual studies. They are rarely used in isolation, and while the examples provided are quite cut-and-dry, there are certainly no binary rules where the only potential outcome is grouped or ungrouped elements. You'll almost always use a diverse amount and degree of these principles. For example, putting similar-looking elements closer to one another in the same bounding box and aligned across the horizontal axis makes use of many principles in a single layout section.

Furthermore, you'll rarely have a single level of hierarchy to communicate—dense interfaces are likely to feature many groups which are, themselves, composed of smaller groups, and so on. Fortunately, these principles have been shown to be impressively scalable and can explain groupings far more complex than you're accustomed to showing, or seeing, in even the most complex interfaces.

Visual field perception as a whole gives us an incredible jumping-off point to explore many other aspects of perception, especially when it comes to cataloging and comprehending the world around us. While conclusions like *putting items in the same rectangle shows they're related* might be just a touch obvious, understanding that we codify seemingly-discrete visual qualities of objects and infer things like relatedness, action possibility, and interoperability can be a hugely empowering notion.

Let's look at two concepts that expand on visual field perception. Firstly, let's look at *contrast* and how it's used to provide the amplitude, or degree, to which we're likely to apply a perception principle and how it's fundamental to communicating hierarchy. After that you'll dive into *signifiers, convention and metaphor*, expanding on the principle of similarity and how to create cohesion, imply interrelatedness, and even harness a kind of distributed cognition. Putting all of these concepts together gives us the constituent concerns of almost any visual design decision.

Contrast

Contrast is one of those concepts that's often easier to show than it is to describe. In the simplest terms, contrast dictates the degree to which any object or stimulus *stands out* from other objects and stimuli within an environment. We might describe a light gray rectangle on top of a white background as "low-contrast" whereas an animated element within a simple, static environment will almost definitely be considered "high-contrast."

Managing and manipulating contrast in contextually appropriate ways is a fundamental design skill. Contrast is both conducive and disruptive, too. A good baseline of contrast between text and its background is integral to creating an optimal reading experience. Buttons need to stand out from other objects to highlight potential actions. Depending on how you use it, contrast can either emphasize or disrupt many of the Gestalt principles already explored.

While we use Gestalt to effectively communicate groupings, we can take certain principles and dial them up or down to present different levels of contrast. Similarity is a great example of this, where a discrete group of items can be made to stand out simply by making them unique. How unique we make them will depend on how contrasting we want them to be, which will in turn depend on their relative priority compared to all other elements on our page.

Figure 2-14 shows an abstract example of a simple posts screen where each post element has certain shared properties: they're all rounded rectangles with the same border radius and shadow (similarity), arranged with the same spacing and structure (proximity), and scrollable or animated in the same way (common fate). We want to make a group of featured posts stand out from this baseline, so we use a big, massive gradient because we're designers.

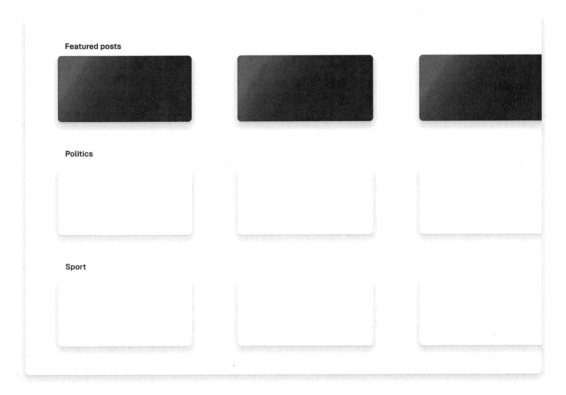

Figure 2-14. *Using contrast to make a group of similar objects stand out from their surrounding environment*

Aside from our stunning and beautiful gradient, we've not changed much. "A post is presented as a rounded rectangle with a shadow and arranged horizontally into a post group" is a design principle that we haven't broken. We've simply applied similarity in a way that makes one group stand out from the others.

On the flip side, let's say we want to subvert similarity. We have a single object that's more important than others on the page, let's say a single featured post among a list of standard posts. Here we have a similar setup to the first example, using similarity to create a baseline. In this case, however, we're focusing heavily on a single item, making it the most unique (or least similar) element on the page (Figure 2-15).

From the blog

My wonderful blog post

Twas brillig, and the slithy toves did gyre and gimble in the wabe. All mimsy were the borogoves, and the mome raths outgrabe. Beware the Jabberwock, my son! The jaws that bite, the claws that catch!

Figure 2-15. *Using similarity to group items and then disrupting it by using a unique element*

Here, we only have a single feature post to worry about. We've created a baseline of grouping and visual perception with our normal posts, arranged into a grid (proximity) and carrying the same designed properties as before (similarity). Here, though, highlighting a single element gives us a little more freedom, allowing us to break out of our grid and use different sizes, shapes, and aspect ratios for our featured post object.

While these are basic, abstract examples, they illustrate how contrast can be a product of breaking away from an established baseline, whether through taking different approaches to grouping to ensure one group stands out from another, or through creating unique, novel elements that break out of your established groupings and qualities. While I'm sure you're not learning something new when I tell you that "unique things stand out," there's a depth to understanding contrast that might not be immediately apparent.

The von Restorff Effect

Contrast is how we communicate importance. Regardless if we're assessing colors, layout, typography, animation, language, loudness, intensity, shape, or any other tool of our trade—effectively making important things stand out at the right time and to the right degree constitutes the practical layer of design.

Figure 2-16. *An example of the von Restorff Effect in action. The red chilis are more easily noticed and more memorable*

The von Restorff Effect, also known as the "isolation effect" and discovered by Hedwig von Restorff, is a visual bias theory that suggests that, when presented with objects in an environment, the *most unique* objects will be easier to notice and recall. At a glance at the photograph in Figure 2-16, you probably very quickly noticed the red chilis. There's also a good chance that, if you were to look away, you'd remember their features to a notable level of detail. However, the green chilis likely almost blurred into one another even though they're as varied in shape as the two red ones. In the presence of much more contrasting stimuli, they're grouped, homogenized, and disregarded. This bias is probably the component of cognitive psychology most attuned to understanding the technicalities of visual design, so much so that its ubiquity makes it essentially common sense: *when something stands out from its peers, we remember it better, and we deem it more important.*

If we view contrast as one of the fundamental conceptual elements of design, the von Restorff Effect—along with Gestalt—forms our perceptive primer into making informed visual design decisions. Just like Gestalt, this isolation effect only works well in an environment of limited stimuli. If we look at the dozens of ways we can make an element contrast with its neighbors and surroundings—vividity of color, size, spacing, framing, motion, and countless others—it may seem intuitive that the busier an element's surroundings are, the more work we have to do to make it stand out, thus the more cognitive effort we require from people to process that information.

Limitations of Contrast

In exploring the notion of contrast as a means of communicating importance, I hope it's somewhat clear that often the easiest way to add contrast to an element is to reduce the perceived importance of its surrounding elements. Just as attention-grabbing is best done to the backdrop of a harmonious and considered environment, so too must contrast occur in an environment free from chaos. There exists a very real situational and individual threshold for contrast to be noticed and a curve of rapidly diminishing returns when we try to make something stand out in a sea of increasing chaos.

The science of—and abundance of theories surrounding—contrast is infuriatingly complex. It's one of those phenomena that we understand conceptually and qualitatively a lot more readily than we do explicitly or quantitatively. That is to say, it's much easier to note that "contrast describes the perceived prominence of one or more elements in relation to their surrounding environment" than it is to actually quantify the *degree* of contrast those elements might possess. Various attempts have been made to provide contrast equations and standards, with the WCAG's exhaustive and well-documented list of acceptable contrast ratios for accessibility probably the most well-known to us as digital designers. While this kind of element-specific approach to contrast, alongside formulating integral rules and guidelines for your interface and style guide's approach to visual contrast, is an important part of any design process, the role of contrast in your initial perception of an environment is conceptually a very different practice.

The Weber-Fechner Law tells us something that I feel is already pretty intuitive: the more stimuli present in an environment, the more impactful any change must be in order for it to be perceived. This law (more accurately, a combination of two interrelated laws) can be applied to many aspects of human sense and perception, and it suggests that our threshold for perceived change is logarithmic, not linear. Figure 2-17 shows this in action. It's quite clear that there are fewer shapes in the top left image (5) than there are in the bottom left (10). However, with a much more cluttered group of shapes, such as the 50 in the top right, the same increase of 5 in the bottom right is barely, if at all, perceptible.

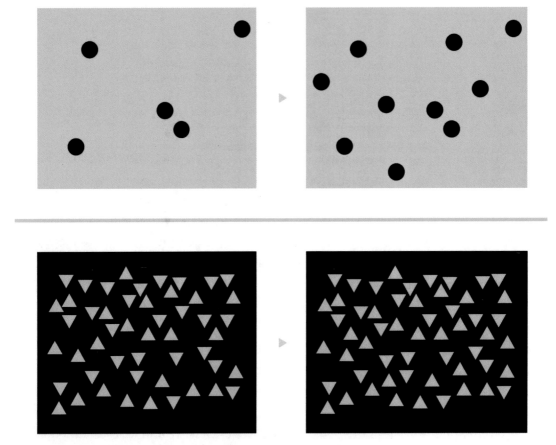

Figure 2-17. *The number of shapes changing is obvious between the top groups of shapes, but may not even be perceptible between the bottom*

This simple concept of perception portrays just how important a stable, calm, and distraction-free interface can truly be. By taking a minimalist approach to the number of stimuli present at any one time, we're able to introduce new concepts and convey importance with much more ease than we could in a poorly designed, distraction-riddled interface. Of course, every interface and product out there has its own baseline at which it can potentially operate—the magnitude of which is vastly dependent on the depth and complexity of features, the personality and tone it's trying to portray, and even the device and external environment in which it's used.

Having a balanced and cohesive baseline and then adding or changing elements to stand out to communicate their importance in a given context is core to design. However, what happens when we highlight the wrong things? Using contrast to bring an element to someone's attention is, at its core, a distraction. If that element's *visual* importance doesn't match its *functional* importance, we've basically manufactured cognitive dissonance. We're saying, *"Hey! Quick! Look at this! It's what you need to see right now!"* and it's hard to ignore that. If this loud, high-contrast, shouty element is actually important, then we're helping people towards their goal and can feel good about ourselves, for a while, as a treat.

However, if the loud, high-contrast, shouty element is a full-page takeover advertising whitening toothpaste or the latest derivative loot-box mobile game or whatever else people are shilling on the web these days, it's absolutely going to make people annoyed, tired, weary, and no closer to their original goal.

This is why modern online advertisements are so egregiously annoying. They bounce and auto-play and shout and trample all over an interface—and they almost always mean nothing to us. Even in interfaces that don't monetize attention through advertisements, we'll often encounter various kinds of upsells and in-app purchases. An attention-grabbing stimulus that is not intrinsically important to the person who perceives it is, quite simply and by definition, a pointless distraction. The more of these distractions you have, the more you dilute your interface and the more you run the risk of your actual important elements being missed due to your living on the tail end of the Weber-Fechner Curve.

It's not just crappy adverts that lead to cognitive dissonance or frustration, though. Sometimes we can be over-eager in highlighting or dimming elements, leading to situations where someone's intended action is more difficult to find because it clashes with the action we *expect* they want to perform. This kind of mistake is abundant in product design, where we tend to prefer nice, neat user flows to messy, open-ended system diagrams—leaving us with unwise assumptions and overly-linear interfaces. Like everything else in design, there's art in the middle ground.

Convention, Signifier, and Metaphor

In the previous chapter, you took a look at how we group objects based on their qualities and affordances. Earlier in this chapter, you saw how to use the Gestalt principle of similarity to do this with visual elements in an environment. But while we might look at a bunch of elements that all have similar aesthetic attributes and think *"Hey! These things might all behave the same way"*—what actually informs *how* we expect them to work?

Conventions, signifiers, and metaphor are intrinsically linked concepts that are often confused with one another when it comes to explaining the kind of distributed cognition that people bring to digital interfaces. The idea of *affordances* will also often be thrown into the mix but, just to save us all some time, the possibility that you'll be dealing with an actual affordance as a digital interface designer is almost zero. An affordance is something we intuit from our physical environment. It's an overused misnomer and almost always either refers to a convention or a metaphor.

I'll discuss the idea of *mental models* in much more detail in the next two chapters, but just to introduce a simple definition for now: a mental model is an explanation of all the things that a person believes to be true in a given context or within a certain system. Mental models greatly inform our expectations; as we encounter events and objects that adhere to our mental models, we start to build up mental schemas that govern how we perceive the world. It's important to understand that everyone brings their own unique mental model to your product, and a huge part of your job is deciding where you want to align—or subvert—your designed model with the observed mental models

Convention

A convention is a rule or norm that's generally agreed on within a group. Language, for example, is a convention with specific rules and parameters for things like grammar, sentence structure, and word order. Social netiquette, too, is a kind of convention for setting a baseline for acceptable interpersonal relationships within a group or community. UI conventions—which we'll naturally want to focus on—are repeatable interaction patterns, governed by explicit and implicit rules that are generally accepted as common best practice. Think about how a rectangle with a border, a placeholder, and a label above it automatically makes you feel as though you can click inside it and type. Spoiler: It's a text input!

Mindful Design Principle: Lean on Convention   *Most designers will have a temptation to over-innovate. That nagging feeling that things need to be unique, that new paradigms need to be set, or that existing patterns are problematic and new solutions are required. This isn't the case. Conventions are conventions for a reason. They're accepted interaction patterns that inform expectations across a broad spectrum of devices, communities, and product ranges. Use convention to limit the cognitive overhead of your UI, giving you the room to innovate where you really need to. Maybe your product's main selling point is a whole new type of code* *editing experience: innovate around that! Present information in novel ways and promote a new paradigm for interaction within the confines of the code editing. You probably don't need to innovate around user management in your code editor, though, so keep it conventional, and let your key features shine.*

Signifiers

While conventions present us with a standard, broad set of expectations that are commonly shared between users, signifiers represent the finer details and specifics of how we communicate things like state and interactivity *within* our interface. We might, for example, highlight a text field with a red border and append some kind of "warning" icon to it to show that it's in an errored state. Or we might disable a button and change its text to "Saving..." to communicate the liminal state between submitting changes and having them persist to a database.

Signifiers let us convey *meaning* within our interface, and if we ensure consistency and cohesion between signifiers, we can leverage the similarity principle to present updates and meaning in highly predictable ways. By repeatedly and effectively signifying interactivity and state, we allow people to infer *action possibility* within a designed environment—this is an incredibly powerful concept.

Mindful Design Principle: Always Communicate State   *The state that your system or elements are in is the most critical piece of information you can communicate when designing interactions. System state refers to the global context your entire app might be in at a given time—for example, correctly highlighting the current mode of a complex, multi-modal UI. Element state refers to the independent state of an element or group of elements—think replacing a button's text with a loading spinner to indicate a "submitting" state.*

Always communicate state. If an input is erroneous, communicate a consistent error state. If something is loading, disable interaction where needed and show a loading indicator. If you're presenting a complex multi-form flow, highlight progress and what step is currently active. Too many UIs poorly communicate changes to state, and it's the easiest way to confuse and disrupt people as they progress towards a goal.

Metaphor

Metaphor is probably the most straightforward concept to grasp when it comes to visually informing mental models. It boils down to borrowing concepts from the physical world and creating a digital representation of them. A good example of this is how the idea of physical folders and documents informed the now standard approach of files and folders in modern day graphical operating systems.

Buttons are another good example of conventional UI elements that started life as an act of real-world mimicry. While modern buttons don't necessarily look like carbon copies of real-world buttons (think the raised, clearly-pressable buttons on an arcade machine), the buttons in early operating systems borrowed heavily from their real-world counterparts.

As people interact with your product, they'll constantly be building and reinforcing their mental models of what's possible and what they can expect from any given interaction. Signifiers can exist solely within your product—such as a unique interaction pattern that you repeat consistently, or in how you communicate system or interaction state—while conventions exist more often as a kind of distributed cognition—such as how most people expect colored (traditionally blue) underlined text to act as a link. Metaphors bring facsimiles of real-world qualities and affordances into the digital realm, allowing you to leverage common mental models instead of trying to establish brand new conceptual models for your interfaces.

When you use convention, signifiers, and metaphors in your work, you're focused on presenting a model of our system that's predictable, that communicates action possibility, that transparently communicates system state, and that is learnable and codifiable. People should be able to enter your designed environment, feel as though they can achieve their goal, and be guided towards it. One place where this is done exceptionally well is in video games.

Video Games As Designed Environments

Video games and product design might seem worlds apart in terms of output, but we share a wide array of problems, challenges, and considerations with our game design brethren. A video game level is as close to an atomic example of a designed environment that we're likely to see. A player jumps in, has a goal they want to achieve, and must try and do so within the constraints of the designed environment. There are conventions—such as industry-standard concepts like movement controls and signifiers like health bars to show how much damage your character can take or timers to show how long you have left to complete a challenge—aplenty.

You'll explore the ideas of communicating and introducing learnable UI concepts later in this book, but something to take away now is that you can, to a degree, introduce and communicate the use and importance of any interface paradigm (color, depth, typography, etc.) to someone in a way that "marks" that paradigm as meaning a specific thing, or conveying a specific use. Video games are wonderful at this, using abstract and idiosyncratic icons to represent complex tasks or concepts. One game that does this wonderfully with color alone is *Horizon: Zero Dawn* in its frankly masterful use of the color yellow.

At some point in your first few minutes with *Horizon*, you're shown a ladder that you can climb. This ladder is bright yellow and contrasts notably with the natural, earthy, and lush palette of Horizon's environments. The vividity of the ladder's color and the fact that it's isolated from its surroundings makes it stand out—and as part of your onboarding into the game and the affordances you associate with the ladder (you know, from your exposure to the world, that ladders, rope, etc., are all members of the functional category "things we can climb"), you're taught, quite effectively, that you can climb this. Figure 2-18 shows how such a contrasting color can signify meaning.

Figure 2-18. *Horizon: Zero Dawn (Sony Interactive Entertainment America LLC, Guerrilla B.V.) using yellow as a signifier, allowing us to attach meaning and causality to the color*

Later on, as the game opens up and becomes less linear ("open world" games generally allow for unrestricted exploration of an expansive map), you start to notice little yellow notches in mountains and ledges tailed in scuffed yellow paint. Of all there is to love about exploring Horizon's world, for it's a wonderful environment brimming with small details to appreciate, this is the thing that really stuck with me. From that initial onboarding experience I had, I was able to deduce that yellow means climbable. And every time I tried it, and it worked, I felt good as heck. By planting that seed in my head and "marking" things quite naturally—you're never presented with a big *you-can-climb- this-you-know?* tooltip or anything that runs the risk of ripping you out of the fantasy world you're in—Horizon was able to present to me an environment that felt truly empowering to explore.

By refusing to patronize its audience, yet still clearly communicating what is and isn't climbable, the game offers a masterful insight into the human mind's ability to catalog and codify concepts together with simple perceptual cues. Without ever being told it, we intuit that yellow means climbable, and this is reinforced every time we try it and successfully prove our intuition correct. We're never patronized by over-explanation. It's assumed we'll understand their inference, and it *feels* like we're making our own discoveries, with just a nudge here and there from the game's UI and design decisions.

To me, this experience, and countless others like it, embodies a very important concept when it comes to color: it's almost useless without context. In seeing something that contrasts with its environment and being able to interact with an object of that color in a specific and consistent way, we're able to manufacture our own, very specific, affordances. In *this* environment, in *this* situation, *this* aesthetic communicates *this* effect. Importantly, we generally codify that aesthetic-effect relationship within the confines of that environment. I didn't take my learnings from Horizon and apply it to different environments; the *climbable* association I had with yellow in the game didn't translate outside of its bounds, and I never encountered any embarrassing situations where I was compelled to acrobatically scale every McDonald's sign I saw. I was simply shown a relationship between aesthetics and effect, and I codified that relationship in that distinct environment.

One of our most intriguing and powerful heuristics is our willingness to accept a simpler signal as a proxy for a more complex one. This can quite often have us falling short on the more philosophical or contemplative issues in life, but as a tool of cognitive economy, our ability to associate a visceral stimulus with something as complex as a series of performable actions is pretty wonderful.

Mindful Design Principle: Communicate Action Possibility   *Action possibility is just that: the possibility that an element can be interacted with to perform a specific action that instigates a specific result. By using convention and signifiers, and being consistent and repetitive with their usage, we can hint at possibilities within an environment without having to be overt or signpost-y. Action possibility is an incredibly important component to forming mental models, and when done well, can be responsible for some of the most seamless, explorative, and rewarding experiences we design.*

Perceptive Design

Visual perception governs the efficacy of a huge range of design decisions and gives us some of our most fundamental tools when it comes to placing elements on a screen. Gestalt shows us that we perceive a visual environment in groups, further reinforcing the innate categorization and chunking that our brains use to save mental energy when processing our environments. Contrast shows us that uniqueness and magnitude can bring elements and objects to the forefront of our attention, with the von Restorff Effect explaining why objects that differ most to their neighbors are more noticeable and more memorable. The Weber-Fechner Curve shows us that the impact of uniqueness and change is correlated to the density of a given environment. That is to say, the more cluttered or chaotic and environment is, the harder we have to work to make something stand out.

You also looked into how things like convention, signifier and metaphor can be leveraged to provide visual cues to communicate concepts such as system and interaction state as well as action possibility. Finally, you explored how visual cues such as color can be used to signify learnable, repeatable concepts within a discrete environment, looking at how video games use color in their environments to signify certain action possibilities. Through consistency and repetition, these concepts are codified by the player, and the visual cue is used as a heuristic for a much more complex concept.

These concepts do a lot of heavy lifting when it comes to explaining why simpler, more conventional interfaces are often the most usable. However, contrast is fun, and certain interfaces can and should have some personality to them. Simple and conventional is also often, well, *boring*. Using high-contrast elements, using animation to give your UI some personality, bringing across illustrations and brand assets to create cohesion across product ranges: all of these things bring some soul and craft to our work. Oftentimes, it's better to see simplicity as a baseline from which to build. Start serene and slowly add elements or flourishes to a tasteful and appropriate point. Remember that the brain wants to conserve energy, and you can facilitate that with good grouping, conventional patterns, and clear signifiers. But if you do the basics well, you give yourself the headroom to surprise and—whisper it quietly now—even *delight* when and where appropriate. Like so many things in design, it's all about balance.

CHAPTER 3

Learning and Memory

In its most reduced model, learning is simply the transmission of information from sensory input into long-term memory, with a few checkpoints along the way. In a wider sense, there are infinite ways in which we can learn things and seemingly infinite categories of learning we can partake in. Furthermore, learning is not *just* about committing a fact to long-term memory—learning a skill is as different from memorizing a fact as it is from developing a habit, yet all can be viewed as some form of learning or memorization.

Some things, like our native language, are codified early on in life, without us really having a choice or making a conscious effort. Others, like playing a musical instrument or riding a bike, require enough deliberate practice for us to eventually treat the act as one of muscle memory. As discussed in Chapter 1, the ability to delegate complex tasks to our subconscious plays a large role in cognitive economy. Once a task requires little to no conscious attention, it becomes less taxing to perform, allowing us to apply focus elsewhere—should we need or wish to—while we perform it.

This process—known as *automaticity*—is integral to developing skills and habits. Repeatable actions with predictable outcomes soon become ingrained, and the neural networks responsible for performing these skills and tasks, or for reciting information, become more easily activated and accessible. While we don't necessarily lose the ability to perform certain skills after not doing them for a while—we literally have an idiom of *just like riding a bike* to explain the phenomenon of our ability to perform certain tasks or skills after long periods without doing so—these skills can be subject to *fading*, which is just as it sounds: a reduced capability, or a need for much more focus and attention than before, to perform certain skills or tasks.

Yet the role of cognitive economy in learning does little to explain the complex emotional and motivational structures behind the vast majority of our decisions or desires to learn something new. This is where goals come in to play. Aside from facts we pick up and remember seemingly at random, the overwhelming majority of the knowledge, skills, and habits we learn and develop over time are preceded by a *goal*.

© Scott Riley 2024
S. Riley, *Mindful Design*, Design Thinking, https://doi.org/10.1007/979-8-8688-0143-3_3

Sometimes that goal involves simply understanding more about the world we live in—studying biology, for example, to satisfy an innate curiosity of how the body and its systems function. Other times, that goal is more tangible or emotional in nature. We may fall in love with a piece of music that inspires us to learn an instrument, which unto itself might reveal many different goals—reaching a level of proficiency to play that particular song or creating our own music in the vein of that piece. Almost every musician I know, including myself, can trace their musical career back to *that one song* that led to decades of deliberate practice sparked by a single emotional response.

Our goals are also almost always unique to and intrinsic to us. We may learn Japanese due to a desire to travel to Japan and engage more deeply in the culture there. We may learn to use a drill so that we can put up a shelf in order to display our favorite books. And we may even try to learn how to do a sick backflip to impress our attractive neighbor. (The last one is *definitely* just a hypothetical example, I promise.) While I'll cover some of the neuroscience of learning, and indeed most of what I discuss will be through delving into the inseparable relationship of cognition and emotion when applied to learning, I want to make clear that the *goal* behind the need or desire to learn is just as—often more—important than the processes of learning themselves.

Goals

A quick aside, while we're on the subject of goals: *never* conflate the internal, organizational goals of your company or product with the motivations of people. If someone uses a product to send money to others, their goal is not necessarily to "perform a bank transfer" and it's absolutely not to "tap the *transfer* button, input the transaction details, and then tap *send*." We're often far too guilty of conflating interactions with goals, but there's always something deeper, something further removed—physically and metaphorically—from the screen that should inform our thinking. Frameworks like *Jobs To Be Done* go some way to helping us avoid this, but conflating success metrics and KPIs with actual human motivation and goals is something that far too many inexperienced designers and product people do.

Why does someone need to transfer money? Perhaps to split a bar tab with their friend. How would your app change were you to design around that potentiality? Perhaps they send money to pay off a debt, or to pay a seller on an auction site, or maybe it's a charitable donation—all unique goals that one would expect to be framed and executed uniquely, with the utmost care and specificity. Whatever the product, without understanding the real-world goals that inform its features, we limit ourselves to designing around the shallowest potentialities.

More often than we'd like to admit, a person's goals when using our work are far, far removed from actions that actually take place within our interfaces. We need to become more comfortable with accepting and embracing transience in our work. There's *always* an external driver to the actions that occur in our interfaces, and often the best thing we can do is to design so effectively for seamlessness that our interface becomes invisible. There is absolutely no shame in creating a wonderful environment for the "just-passing-through" crowd. A product or service that lets people pop in, do what they need to do, and enjoy the fruits of their labor is an all-too-rare find in this age of *stickiness*, *mindshare*, and *habit-forming*.

Indeed, the modern-day fetishization of attention far too often distorts our vision for our work. It suggests that the more *engaging* our products are, the better they can be perceived as performing. At best, this is a gross abstraction; at worst, it's just categorically wrong. Generally, people aren't looking for *engagement*; they're looking for solutions to their problems. They're looking to be enabled and empowered in their pursuit of a goal. At the risk of generalizing, here's a hypothesis: *most people want to engage with their banking app about as much as they want to engage with their alarm clock.*

Even for media-streaming products such as Netflix and YouTube, our goal is not to "engage with the app." It's *escapism*, or *education*, or just outright *entertainment*. The fact that roughly 94% of my interactions with Netflix involve scrolling through with my partner and taking it in turns to say "Nah, not tonight" to every suggestion we see doesn't mean Netflix has created an engaging interface. It means that, firstly, finding a good show is *hard work* and, secondly, the interface is *apparently* doing a poor job of presenting us with viable solutions to that problem.

Mindful Design Principle: Acknowledge Real-World Goals   Your product's KPIs and success metrics don't matter one bit outside of your team or your company. People come to your product with their own goals and motivations, and if they achieve what they came to do, observe their success in the real world. People don't want to "click X button" or "perform Y action;" they want to finish a job, or show their love, or express their creativity. Your product is not an island.

So, this puts us in a bit of a conundrum. As you're about to read, repetition is key to learning. Learning something well enough begets automaticity. Automaticity reduces the mental energy and focus required when performing that task. So, people should use our stuff *all the time*, right? Well—and you're going to get sick of me saying this—it's again all about *balance*.

How We Learn

While the most interesting and challenging aspect of designing around the human learning process lies, in my opinion, in the creation of a positive and enriching environment, it'd be remiss to not explore the basics of our learning processes first. The subject of human learning is extraordinarily broad with wide-reaching implications. Thus, the science of learning and memory is rife with debate, controversy, and ethical considerations. With that in mind, I'll cover some of the basic principles of learning and then zone in on where we can really make an impact with our work while leaving the shouting and debating to the professionals.

As mentioned at the beginning of this chapter, learning can be (over-) diluted into the act of transferring sensory data into long-term memory storage. Broadly speaking, we hear or read a fact or observe a technique and, through some form of practice or repetition, we commit it to memory. This process involves said sensory data traversing a few checkpoints along the way, with data loss or corruption often occurring between each stage. Furthermore, for most humans, this process is rarely a straightforward A-B-C flow of information; it's almost always a messy and chaotic back-and-forth between our different memory storage and retrieval structures.

Our brain is a living ecosystem of neurons and synaptic connectors—a universe wherein stars burn out and are born anew. If we were to observe the light show of the brain's neural activity during learning, it'd be akin to watching a time lapse of our galaxy shifting over millennia. As we learn and meditate on new information, connections between neurons are reinforced, allowing them to better communicate. New connections between neurons are formed, existing connections are occasionally dimmed, and new neurons themselves may even be created. The more often a neural network associated with a specific task is strengthened and activated, the more efficient it becomes. This shifting structure at the brain's cellular level is known as *plasticity*—the idea that our brains are living, malleable things, brimming with life and complexity, constantly changing until the day we die.

It's this neural strengthening and cellular rearrangement that allows us, over time, to relegate the performance of certain tasks to the back of our mind. Essentially, when the neural network used for a certain task is strengthened enough through consistent engagement, it allows for a level of efficiency in neural communication that requires very little conscious thought. When this happens, our default mode network is able to engage, we pay less attention to the task, and we can perform it intuitively and seamlessly. When discussing this journey from stimuli to stored memory, you'll often encounter three key concepts: encoding, storage, and retrieval.

Encoding

Encoding is a cognitive process that involves taking information from our environment and, essentially, *formatting* it in a way that makes it easier to store and retrieve later. We can see encoding as an extension of our attentional system—it's selective, and there needs to be a degree of salience to a stimulus for us to focus on it to encode it in the first place. Once focused on a stimulus or piece of information, we will more often than not perform some form of *re-coding* to help with memorization. Sometimes recoding is a conscious effort to help us remember something, such as creating a mnemonic, like how we might be taught to remember the planets as—and I'm going to show my age here—*My Very Easy Method Just Speeds Up Naming (Planets)*, with the order representing each planet's proximity to the sun. (Mercury, Venus, Earth, Mars, Jupiter, Saturn, Uranus, Neptune and ... the now-famous Not A Planet, Pluto. RIP little fella.) Other times this re-coding is subconscious, and we're attaching information to events and contexts without really being aware of it.

The re-coding process is also prone to error. When we allow certain information to be attached to certain events or existing memories, we can color both the new information and the older memories with new contexts and connections. This is where the phenomenon of unreliable memories comes from—everything from our existing biases and schemas through to unrelated stimuli from the environment in which we encoded can distort the information and memories that we store. Often, we're better at misremembering what we *inferred* from an experience than we are at remembering the experience itself.

All memories must be encoded, but not everything we encode will be memorized. There's no hard and fast rule that tells us what kind of encoding or recoding guarantees a successful or failed storage of memory. There are, of course, ways to give our brains the best chance.

Storage

While encoding information lets us perceive and recode signals into something our memory system can deal with, storage explains how we pass this information through the various layers of memory, eventually cataloging it in our long-term memory.

Storage starts at the sensory level. While most people will be familiar with the concepts of short-term—or working—memory and long-term memory, this sensory layer of our memory system is often overlooked. Our sensory memory lets us hold a stimulus in our memory for a very brief period of time, even if it is no longer present. For visual information—otherwise known as iconic memory—this is usually a fraction of a second and provides a kind of sensory buffer, allowing us to perceive a coherent sequences of events—similar to how we can watch a movie recorded at 24 frames per second and perceive it as one continuous sequence rather than a disjointed series of extremely rapid individual frames. Alongside iconic memory, we have echoic memory, which is essentially the same concept but applied to sound. We have a much higher capacity for echoic memory, usually up to a few seconds, and this is integral to our ability to comprehend language, engage in conversations, and follow spoken directions.

Storage occurs next, at a more active level, in our short-term memory. Otherwise known as *working memory*, our short-term memory is where we store information during cognitive processing. Our working memory is limited in capacity, especially when compared to our long-term memory—assumed by many to be infinite—and presents some limitations that we have to be extremely mindful of when designing. When information is being held in our working memory, it can add a cognitive load. Asking people to keep too many things in mind, or make too many decisions at once, can result in their working memory capacity being exceeded, potentially resulting in cognitive overload, stress, and anxiety.

All the concepts we explored in Chapter 1 with regards to the cost of distractions apply just as much to the cost of storing information in our working memory. And just like how the threshold for attention switching and focus differs for any individual, so too does the capacity of any one person's working memory. Similarly—and intrinsically linked—to our ability to hold focus, our capacity for working memory can also be influenced by external cognitive impairments, neurodevelopmental disorders, and mental health issues. Anxiety and stress, ADHD, depression, generational trauma, dyscalculia, poverty, and even the knowledge that we have an unread email in our inbox can all impact our capacity to hold information in our working memory.

You might have encountered *Miller's Law* in your studies or career. It's an often-cited concept, also known as "magic number 7," that suggests a rule of thumb of four to seven items as a capacity for our working memory. This often gets translated into quirky design principles like "limit your navigation to a maximum of seven elements"—which is somewhat useless, unless viewed in its vaguest form of "don't present too many options." While we *can* store single items in working memory, it's not a cut-and-dry capacity where one item takes up one slot. More often, when we talk about capacity, we're actually talking about *chunks* of information. This is where we get back to our good friend, grouping. (I told you it was going to come up a lot!) By splitting information up (think about how we can use Gestalt to visually group related elements), we can create a *chunk* of information. An elementary example of this is a phone number, let's say 5554206969. While there are ten digits to this number, it doesn't *necessarily* mean we need ten "slots" of working memory to hold that number in our heads. In fact, phone numbers across the world are almost always hyphenated—prechunked, for our convenience. Our totally fake phone number, were it printed in a phone book or displayed on a contact page, would quite likely be presented as 555-420-6969. Much nicer. This gives us three *chunks* of information to hold in our memory:

- Chunk one: 555

- Chunk two: 420

- Chunk three: 6969

Some people will argue that the length of each chunk *also* should adhere to Miller's Law—that is, no chunk should exceed seven characters—but there really is no hard and fast rule when it comes to working memory chunking. As mentioned, there are myriad circumstantial, mental, and physiological reasons why someone's working memory might be seemingly limited or expanded when compared with a stereotypical average—if such a thing exists. The type of information being processed will also have an impact. Some people have an incredible knack for remembering numbers. To them, perhaps even the non-chunked phone number is trivial to hold in their working memory. A person with dyscalculia, though, might struggle to keep even a three-digit chunk in their working memory. That doesn't mean that they'd naturally be bad at remembering a sequence of playing cards or a list of countries and capital cities.

Rather than having a reductive "only show four to seven items" approach to design, what we really want to do is *limit the need to hold chunks of data in working memory*. There are a few ways we can achieve this, and I'll touch on them very soon, but let's get that out of our working memory, for now!

The next stage of storing information is our long-term memory. This is where we consolidate information from our working memory into a more solid, retrievable state. What actually happens during this consolidation is quite incredible: our brains manipulate our nervous system—reinforcing and creating neural connections in the same vein we'd leave a Post-It on our monitor to remind us of an important note. These memory traces—also known as engrams—can sound like the stuff of science fiction: if the brain manipulates the nervous system to leave *notes* for itself, could we reverse engineer them to replay memories? That's dystopian as heck, though, and we'll save that one for the neurobiologists. What we need to be aware of is that, although memory traces sound sophisticated, they're just as fallible as our encoding and recoding, and just as liable to accidental falsehoods and embellishment as the rest of our memory process.

For something to be stored in our long-term memory is for it to transition from a fragile, fleeting object of focus to a solid, codified concept in our brain. This usually requires a deeper level of processing. We don't tend to make strong connections from weakly-held information, and many facts and occurrences are only truly memorable because of the context at the time of noticing and encoding the information. This can stir up a fair bit of cognitive dissonance for us as designers. We know that deeper levels of processing require more conscious effort and more cognitive resources, but if we want something to be learnable, we almost have to strive for slower, more methodical interactions.

Retrieval

Information that is stored away in our long-term memory isn't just immediately and miraculously retrievable. How many of the things you've felt, experienced, and learned recently do you think you'll remember in ten years' time? Or how much from ten years ago can you remember now? For most people, stored information does not necessarily stay as retrievable information.

Retrieval is a broad term for how we access previously-stored information. Through a process known as *ecphory*, we're theorized to be able to reawaken memory traces, helping us recognize, recall, or relearn information we previously cataloged. Essentially, we're bringing stored information back into our conscious awareness.

Retrieval often happens in response to a cue—an external or internal trigger of sorts—that allow us to access certain memories or stored information. We call this kind of retrieval *recognition.* We notice some aspect of our environment, or we feel a certain emotion or other type of interoception, and it triggers a memory of some kind. This is often related to the context or environment where encoding and storage occurred, like how going to your garden on a sunny day might trigger a reminder of a conversation you had at a family barbecue.

Retrieval and recognition are key when it comes to signifiers in our interfaces. Provided that the signifier was observed at the point of encoding, it's quite probable that future encounters with this signifier will act as retrieval cues. Think about the video game example from Chapter 2, where yellow was used to indicate climbable surfaces. While the first encounter with this concept was novel, provided that encoding and storage worked at least somewhat well, the next encounter with that signifier then becomes a cue for recognition: "the last time I saw this yellow, it meant that I could climb the surface."

As you've seen, this process of encoding, storage, and retrieval is far from perfect. It has to happen countless times for a single stimulus to work its way through our attentional system, into our short-term or working memory, and finally to our long-term memory. All of that is only half the equation, too, as a memory lays dormant until we need to recall it, with this recall requiring a similar chain reaction of lighting neurons and synaptic activity. This results in some fascinating phenomena where memories that are stored are almost always slightly removed from the "pure" sensory input at the beginning of this chain reaction. We rarely remember anything in verism, seemingly relying on an acceptably low level of corruption to inform the truthfulness of what we recall. As you can probably guess, this opens up a scientific and philosophical minefield with implications ranging as far and wide as the objective trustworthiness of witnesses to crimes, the effectiveness of traditional educational exam structures, and the legitimacy of psychedelic experiences.

Designing for Intuition and Predictability

You've seen a lot of challenging and competing concepts already in this chapter. Firstly, you know that practice and repetition allow for automaticity, which in turn allows us to perform tasks and skills that were previously arduous and taxing without even consciously thinking about it. You also know that learning requires deeper levels of processing and more meaningful interactions. However, this all seemingly flies in the face of wanting to create simple, low-impact interfaces. How do you take these concepts and use them effectively and responsibly? The answer, rather paradoxically, is to start from a position of not really *needing* learnability.

Meeting Expectations

In the previous chapter, you looked at conventions and signifiers in some detail. Conventions are integral to providing a usable experience that doesn't require learning. While you still have to consider things like working memory capacity and limiting options, and you would quite likely benefit in some way from a person remembering their experience with your work, you don't have to worry about presenting novel concepts. Conventions by their very nature require little learning; they're accepted norms, after all, and it's quite likely that people who find their way to your product use other products where these conventions also exist.

You also know that signifiers help convey potentially complex possibilities through much simpler abstractions. While the first few encounters with a signifier *will* require some kind of encoding, re-coding, and storage of the represented concept, future encounters with the signifier will require much less cognitive overhead, provided that they're consistent and predictable.

And it's this *predictability* that you're most interested in when it comes to creating interfaces that can be intuited rather than learned. Whether it's through convention, past experience, or exposure to your signifiers and system concepts, people will build expectations about what is possible in an environment and what certain qualities of certain elements might signify. It's here that you encounter one of the most important concepts you'll see when it comes to design cognition: the humble *mental model.*

Mental Models

A mental model is the culmination of all of the assumptions and intuitions an individual holds about a system, including how its constituent parts perform and combine to make up a *whole*. Mental models are often simplified, zoomed-out assumptions (Norman, 1988) and rely heavily on heuristics and often metaphor. We tend to form mental models of many of the core aspects of our lives, including social dynamics, sociological and political ideologies, economics, and scientific and mathematical utilities. Our mental models have a huge say in how we perceive the world, yet they are flexible and malleable in nature, constantly shifting as we better grasp the world around us. We can also quite easily use our mental models to our own detriment.

Far too often we limit our perception of situations in our life based on a number of our existing mental models. Our worldview biases our perspective and can often lead to myopic reasoning, stubbornness, and dissonance. In the same vein, our unique combination of mental models can result in some quite innovative and refreshing ideas. Approaching a visual design problem with the mental models of cognitive psychology, for example, can lead to some rather creative, human-centered work. Similarly, approaching the same problem with the mental models of an economist might lead to a very different, equally interesting result.

Most importantly, mental models inform what people *believe to be possible* within a system or environment. Part of someone's mental model of a shopping site might be *if I click the Add to Cart button, this item will go in my shopping cart* or *if I click the Publish button, my work will be live straight away*. It might also be something much vaguer, like *I could use this to edit my next video project* or *I can invite my whole team to this and collaborate in real time*. This might never be expressly or explicitly communicated to someone, but it's inferred and expected by their previous interactions and perception of the interface or environment they're exposed to. As we adhere to these expectations, we're able to present intuitive, seamless environments. Imagine how you'd feel in an environment where every expectation you had was in some way incorrect—say, a hard wooden floor was suddenly bouncy and squishy, or a glass full of ice and water was somehow hot to the touch. Think how disorienting and confusing this would be to navigate. Suddenly hot things are cold and cold things are hot; every interaction is a surprise, and you cannot trust your intuition or predictive cognition. This would be a disaster to have to navigate, and you'd use a huge amount of cognitive energy to process the levels of dissonance to which you've been exposed.

This is the kind of environment we create when we defy convention too often. When *everything* is a novel experience, nothing can be predicted, and we create an environment full of dissonance, with possibilities and interactions that must be learned and memorized to be effective. The backbone of seamless design is the idea that intuition outdoes memorization. This idea forms the very basis of usability, and we rely on it every time we turn on a device and attempt to navigate designed environments. Thus, when we explore the need for learnability, we should assume that we've already ruled out the potentiality of making something intuitive. That is to say that either (a) the concept we're conveying has no universal signifier or intuitive mental model around it— think early touch device or newer, purely gestural interfaces—or (b) that the unintuitive mental model we're proposing represents an advantage that makes it worth learning. As you explored in Chapter 2, the acceptance among a population of a particular pattern or signifier portrays an extremely valid argument for convention; however, countless innovations, including the touch interfaces that revolutionized modern technology, would have never occurred if we *always* relied on or settled upon such conventions.

Common Mental Models

Many of the most universal interface concepts exist to provide an intuitive experience by making use of heuristics and real-world metaphors. Ideas such as the file and folder structure seen in most operating systems—or even the copy/cut/paste edit actions we see as universal when dealing with data such as text or images—are stellar examples of taking somewhat universal concepts from the real world and abstracting away the complexities of a system to present a more intuitive, predictable model. Let's take a look at some of the key concepts we encounter in digital products and how they've been abstracted in ways that encourage the forming of predictable mental models.

The Storage and Retrieval of Files or Data

A classic example of a conceptual model creating a predictable mental model is that of a computer's folder and file structure (Figure 3-1). While our data isn't actually stored on tiny sheets of paper and placed in tiny physical folders inside our computers—as fun as that imagery might be—we recognize the metaphor and can build up a mental model to help us intuit behavior and possibilities within this conceptual model. The mental model here usually includes things like "this data (documents, website, etc.) lives in this container (folder, tab, etc.)." For the most part, an underlying model of the deeper system is not required, and we defer to the simpler, more recognizable conceptual model.

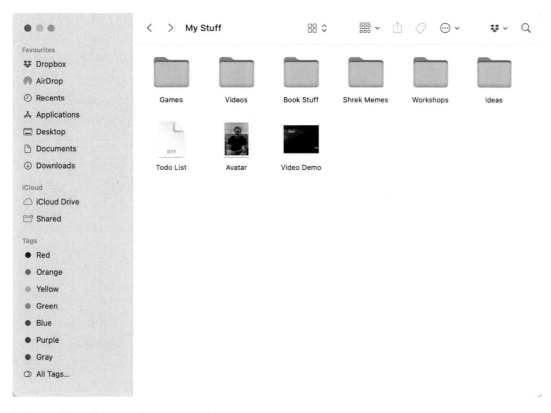

Figure 3-1. *MacOS's file and folder structures*

While a computer doesn't have a bunch of physical folders that store physical documents, the design of the interface abstracts the system's storage into an understandable model of the real world. Even if someone *was* to believe that computers performed this physical storage on our behalf, it really doesn't matter that they're wrong. Their model of the system is effective enough for them to never have to question its deeper workings. For someone who has to deal with the inner workings of a system—say, a computer technician or an operating system engineer—their model will be clearly different. In this case, they likely must have a deeper understanding of the machinations of the system—that is, the fact that computers use digital storage, encoding, and decoding for data storage and retrieval—as opposed to the shallower understanding provided by the file/folder metaphor.

Similarly, when it comes to storing and retrieving data within, for example, a web or mobile application, the metaphors used to communicate an adequate model of the system don't necessarily need to inform people of the underlying server or database structure. In fact, one of the biggest mistakes we can make (as touched on in Chapter 1) is assuming that people external to our organization will have a similar understanding of our category structure as us and our teammates. This also applies when communicating the models of our systems. If we assume that the underlying data structure, such as the schema of our database, is the best way to structure data externally, then we run the risk of communicating a too-technical, overly literal model. Where data is stored and how it's sent there is usually of no concern to someone who just wants to manipulate or store it. An extremely common oversight is to not abstract your system's structure into a clearer conceptual model. Sometimes this can be as simple as renaming a verbose error message to a more straightforward *Oops! That message failed to send. Try again!*— other times it can be obfuscating huge chunks of your system model behind simple and effective metaphors, just like the file and folder model we're so adept at navigating.

Sending and Receiving Communication

One of the most successful conceptual models is that of the humble email inbox. Similar to the file and folder structure explored above, email inboxes mimic a real-world concept—although I can't say I've ever actually interacted with a real-life inbox—and adheres to a set of qualities observed in the real-world object to ensure familiarity and predictability. A real inbox on your desk contains letters, notes, and other forms of information that might be relevant to you.

In the *olden days*, when you'd sit down at your desk to work—if you were a *very important business person*, at least—you'd find your inbox full of things that might need your attention. You might then quickly glance through everything in there, file away items of importance, discard stuff that doesn't matter or doesn't need to stick around, and even label or mark up certain items that might require further action. You can do all of this in many digital inboxes too. Take Gmail (Figure 3-2), for example: you have a list of messages, sorted by most recently received (just like your latest message in a physical inbox would be placed at the top), alongside the ability to do things like archive, delete, annotate, and reply.

Figure 3-2. *Gmail's inbox broadly behaves like an old physical inbox you'd find on someone's desk*

This inbox model became so universally adopted that it's essentially the default structure for all types of messaging applications. However, as the world moves towards more real-time communication, and more and more of our interactions take place in the digital sphere, messaging applications have brought in other conceptual models to embrace this more ephemeral, transient means of digital communication.

A great example of this is *emoji reactions*. Seen commonly in workplace apps like Slack, and making their way through almost every personal messaging application in recent years, emoji reactions provide a conceptual model that's somewhat akin to *body language*. This might sound like a strange claim, but think about it: when we have real-world, face-to-face conversations with people, we almost always communicate feelings—agreement, disagreement, disgust, adulation—through our *physical* reactions just as much as our *verbal* ones. If we see a message thread as more akin to a conversation than the stuffy confines of a business inbox back-and-forth, then we are almost completely missing this kind of conversational metadata that we provide through body language. Emoji reactions (Figure 3-3) give us a lightweight and more immediate means of expressing wordless response. While not *specifically* a mental model of any kind of real-world object, they bring a facsimile of an extremely important real-world concept into the digital realm.

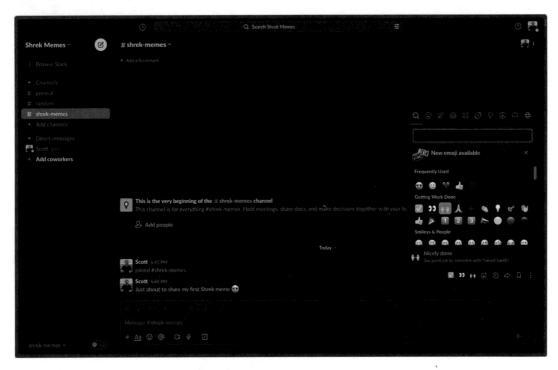

Figure 3-3. *Emoji reactions in Slack*

The Creation and Manipulation of Media

Design products, like Figma in Figure 3-4, portray a "canvas"-centric interface containing features such as a pen tool, pencil tool, and various shape-drawing options.

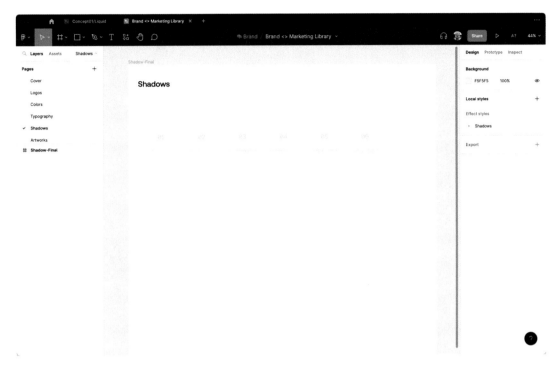

Figure 3-4. *Figma's canvas-centric model and shape-drawing tools*

This makes Figma, and design tools like it, conducive to a mental model of the tools we use to create and draw in the real world.

Adobe's Lightroom (Figure 3-5) uses language and concepts related to the analogue world of developing film photography, again allowing for the application of a real-world mental model.

Figure 3-5. *Adobe Lightroom*

Lightroom has distinct modes such as "Library" and "Develop," using labeling that would fit the mental models of someone already familiar with the medium. If you remember back to Chapter 1, you'll also appreciate how the splitting of the app into these modalities is great for chunking and plays into our natural proclivities to categorize and group objects in our environment.

Finally, Blackmagic Design's DaVinci Resolve (Figure 3-6) provides tools such as a "razor" tool—harking back to the days where movie reels were manually sliced and spliced.

Figure 3-6. *Blackmagic Design DaVinci Resolve*

These, of course, only begin to scratch the surface of some of the ways complex interfaces communicate conceptual models, but it does show how such interfaces harness potential real-world metaphors, especially in the realms of media creation and manipulation.

Designing Learnability

Modern products and interfaces are often hugely complex beasts—there's no changing this. Often the best we can do with our skills is to ensure that this inherent complexity is managed and explained in ways that, over time, bridge any gaps in someone's mental model of our systems. This is where the idea of *learnability* comes in to play. While convention and signifiers can communicate many functions of an interface at a glance, there will always be times when we need to work around an idiosyncrasy of our system. In these cases, there's often no means of communication that can 100% intuitively demonstrate a potential action. Herein lies a probable "gap" in a mental model. The system does something in a certain way, which is difficult to explain using conventional interface components, thus creating an ambiguous "smudge" in a person's mental model of the system. Our priority in this situation is to slowly and purposefully bridge that gap—to sharpen the smudge, if you will—so that the human mental model of our system becomes more useful.

So, how do we get there? First and foremost: Start from a seamless and intuitive baseline. Yes, I've said this dozens of times already, and yes, I will continue to say this, but *start simple*. Make sure that you're giving people the best possible starting point by leaning on convention, meticulously designing for grouping and categorization, encouraging focus by limiting distractions, and presenting solid conceptual models full of metaphors and signifiers that you consistently reinforce. If you do this, once you uncover those inevitable gaps and smudges in people's mental models of your product, you put yourself in the best position to ask for the attentive, deeper processing that's required to learn your unique concepts.

I want to present some principles for fostering learnability within a designed environment. This isn't going to be a simple checklist that you can mindlessly pass through, and it requires a lot of top-down enforcement—these are principles for an environment and are broad enough to govern your entire approach to design—but they're essential to providing the kind of environment that sets people up for success when things are different, difficult, or confusing.

Forgive Mistakes

Whenever we encounter something new, we're faced with a certain degree of trepidation that is usually relative to the complexity of the thing we're trying to comprehend. In the case of a relatively complex interface, one of the main sources of worry is that we'll accidentally delete or corrupt important information. A powerful solution to this can be seen in the—thankfully increasingly more commonplace—implementation of *undo* functionality for destructive tasks. When you looked at GitHub's Danger Zone approach to repository deletion back in Chapter 1, you saw an attempt to preempt and inform destructive behavior. What you didn't see is any level of forgiveness *after* the fact. Contrast this with Figure 3-7, which shows Gmail's undo functionality after having sent an email.

Figure 3-7. *After sending an email in Google Inbox, the sending is briefly delayed and you have the option to "undo" the action. This is useful if/when you spell someone's name wrong or accidentally "reply all" with some juicy office gossip*

I think we've all encountered a situation where we've sent an important email only to realize the second we hit send that it contains something less than professional—say, forgetting to attach a file or spelling the recipient's name incorrectly. This "forgiveness" shown by Gmail allows us to rectify our mistake like it never happened. This approach allows us to foster an environment wherein people finding their footing can explore and test their assumptions with less trepidation.

Unfortunately, the "are-you-extremely-very-sure-you-absolutely-want-to-do-this" obstruction is still a super common paradigm in interface design, which means that when we *do* offer undo functionality, it's quite likely we have to show and/or explain that it's possible. The "forgiving" model of change management is a far superior approach in relation to fostering an empowering and positive environment. When we're new to something, we *will* make mistakes—and we don't suddenly become "not new" to something as soon as we've gone through some fancy post-signup onboarding or snoozed through a webinar. How your interface handles mistakes directly impacts the learnability of the concepts within. We spend much of our lives learning through exploration and direct manipulation, and testing how things react and respond. In this modern age, where data storage and retrieval is exceptionally cheap and state management solutions are seemingly infinite, there's absolutely no excuse to continue with archaic, irresponsible handling of such important tasks.

Mindful Design Principle: Forgive Mistakes   ABU: Always be undoing. Mistakes are punished implicitly when actions cannot be undone or reverted. No amount of pre-emptive warning makes up for a lack of post-action rectification. Let people make mistakes, insulate them from their own errors, and never ever ever assume someone is "stupid" because they don't use your interface in the ways in which you expect them to.

Provide Positive Feedback

Enjoyment is one of the most powerful learning tools there is. When we encounter something that makes us react positively, we more readily remember not only the result, but also the actions. Our emotional state has been shown to have a notable impact on how well we remember an activity or action and, especially in a self-initiated, informal learning environment, the intrinsic emotional attachment we have to an object or an idea can be crucial in not only how well we remember it, but also how fondly or vividly. We also remember information more if we're surprised at the point of learning it—something that positive, personality-filled interaction design can actively achieve. This principle is both relatively simple and infinitely complex, namely because we can't ever directly *dictate* the emotion someone may feel at any given time. To some, an animated mascot brimming with energy might be a complete delight, while, to others, it could be seen as tacky and annoying. This is the risk we take when we decide to not go with the middle-of-the-road of our emotional design.

Clearly Communicate State

Application state can broadly be described as a "snapshot" of all the important variables within a system at any given time. These snapshots constitute the purest representation of an application's model and are the most important thing to communicate to someone trying to achieve a goal within it. State is how we let someone know what actions and options are available to them at any given moment. Changes in state are how we let people know the results of their actions or whether or not their actions are still pending. An interface that effectively communicates current state and, just as importantly, effectively transitions *between* states is an interface that is prime for learning.

When we form our mental model of a system through its interface, we're only able to reconcile that model if we actually attempt to *do* the things we *think* we can. If we see, for example, a number field with a range slider under it—sufficiently grouped using proximity, I might add—we might infer that we can change the number by either typing in the input or dragging the slider. However, until we actually *attempt* this change, we simply cannot know for certain. Furthermore, let's say this number and slider represent something such as the saturation of a photograph in an editing app. We're actually reconciling a number of assumptions in one go: first, the assumption that changing the slider will change the number in the input (and vice-versa) and second, that changing either of these fields will result in a perceptible change to the image we're editing.

Let's say we tried to test them, and the change in the image was delayed by a second or two. For the sake of example, let's say it's a rather large image, and processing and displaying this change in saturation takes some time. We're essentially transitioning between three states here: the initial *framed* state, wherein we've made our assumption as to the relationship between controls and their effects; the *transient* state, wherein any of the necessary processing and/or external communication to handle the action occurs; and the *reporting* state, where the results of the attempted action are communicated back to us. When we test an assumption we've made in an environment, the transitions between these states form our reference points. Without these being clear, effective indicators of state, we have little in the way of feedback.

If the transient state was never catered for in our fictional photo editing application (that is, there was no indication the image was loading or processing), we're likely to believe our assumption to be incorrect. Conversely, if we're immediately shown a processing indicator upon making our change, we're clearly shown this transient state and know that we need to wait a short time for our assumption to be proven correct or not. The overall state of an application at any given time presents us with cues against which we're able to make and test assumptions in context—a vital part of the learning process. Without direct, instant changes in state to help us prove our assumptions, we're usually left questioning the interface or ourselves. If we approach an interface with a set goal—which we almost always do—then how well that interface communicates state determines how well we can perceive the status of our goal. It's useless being able to do something if we don't know when it's done!

Maximize Cognitive Economy

I've already covered this from a number of angles, but cognitive economy is especially important when it comes to designing around learnable concepts. The overall complexity of an interface in any state that requires some form of learning is of huge importance as, by definition, learning requires substantial focus and cognitive effort. By operating at the harmonious baseline of as-low-as-possible cognitive effort that we've discussed throughout this book, we allow someone to devote the required amount of attention to the complex or idiosyncratic features we're asking them to learn.

Allow for Exploration and Experimentation

This last point is more of a culmination of the previous five, yet it bears repeating: an interface that can be effectively explored, where assumptions can be tested without fear of failure or negative reinforcement, is far more learnable than a poorly designed, linear interface. The idea of an explorative interface is something that I think is key to modern interface design. Where applicable, if there are multiple possible ways of achieving a specific result, we move away from the need for linear, learned paths—or user journeys— and toward environments that foster exploration and positive attachments.

The most important thing to consider when we want someone to learn our interfaces is that learning is most effective when done in context, with meaningful, observable results. While the far end of the exploration spectrum would look like a completely open, complex, and exciting environment, in interface design, we'll likely spend most of our time operating at the shallower end with "guided exploration" our likely optimal point. By allowing someone to experience *how* things work without removing them too far from their usual contexts (you'll dig into this in the next section on onboarding) and clearly communicating the results of interaction, we put ourselves in the most optimal position to have our interface paradigms codified and better remembered.

In Part 2 of this book, you'll start tying all these ideas together in the form of designing effective environments and dissecting the interactions that occur within them. However, for the sake of the learning experience, it's important that there exists some breathing room within which people can carve their own path through our interfaces and toward their goals. By embracing the idea that we can cater both efficiency and exploration, and judging the balance we need between the two in any given situation, we set ourselves up not only to create a great learning environment, but also to create a great interface as a whole.

Levels of Processing

The "funnel" of memory from sensory input to long-term storage is far from a constant, invariable, or linear process. Instead, it's affected by seemingly infinite variables. Everything from our emotional attachment to the stimuli we're presented with to how long we wait to fall asleep after processing a stimulus can have a huge impact on the "quality" of the memory we store for that particular item. One of the most tested theories of memory "quality" is that—rather than memories strictly following an encoding, or stores/structures, process—they're directly dependent on the *depth* of processing performed at the time (Craik and Tulving, 1975).

In their 1975 study, Fergus I.M. Craik and Endel Tulving posited that when we perform deep, semantic processing—such as giving meaning to or creating associations with new information—we create "stronger" memories that are easier to recall. The implications of this study, along with a study three years prior that formulated much of the early workings of this theory (Craik and Lockhart, 1972), are rather fascinating. The notion that deeper processing of information encourages stronger memorization is the foundation of many learning techniques, such as mind maps and the famous "put-it-in-your-own-words" approach of the Feynman Technique. But what implication does this have on our approach to design?

Do Make Me Think

Quite simply, sometimes we just need to slow down and *think* when we're using an interface. The old adage of purely intuitive and completely friction-free experiences being the pinnacle of usability, while apt and still extremely relevant, doesn't cover all of our bases. For learnable concepts, a certain degree of friction—or at least a slowing down of the fast-paced, bottom-up autopilot to encourage more top-down, deliberate thinking—can actually be a huge help. By gracefully or enjoyably *impeding* progress or thoroughly encouraging someone to interact with a complex feature in a meaningful way, we can go some way to, hopefully, ensuring that concept is better remembered. There's a palpable degree of irony—if not flagrant hypocrisy—in advocating this approach in a book about design's role in cognitive economy, but this is an optimistic, long-game technique. In slowing things down, just a touch, the first few times a difficult or idiosyncratic interaction is taking place, an interface can help us better remember how to perform it during subsequent uses.

Of course, the trade-off here is that the learning *must* be worth the time. Spending energy, effort, and time learning something novel only for the result to be underwhelming or obtuse is a surefire way to create frustration, distraction, and cognitive dissonance. Semantic processing is something that requires more focus and more mental energy to perform. To request this from someone is something that requires heavy justification.

Where and When We Teach

One of the key factors in teaching the concepts of a system is deciding on *when* and *where* we do so. With the typical Create/Read/Update/Delete products and interfaces we usually encounter, we generally have a few key areas where we can provide educational information or take people through guided interactions. When deciding what approach we take in guidance, it's important to avoid anything that remotely resembles information overload. When presented with new concepts, the user is likely to feel some form of blank-slate anxiety, so compounding this by asking for a lot of upfront effort in order to learn our concepts can quite quickly result in someone abandoning our product altogether. Let's explore these key areas of guidance and, in the process, provide a number of "checkpoints" across which we can spread the effort of learning.

Onboarding

While more open, explorative interfaces are key to continued learning and creativity, throwing someone into such an environment without any priming or initial context will almost always be overwhelming. An extremely common practice in modern product design involves taking someone through an initial "onboarding" phase, usually straight after signing up for a service. This phase is often designed to introduce people to the concepts and key components of the product and interface, usually by separating them out in a somewhat linear fashion. It's extremely tempting to use onboarding as a means of communicating *all* of the key concepts of your product and equally tempting to isolate these into their own dedicated "steps." However, we must be careful to avoid de-contextualizing actions. While onboarding is fantastic for set-and-forget style settings, it's important to avoid removing components too far from their usual contexts, and even more important to avoid falling into the trap of mistaking "instruction" for teaching.

As discussed, the more actively we engage with something, the more likely we are to remember it. This makes onboarding that contains some form of interaction essential. While it's common to see flows like that shown in Figure 3-8, simple "stepped" screens that introduce the key features of an app without any actual interaction—labeled as "onboarding"—are really an extension of an app's marketing at best.

Figure 3-8. *Google Drive's onboarding for their iPad app is just three stepped screens of informational content*

While this approach isn't necessarily bad practice, it is pure instruction, which is not conducive to learning and often acts as a barrier to getting up and running an interface.

A technique employed by most onboarding processes is that of *progressive disclosure*. Progressive disclosure, as the name suggests, involves gradually or contextually disclosing new information and features to someone as they progress through the layers of a system. While progressive disclosure is a relatively broad interaction design concept and is not without its downfalls, its use in early-stage onboarding highlights many of its key benefits. If our onboarding process is the only real point in our interfaces where we restrict exploration and impose a somewhat linear flow, it puts us in control of the order in which we "disclose" our information. Again, it's important to be careful not to remove components too far from their usual contexts, but by limiting interactions early on we're able to take advantage of this initial, controlled stage of learning.

Good onboarding will not only introduce the core concepts that form the underlying model of a system, but it will also allow people to explore their usage and causality. As examined previously, testing assumptions is a core component of effective learning, and a solid onboarding phase must still allow for the flow of "assume, test, reflect."

An effective onboarding process will have people using our interfaces to perform real actions with components that communicate their effects clearly. Just as you saw in the previous chapter with Horizon: Zero Dawn's use of yellow as a signifier for climbable objects, discovering this association for ourselves is a powerful way of learning how an interface communicates its causality. Now, unless we're designing a game, we likely lack a lot of the intrinsic motivation that's required for such an openly explorative onboarding process, but we can still garner some valuable insight from it—namely, that we're able to codify and associate causality without much in the way of explicit instruction.

An onboarding process that focuses on presenting key features in context will almost always outperform one that is purely instructional.

In-App Guidance

Aside from the focused, pre-emptive teaching that we often attempt to perform in typical onboarding processes, an often-overlooked form of teaching is "in-app" teaching. There are many possible ways of implementing this approach, but the most common take the form of *interactive tours* and *contextual help*—and often the in-app learning includes both these approaches.

First, interactive tours are similar to onboarding in that they're intended to drip-feed information and progressively disclose features, yet they differ in the fact that they're *usually* only initiated when it's clear that someone wants to start a complex chain of interactions. It's important to note that in-app guidance can *be* your onboarding process. In fact, it's extremely common to forgo a "controlled" onboarding process and present a fully functional interface up front and ready to explore, with in-app guidance scattered around where necessary. This approach to guidance is extremely useful if your surface-level interactions are relatively simple to understand and mostly intuitive, and the complexity of your interface lies a little deeper. You get to present a simple and concise interface up front and then interject when you feel the need arises.

A great example of this can be seen in Adobe Photoshop's in-app guidance. I'd go as far to say this in-app guidance is one of the most effective onboarding experiences of any complex product I've studied. When you first open Photoshop, you're presented with the Learn screen, seen in Figure 3-9. This screen alone utilizes *so many* of the concepts discussed in this chapter. First, the Photoshop team has identified some common tasks that people picking up the product for the first time might want to perform, such as removing imperfections from an image, changing the color of certain objects, and duplicating objects within a scene. This is an application that considers our *goals* from the very beginning.

Figure 3-9. *Adobe Photoshop's Learn screen*

In addition to giving us the option of selecting one of these goals, the preview image for each goal actually shows a before/after comparison so we get to see the type outcome we might expect. This answers some of our most important questions right off the bat. The "try-it-in-the-app-right-now" microcopy is a descriptive, arguably even exciting, call to action.

Once we've selected our example, we're shown the screen in Figure 3-10. It's the Photoshop interface, fully explorable, but with a sample file opened already for us, a Learn panel open on the right providing us with detailed text, and a succinct tool tip telling us what tool to select.

Figure 3-10. *Photoshop's interface with in-app guidance*

In this case, it's the Spot Healing brush tool. As an added bonus, when we hover over the tool in the sidebar, we're shown a video of it in action (Figure 3-11), which allows us to see both its common usage and the potential results we can achieve.

Figure 3-11. *Hovering over any tool for a short while shows an example video of the tool in use*

And once we select the tool, we're given not only instructions as to how to customize it, but also a *reason why* we might want to do it. We're asked to change our brush settings (Figure 3-12), and we're told it's because we "want a brush that'll just cover the splotches on the shirt."

Figure 3-12. *After selecting a tool, Photoshop's interface walks us through configuring it*

This reasoning is so important. By explaining *why* a certain parameter is being changed, not only is the causality of the settings explained to us, it's also related back to a specific goal. In this case, the sliders, or text inputs, will change our brush hardness and size, and the reason we're doing this is to "just cover" the splotches. We already stated our goal when we chose this particular tutorial to follow, so by relating configuration back to that goal, we're left knowing that these settings changes are far from arbitrary practice.

Finally, once we've set and configured our tool, we're shown how to use it (Figure 3-13).

Figure 3-13. *Tool tip instructions on how to use the selected tool*

This is truly exemplary in-app education, and I think the Photoshop team deserves immense credit for their implementation of it. They've just taken us through an educational experience that first focused on our goals, then presented us with guidance, persisted with us when we decided we wanted to go off and explore, explained *why* we're changing the settings we are, and helped us perform the actions we were trying to do, all in the context of the full, unrestricted interface Photoshop provides. We've processed these concepts on a deeper level because (a) they're related to our goals, and (b) we're given some short guidance before actually using them. We've performed the same actions—in the same context—as we would if we were to do this "for real" with our own image and, quite wonderfully, we've been allowed to explore the interface away from the guidance whenever we felt like it.

Contextual help is a very similar concept, the main difference being it generally highlights single interactions, elements, or structures preemptively. The tool tip in Figure 3-14, from Google Docs, provides a good example of contextual help—highlighting the function of the icon while simultaneously showing the keyboard shortcut one could use to perform this action faster in the future.

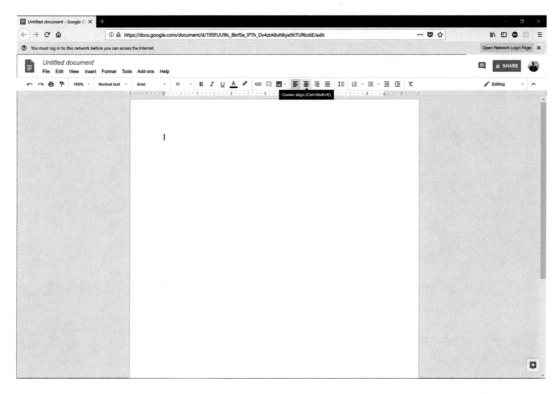

Figure 3-14. *Google Docs' contextual tooltip—describing the function of an icon and also showing the keyboard shortcut to perform this action faster next time*

Contextual learning is great for subtle reminders or pre-emptive hints. Using small tool tips, coupled with excellent microcopy, we can provide guidance and feedback throughout our interface without glaring, attention-grabbing practices.

A rather infamous example of the contextual help approach, which I believe feasibly set the "interactive assistant" phase back by at least a decade, is Microsoft's Clippy mascot from back in the early days of Microsoft Office and its "Office Assistants."

Clippy is an astounding example of attention-grabbing and obstruction gone haywire—even if the underlying goals and ideas were commendable. The goal of Clippy was to assist people with everyday tasks, such as writing a letter, by popping up in the corner of the screen if it "detected" behavior that suggested such activity. I'm going to put what's left of my reputation on the line here: I think Clippy was great. At least conceptually. If the Office Assistants had been designed differently, their process of offering pre-emptive guidance and useful information when deemed contextually appropriate to do so could have been incredibly useful. As it turns out, Clippy proved too much of a pest, its annoyance outweighing its utility, and it was eventually removed from Microsoft's software, leaving behind only a legacy of annoyance and an entire category of dank memes.

Many of the same principles from onboarding apply to in-app guidance. When designing such processes, the biggest consideration remains the level of interactivity. As with onboarding, any tour or contextual guide that is focused around performing actions, rather than explaining them, represents an optimal incarnation. As the old adage goes: UI is like a joke—if you have to explain it, it's probably bad. Or so good the peons will never understand it. Or you're inherently a mansplainer and should work on yourself and your outward displays of insecurity before it's too late to be a good person. Where were we again?

Our goal for this type of interaction should always be to allow for an ideal depth of processing to occur. Limiting actions, or directing focus to a specific setting or interaction, and allowing that interaction to be performed and observed is often far more effective than using up valuable space (both physical and cognitive) in an attempt to explain it. As you saw with Photoshop's guidance, it *is* possible to provide an effective, enjoyable learning experience while checking all those boxes.

Establishing Learnability

Considering what you now know about mental models, memory, and learnability, let's put together a practical framework of sorts. While the following steps are multifaceted and will often involve a wide range of design considerations, here's a general, flexible guideline process.

Understand the Models

The first step in designing a learning experience is understanding the various models that may be applied. Generally, you'll be comparing two archetypical models: the *designed* model, which you're in control of, and the *perceived* model, which is what an individual forms of your system through their interpretation of your interface. Both of these models represent an abstraction of the underlying system structure—the designed model being your ideal structure and the perceived model being a perceptual manifestation or translation of the designed model.

Find the Gaps

This is where traditional research methods are your friends. Conducting early-stage usability testing (with, if you remember from Chapter 1, various distractions and simulations of cognitive load) can give a fantastic insight into which areas of your designed model make sense and which cause dissonance or misconception. You'll also likely intuit—or better yet, have market research that shows—the average technical capabilities of your audience, as well as perhaps the apps and services they interact with on a regular basis.

This research should give you hints as to what areas of your designed model are likely to cause the most friction. Anything that breaks the assumed conventions of the apps and real-world tools your audience already uses is going to require some degree of behavioral change. If you can't afford to test in a good environment, using this market research can still give you a good way to understand the potential blanks between your mental model and your perceived model. Make sure to account for the filter of your own biases and that of your team, and only make these assumptions as a last resort.

Understand the Type of Gap

One last consideration before you actually jump in and start designing some lovely learning environments—you need to have a grasp of *why* this dissonance between two models exists. Is it a **knowledge** gap of some kind? For example, if you were designing an Agile-focused project-management app (because apparently you're a masochist), you need to ask if a chunk of your audience does not have the technical knowledge of how Agile works in order to understand your more idiosyncratic concepts. Or is it a **skill** gap of sorts? While the required mechanical skill to use an interface isn't *usually* taxing, if you're working on a game or game-like product, you may actually encounter this kind of gap between models quite often.

A skill gap generally means that some form of practice or repetition is required, and it puts you into the realm of gamification, which is its own beast all together. Aside from knowledge and skill gaps, there are also various **conceptual** gaps. Perhaps your interface handles a common interaction differently from your competitors' or the interfaces your audience are used to interacting with on a daily basis. In this particular case, it's important to show up front that this is an uncommon pattern, and then highlight *why* it's done differently. Figma has, again, another great example of this. Its vector pen tool is quite different from what you get in Figma's competitors. The first few times you attempt to use it can feel quite strange if you're already familiar with the standard approach. Figma pre-empts this with one of their onboarding tooltips (Figure 3-15) by letting you know that "vector networks" are quite different from what you're used to and why you might want to give them a try.

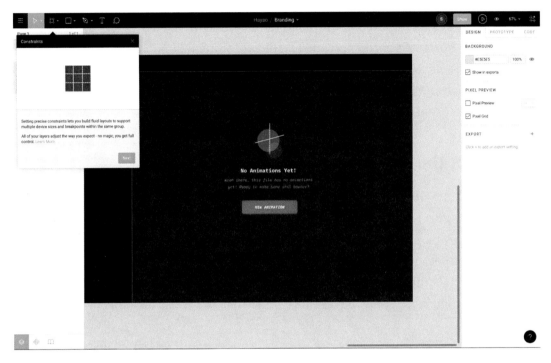

Figure 3-15. *A tooltip in Figma introducing one of its core features*

This not only brings your attention to one of Figma's core features, but it also encourages you to give it a try. Again, my biggest gripe with Figma's approach is there's no "learn-by-doing" to any of this. I'd love to see some form of guided "draw some stuff with the pen tool" process that satisfied a deeper level of processing, but as pre-emptive communication, this approach has its merits. I consider this gap a **convention** gap—a concept or interaction that deviates from standardized convention.

Another conceptual gap emerges when you simply don't have a relevant metaphor or model to apply to a concept. Sometimes, an idea or feature has no real-world comparative and no existing conceptual model—I call this a **null-comparative** gap, but only because I want to be credited for inventing a fancy phrase.

These gaps are pretty exciting because they can often be an indicator of innovation. If you genuinely believe the concept you're trying to convey is important and valuable and there truly exists no possible metaphor or accepted convention, you could be onto a pretty important discovery. Or it could just be a really, really bad idea.

Quite often, the gaps you recognize will be a combination of these. Knowledge and conceptual gaps especially go hand-in-hand more often than not and bridging them requires both providing information and encouraging interaction. The important thing here is not to spend a bunch of time labeling your potential gaps, but to understand the underlying causes behind them. Having this list sets you up perfectly to delve into designing and to asking the most important questions: *where* and *when* do you communicate this?

Decide on the Where and When

I've discussed this step in detail throughout this chapter, so hopefully this is the stage where you can start really utilizing and designing around your knowledge of learning and memory. Depending on the feature and the gap that it presents, you'll want to consider what method best allows you to communicate its use and properties. For important-but-complex features that are usually present in the "default" starting state of the application, it generally makes more sense to tackle these in some form of guided onboarding.

For features that depend on context or application state, contextual help will likely be a great starting point. It might make a lot more sense to only try and teach specific concepts once the context in which they can be performed has been entered (e.g., Photoshop asking us to change our brush settings only when the Spot Healing brush tool was selected).

For more complex, chained interactions, in-app guidance can be extremely useful, especially if it works toward the achievement of a goal. You're encouraged to revisit the relevant sections earlier in this chapter if you want to brush up on any of these learning areas!

Design the Explainers

Now you're really at the fun phase. First, a quick recap on what you've done so far. You've made steps to understand the two models: the designed and the perceived. You've documented potential gaps between the two models. You've attempted to objectively assess whether you *should* bridge the gaps. You've made efforts to understand the type of gaps you might be facing and, finally, you've formulated a plan as to where and when you present the learning information. All that's left for you now is to actually design this stuff.

When doing so, remember that learning by doing is one of the most powerful methods of learning, and I encourage you to, wherever possible, allow for real interaction during your guidance. Exploration will play a role in this too. Quite often you may defer to someone by presenting your concept to them and allowing them to test their assumptions against it. *Always* remember to explore the goals that may underpin these interactions too. If you can link the concept you're teaching back to a possible intrinsic goal, this interaction and its results will be far more meaningful.

This stage is where everything from the previous chapters comes into play—along with your own design skills and the constraints of any style guides or design systems you might have in place. When implementing in-app guidance especially, the Gestalt principles and the von Restorff Effect will greatly inform how you might group a component with its "explainer" and differentiate the explainer from the rest of the environment. These principles go a good way to describing why the typical "tool tip" approach is so ubiquitous in onboarding and guidance design. Your knowledge of attention will also be universally important during this process. As you explored earlier, some creative slowing down can help with learning and memory recall. Although I despise the term, onboarding and in-app guidance can feasibly be described as "attention manipulation" as, in their essence, these experiences attempt to encourage some degree of linearity in our focus.

As is the universal caveat, these processes need to be approached responsibly and with great care for the people we wish to have follow them. Remember the impact that design has on the voice and character of a system. Coupled with excellent microcopy, design can imbue a personality and positivity into our guided interactions that can have a notable impact on retention and recall of information. Finally, and at risk of sounding like a broken record, this guidance should form part of an interface that is operating at a baseline of low cognitive load and clear state communication and is as devoid of overt complexity as is possible. Plastering an already-chaotic interface with tool tips and explainers rarely ends well.

Summary

In this chapter, you explored the various processes behind human learning and memory. I discussed the idea that an active decision to learn is almost always accompanied by a goal of some sort—learning an instrument so you can play your favorite song, for example. I also discussed the important differences between a "learnable" interface (an interface that is designed to be learned) and an educational interface (an interface that is designed to teach), and I limited the discussion primarily to the learnable. Educational applications often involve a highly specialized approach, usually involving an exploration of the intrinsic motivation behind the decision to learn. The design of such would be (and indeed is) the subject of its own entire book.

You first explored that learning, broadly, can be seen as the transference of information from short-term or working memory into your long-term memory structures. This flow is rarely a simple, linear process. You saw the brain as a network of neurons and synaptic connections, with various neural pathways being activated and strengthened through practice and repetition. Through consistent practice, acts and concepts that seem difficult and complex at first can become second nature over time.

The bulk of this chapter was spent discussing the notion of mental models and their resolution against the underlying model of a system. Mental models are abstract representations of how we see the world. Underpinned by our schemas, they represent how we may form our expectations and understanding when interacting with a complex system. Various applications utilize expected mental models to communicate features and functionality. You saw this with the razor tool in video-editing suites and the pen tool in design applications.

I raised the idea that the learnability of an application is largely dependent on how you reconcile the system's underlying features against the mental models that a user might carry into its use. By finding and acknowledging discrepancies that exist between the actual, system model and a person's assumed, mental model, you can look to purposefully bring mental models closer to usable abstractions of the system's workings. You explored that, to do this, the environments you design should forgive mistakes, provide positive feedback, clearly communicate state, maximize cognitive economy, and allow for exploration and experimentation.

You explored where and when to teach the learnable elements and concepts of the interfaces, including linear onboarding processes, which use techniques such as progressive disclosure to slowly introduce people to the more idiosyncratic interface elements. You looked at in-app guidance via Photoshop's fantastic goal-based instruction.

An important consideration when designing learnable interfaces is the general depth of processing that occurs in the learning of an interface element. Shallow processing, often in the form of simple explainer copy or tool tips, can result in poorer learning than deeper processing, such as how Photoshop has us achieving our goals and actually using the elements we're attempting to learn. Shallower processing requires much less cognitive effort, but sometimes we just need to slow things down and ask for a deeper level of processing. This further highlights the importance of ensuring our interfaces are not full of overly complex, esoteric elements that require deeper processing to learn.

Finally, I discussed a framework of sorts to find and understand any gaps between a system's underlying structure and the broad mental models that people might possess based on our design work. This revolved around understanding the system and mental models, finding the gaps between the two, deciding whether a feature's presence justifies the work required to reconcile any gaps, understanding the type of gap (knowledge, skill, or conceptual), deciding where and when to teach the knowledge necessary to bridge the gap, and finally designing the explainers themselves. You'll explore how this process can fit in around various stages of the design process in Part 2.

If you only focus on one thing from this chapter, I propose getting comfortable with the idea of system models, conceptual models, and mental models. Understanding that designers present a conceptual model of a system and that users reconcile their own mental models (and any knowledge they might have of the underlying system) against this is a key factor in designing both intuitive and learnable interfaces. Remember that mental models encompass what people *believe to be possible* within an environment, and that adherence to—or divergence from—these expectations and beliefs can make or break an entire experience.

CHAPTER 4

Expectation and Surprise

Throughout our design process, we need to contend with user expectations. You've already explored how expectations can be shaped by past experiences and accepted conventions, which shape the mental models users bring to our product. The flip side to expectation is *surprise*. It's an emotion that holds a lot of weight, and one that is bandied around in the design world without much thought beyond the surface-level cringiness of overzealous pushing for *surprise and delight*. We should be able to intuit this from our own lived experiences: not all surprises are good. In this chapter, you'll explore the various forms surprise can take and how effectively balancing this against conventional expectations can help you build products that are both seamless and meaningful. But how does surprise even come about?

Our brains are, at least to a degree, prediction machines. As we make our way through life, we start building up schemas and mental models that help us to make sense of the world, make assumptions about how it works, and make predictions about how things in our environment will behave or respond to interaction. While we might want—and often *need*—to believe that these learnings and assumptions are correct, even immutable, we're realistically making a lot of subtly (and not-so-subtly) incorrect assumptions and predictions all the time.

One thing that's fascinating about this area of cognition is that we're *always* updating our understanding of the world. We don't just decide that something is true one day and then live with that fact until we die—even the most conservative, stubborn people still can't escape cognitive inference. Rather, we use our past experiences and a cumulative knowledge of our world to frame subsequent events. If we encounter something we're in any way familiar with, we bring to that encounter certain expectations as to how that thing will behave. Even if we're intimately familiar with our subject, there's an infinitesimal chance that our expectation or prediction will be one hundred percent correct. Our brains are not computers, and there's *always* a margin for error. When this

© Scott Riley 2024
S. Riley, *Mindful Design*, Design Thinking, https://doi.org/10.1007/979-8-8688-0143-3_4

happens, we take that unexpected behavior or information and file it away for future reference. Thus, the more we encounter or interact with something, the higher the fidelity of this mental "store" we have of it and all things related to it.

What Is Surprise?

Surprise is an emotion and is usually the result of some kind of prediction error or schematic violation we experience. We feel surprise to varying degrees whenever we experience something that we don't *expect* to happen. If you remember back to Chapter 1, you explored the idea of a startle reflex: a sudden reaction to unexpected stimuli in our environment that results in our attention being immediately pulled away from our current focus (or current daydreaming) to the source of said stimuli. While the startle reflex could definitely be viewed as a *kind* of surprise, it's more of a defense mechanism than an emotion. Surprise, as opposed to being startled, is multifaceted and much more complex. Depending on the stimulus or information that surprised us, the delta between our expectation and reality, and how important we deem the new experience to be, surprise can be anything from mildly novel through to harrowingly disturbing.

Surprise is what happens when something is sufficiently incongruent, novel, or unexpected such that it may elicit an emotional response within us. When something is sufficiently surprising, it is brought to our attention, just as if a stimulus was emotionally relevant or in some way important to us. Many times we'll encounter something that only slightly deviates from our expectations. Let's say we leave the house and give a wave to our neighbor across the street. We might reasonably expect that neighbor to return the wave with a quick "hello," especially if they regularly greet us as such. If they instead greeted us with a "good morning," while it's not precisely what we expected, we're probably not going to be sufficiently surprised to pay this any heed. However, if our erstwhile amicable neighbor instead ignored us, or even hurled abuse at us, it's quite likely that we'd be surprised to a notable degree. Just like our brains can't go alerting us to every stimuli we encounter—lest we become so overwhelmed with our surroundings we shut down—neither can they go about bringing every minor deviation from our expectations to our conscious attention. We're simply not that good at predicting things, and surrounded by so many inherently unpredictable things, that we'd spend the rest of our days pulled from one stimulus to another.

So, while predictions are always being made, and while expectations will always frame our understanding of the world, there's a threshold below which our brains are happy to just proceed, codify the discrepancy, and stealthily update the models we hold about the world. Beyond this threshold, however, is where things get fun.

Surprise As Novelty

Many artforms, especially those that play out over time, like movies, music, and video games, masterfully play around with our expectations. As we build up our schematic understanding of how something—let's say music—works, we become more readily prepared to expect or believe certain things. Many westerners grow up on a musical diet of structured rhythms in a 4/4 time signature, simple melodies, repeating structures, and predictable harmonies. Through repetition at the macro—in this case, over years of listening to music—and micro—within the confines of a single song or album—levels, we're left expecting to hear certain things when we listen to a piece of music. As an example, many songs are made up of just a few repeating parts that dictate the pieces' *structure*. If we look at western popular music, an extremely common song structure is as follows:

- An **intro** where certain rhythmic, melodic, or harmonic themes are presented and built on.

- A **verse,** where the energy is usually lower and subtler musical elements are used to build up to …

- A **chorus**, quite often preceded by a **pre-chorus** where we experience a crescendo of sorts. This provides the main hook of the track and is usually the part we remember most.

- Another **verse**, similar—often ostensibly the same—as the first.

- The same **chorus**, again often preceded by the same **pre-chorus**.

- A **bridge**, usually a standalone section that deviates most dramatically from all the other parts.

- An **outro**. A denouement to bring the song to a close, often repeating chorus or verse elements to ground the song again in its memorable parts.

This structure, or very slight deviations of it, can be attributed to an astonishingly wide range of modern popular music. It works. Artists know it, record labels know it, producers know it, and we know it.

This predictability isn't necessarily *bad*—it would be doing a lot of talented people a huge disservice to claim such—and while many people don't like or appreciate seemingly formulaic music, there's a reason this structure and the various conventions found within are so prevailing. Musical predictability—that is, the piece we hear adhering to our expectations—feels *nice*. It's comfortable, and while it might initially feel tropey or lacking creativity, there's still a *lot* of subtle surprises, even in the most predictable genres of music. No two choruses are the same, and oftentimes the most memorable hooks from pop tracks come as a result of a low-key verse erupting into a jovial, intense, or otherwise impactful chorus. There's *just enough* schematic violation to keep us listening, but not so much that we're left contemplating the very definition of *music* every time we spin a record. The flip side to this is that it can often feel like once you've heard one song by a particular artist, you've heard them all. We like comfort *and* novelty, and artists are always challenged to find a balance somewhere between the two.

Some people consciously seek out more challenging music where simple, even time signatures are replaced with odd or compound signatures, or where structures are regularly nonlinear and where constituent parts are oftentimes not repeated at all. Now, complexity doesn't magically make music objectively better, but such people might be seeking something more intellectual—eschewing danceable rhythms and singalong potential for rhythmic complexity or lyrical verbosity. In reality, there is no *right* way to enjoy art. While fandom and snobbery can provide their own intoxicating blend of social belonging, schematic adherence, and parasocial relationships, even in the confines of one artform, like music, many different levels of schematic violation are enjoyable to many different people, for many different reasons.

We see this all the time in movies, too. Sit down to an 80s action movie like *Lethal Weapon* or *Beverly Hills Cop* and you know exactly what you're getting: a short intro to set the scene; an action-packed, spectacle-filled middle; and a satisfying end. And lots of explosions. And Danny Glover saying he's *too old for this shit*. Alternatively, jump into a psychological thriller or murder mystery and you're going to have a much less predictable experience. In fact, that's *exactly what you want*—sitting down to a three-hour, tension-filled movie screening only to guess the killer after the first five minutes means you're either a genius detective or the movie sucks. Or both. In a roundabout way, you're *expecting the unexpected*, so imagine the chagrin if you get something bland

and predictable. Thus—deep breath now—by expecting the unexpected but getting the expected you're actually getting what you didn't expect and this feels bad. But if you expected the expected and got the expected, then you're getting what you expected and this feels good. Got that? Perfect.

Needless obtusity aside; the main point here is that our threshold for *enjoyable schematic violation* varies tremendously and contextually. Sometimes we want nothing more than to be surprised, to be taken on an emotional rollercoaster, to be challenged intellectually, and to experience the abundant spectrum of human capability. Other times we just want to eat popcorn and watch explosions. Or dance around the kitchen to Beyoncé.

Consider too that surprise is, by our very nature, attention-grabbing. The more prediction errors or the deeper the schematic violation we experience, the more our attention is grabbed. And just as we don't want to spend all our lives in task-positive, focused mindsets and conversely require daydreaming and downtime of the default mode network, so too do we seemingly need *comfortably predictable* media as much as we need to experience art that shifts our perceptions and poses difficult questions. Surprise is the fulcrum of these experiences, but that doesn't mean that we need to manufacture or seek it at every possible turn. That's just exhausting.

Prediction and Cognitive Economy

One fascinating aspect of the brain's approach to energy conservation can be found in how it *predicts* outcomes. While the biases and heuristics touched on in Chapter 1 show how we conserve energy in decision-making by deferring complex processing to more immediate heuristics, that's not the only way our brains take shortcuts when assessing our environment.

The theory of *predictive coding* proposes that our brains are constantly making predictions as we process our environments. When the brain receives sensory input, it's ticking away and predicting outcomes, so that when these outcomes are satisfied, a lot of the hard work has already been done. Our brains don't always get predictions right, though. Sometimes we don't have a sophisticated enough experience with the stimuli we're experiencing. For example, if you'd never seen a dog before, how could you possibly predict its behavior? Or what noise it might make? It's a novel experience—which our brains often *love*, by the way—and you're on new ground, constantly updating your schematic understanding of this furry friend in front of you. If you have a certain experience with this dog, it will shape the predictions made during your next encounter with a dog, which could go very differently. Maybe your first encounter was with a boisterous, overly-friendly dog: lots of tail wags, lots of excited barking, lots of jumping up and affection. If your next encounter is with a more timid or reactive dog, you're going to be surprised when certain predictions aren't met. Maybe this dog shies away from you or shows its discomfort by baring its teeth. Now you have two radically different experiences with the same animal. As you encounter more and more dogs, you'll start to build a more sophisticated understanding of their behaviors, thus giving you a much deeper "pool" from which to base your expectations and inferences.

This process makes use of *Bayesian inference*, a fancy phrase that basically means *using stuff you already know to predict what might happen now*. The more we interact with a diverse range of dogs, the more we build up a pool of knowledge from which to make our predictions, and the more we interact with any specific, unique dog, the more their specific, unique behaviors will contribute to this pool of knowledge. Essentially, we combine what we already know with what we're currently experiencing to make predictions on the fly.

Some predictive coding studies even suggest that the brain preemptively engages neural networks associated with *future* outcomes. If you reach out to touch this book—or whatever device you're reading the digital version of it on—your brain will actually start activating the neural networks associated with the sensation of touching it *before* you have the sensory experience of doing so. This is known as *motor-sensory prediction* and it relies on your past experiences with similar objects and interactions to predict or infer any subsequent stimuli. Unless you've skipped randomly to this page, you've probably touched this book and turned many pages (or touched your reading device and pressed many buttons to scroll through the content) since you picked it up (thanks for that, by the way). You're not likely to have a suddenly different experience with this page than with any other page, or with this book in general compared to other books. There aren't any pop-up surprises or glitter bombs or anything *exciting* like that here, so there's not going to be any prediction errors aside from the odd unfortunate papercut, or if you accidentally drop the book on your face trying to stay awake. In many situations, though, results and outcomes are far less rote or predictable, and that's where things can really take us by surprise.

Surprise as Prediction Error

While our brain is making all of its predictions, it appears to be actively seeking out *more surprising* outcomes. If there's enough of a prediction error, the stimuli responsible for it will eventually be brought to our conscious attention. Thus, to state the completely obvious: *surprising things grab our attention*. Shocking revelation, right?

There's actually a lot to unpack from that ironically quotidian conclusion, though. Firstly, you know that when something is brought to our active attention, we're more likely to codify it into our long-term memory. Additionally, you also know that we're more likely to interact with the source of the stimuli at a deeper level. Finally, you know that for every switch of attentional focal point, we deplete our mental resources. So *surprising events are inherently more memorable, more learnable, and more costly to experience.*

This presents something of a quandary: by actively subverting someone's expectations or predictions we can seemingly improve the chances of information being retained, concepts being learned, or experiences being remembered. What's more, the bigger the delta between the prediction and the experience—that is to say, the *size* of the prediction error—the more impactful the experience. Imagine how you'd feel if, after years of sitting on the same chair, one day you went to sit on it and just completely fell through it as though it was a holographic projection. You've had the same experience every day for years, and then suddenly something so overwhelmingly *not that* happens. While your first reaction might be to wonder who has the unique combination of malice and technical knowledge to pull off such a prank, one thing is for sure: you won't be forgetting that experience any time soon. The difference between prediction and reality was just too stark.

It's not just the experience or stimuli itself that's more memorable during surprising events, either. Many people have reported being able to vividly remember highly specific details of their surroundings or associated events during an extremely surprising world or life event. I still remember explicit details about where I was, who I was with, and what I was doing when I found out that Donald actual Trump became the actual President of the actual United States of America. An almost violently shocking experience with immense implications. Not only was this event itself understandably memorable, but the cataclysmically dumbfounding moment made everything around it more memorable too. Many people have similar experiences to share; remembering in vivid detail where they were when a notable—and notably surprising—world event happened.

Schemas

In Chapter 1, I spoke about the mind's need to categorize. As a result of categorizing, we create and reference various *schemas*. A schema is a mental structure that consists of "rules" against which we can judge objects or stimuli from our environment. Schemas are similar, at least in definition, to the mental models covered in Chapter 3. They both represent structures of the mind that allow for relation, abstraction, and categorization.

To hopefully disambiguate: when I talk about mental models in this book, I'm talking specifically about a person's perception and understanding of an underlying *system*. While "system" is a vague and all-encompassing concept, most of the time this will refer to *the thing you're designing*—namely a product, service, or platform. A mental model in this context is a cognitive structure that a person uses to make sense of what's in front of them. It informs their expectations and beliefs about what is possible within their environment, what actions they can perform, and even what they can achieve with the thing they're using.

Contrast this to schemas, which represent a broader set of rules, abstractions, or features of a category. Schemas also inform our expectations, but they're broader and usually refer to how we navigate the world. Sometimes schemas are described as mental models that have made their way into our long-term memory. There's nothing particularly *wrong* with that definition, but for our purposes, it's better to have these specific definitions—schemas, if you will—to avoid mixing concepts. Just know that if you do go off and do your own research on either schemas or mental models, you'll likely want to broaden your definitions from the ones presented here.

When it comes to categorization, schemas represent all the different characteristics that might describe members of a particular category. We subsequently use these rules and characteristics to classify something as a *member* or *nonmember* of said category (technically this is not a binary yes/no classification; more on that in a sec). This approach to categorization allows us to quickly make decisions and predictions against objects and stimuli in our environment—based on traits like physical appearance, tactile response, and auditory input. Furthermore, in developing rules and expectations for categories, we also appear to form *prototypical* members of categories based on our schema.

As part of an important and intriguing series of experiments around categorization starting in the 1970s, Eleanor Rosch presented and evolved her Prototype Theory. The Prototype Theory suggests that, rather than simply having a binary yes/no determinator as to whether or not an object or stimulus is a member of a category (it either meets the rules or it doesn't—also known as the *Aristotelian Model*), we adopt the notion of *prototypes* (Rosch, 1973)—basing category membership on comparisons to central members that most closely adhere to the schema of our categories. Rosch's examples include the category of *furniture,* where it was shown that objects such as chairs and sofas are deemed "more central" (Rosch, 1975) to the furniture category than, say, stools or lamps. Thus, we can position chairs and sofas as "privileged" members of the category against which membership can be weighed for less prototypical potential members.

The implications of this approach to graded categorization are substantial. The idea that categorization is central to our comprehension of the world is rarely disputed, but the idea that we compare *members* of categories to help determine the validity of other prospective members presents some fascinating insights into our nature. Particularly, it goes some way in explaining why our existence and understanding of the world is so inundated (and often plagued) by stereotypes and archetypes.

By using prototypical members of a category as a heuristic determinator as to whether the thing we're analyzing *belongs* in that category, we invariably form—often incorrect and often damaging—stereotypes for members of that category. While instantly jumping to a small chirpy sparrow or robin as opposed to a big, gangly ostrich when asked quickly to "think of a bird" doesn't contribute to a damaging worldview at all (unless you're an ostrich), jumping to the image of a young woman when asked to "picture a nurse" or an old, white man when asked to "think of a scientist," for example, really does.

The combination of schemas and prototypes should lay clear two straightforward, but apparently controversial, reality checks. Firstly, schemas are—in part—social constructs; sculpted and framed by our lived experiences. Everything from the people we meet to the media we're exposed to form the guardrails and constraints between which we view our world. Secondly, that schemas and prototypes are *fuzzy* concepts by nature. They're *supposed* to be challenged. To be molded and remolded as we journey through our lives, enriched by other people, cultures, and experiences. Spending your life so completely invested in immutable schemas that dictate how you understand the world is the literal definition of close-mindedness, often to the point of complete bigotry: the refusal to acknowledge the agency—or even the existence—of people or concepts that don't fit into a neat, comfortable definition of how you categorize the world around you.

Refuse to accept a same-sex couple because it doesn't fit your neat definition of what a *couple* or *marriage* represents? Congratulations, you're a bigot. Refuse to acknowledge the womanhood of a transgender woman because she doesn't fit your schema of a *woman* (usually—and let me be clear, very incorrectly—translating to someone born as a biological female)? Well done, more bigotry. Perturbed by the notion that the gender binary in general is bullshit because you have immutable rules that someone is either male or female?

You guessed it. The notion that *humans often struggle to reconcile schematic violation* is neither false nor an excuse for being a shitty person. Every human to exist on this planet has had to contend with their understanding of the world and their environments being challenged, reframed, and oftentimes completely torn to shreds. How we deal with that is what defines us as people, not the fact that it happens.

Schemas, for better or worse, appear to form the basis of how we categorize objects and stimuli in our environment. However, another key area of schemas—and the area that is pertinent to the discussion of concepts such as surprise, tension, and anticipation—is that they greatly inform our *expectations*. In fact, schematic violation is key to one of the most visceral emotions we experience—*surprise*.

Surprise as Schematic Violation

At the surface level, schematic violation and prediction error are basically the same. You have set expectations, you encounter something that does not meet those expectations, and you act accordingly in the face of a surprising event. The differences between the two are subtle, but understanding both is key to forming a functional understanding of how expectations are built.

While prediction error occurs when reality does not match a prediction we've made, schematic violation occurs when our knowledge or beliefs are challenged. Thus, prediction errors and the resulting updated reality help our brains build that pool of lived experience to then use for later, more accurate predictions via Bayesian inference— the process of making predictions based on our prior beliefs and perceptions. Schematic violation, however, forces us to consider expanding or reassessing our categories and their prototypical members.

Going back to the Donald Trump example (yes, I know and yes, I'm sorry) from earlier. This can be seen through the lens of schematic violation. We all likely had a schema for what a U.S. President should be. Some of it was rooted in bias, a lot of it was rooted in media representation of the supposed values and integrity we expect from such a position (patently false; George W. Bush was a thing), and much of it was likely rooted in the previous and incumbent presidents. Before 2016, my schema for a U.S. President would have looked something like *neocapitalist, media-trained, career politician, well-spoken, intelligent* (sometimes: again, George W. Bush was a thing), *diplomatic*, and a few other specifics that aren't really fit for a book of this type. What it definitely didn't include, though, was literally *anything* the orange man with tiny hands encompassed. This was an unadulterated schematic violation. It took many people's ideas of what a U.S. President *should be* and flipped them on their head. A candidate who ran a campaign that was staunchly right-wing, populist, racist, sexist, ableist, and patently unhinged *actually won*.

To get away from the depressing political examples, let's have a palette cleanser: *bulls can't see red*. Either you knew that, in which case shut up, no one likes a smart ass, or you didn't, in which case, you're probably surprised (Yes, it's true! Only primates can see the color red.) and you might even be more likely to remember that pointless fact if you previously believed the common myth that red drives bulls crazy. Many of us are unfortunately exposed to footage of red-wielding *matadors* or *bull runs*, and often popular cartoons and other media depict bulls getting sent into a rage just by glimpsing something red. But it's all false—turns out getting thrown in a ring with a strange man in tight pants when you just wanted a normal day is actually frustration enough—and the repeated exposure and schematic association of *bulls* and *red things* makes a rather innocuous fact surprising and, thusly, memorable. If I told you that *otters* can't see red, for example, it perhaps wouldn't be anywhere near as surprising.

In these cases, we're not really dealing with *predictions*, at least not at the cognitive or neurological level. We're talking about *challenges*. Events or encounters that take what we believe to be true—what we expect—and go against that in some way. Some are just factual and thus challenge schemas that we've built through exposure to falsehoods. Others are more nuanced or intrinsic and go against more institutional beliefs we might hold. Either way, we're taxed with expanding, updating, or completely reassessing the schema we hold in our minds. Bulls and U.S. Presidents will never be the same again.

Understanding Expectation Through Abstraction Models

If you recall, a mental model is an abstraction that a person makes in order to understand a system, an environment, or the world around them. Mental models inform *what we expect* when we interact with an element or *what we believe to be true* about a system or environment and they broadly exist as an internalized, simplified model of any given system.

While mental models might be the most important abstraction model to us as designers, they're not the only ones we'll encounter throughout our careers. In fact, in order to design effective mental models, we often have to build abstraction models ourselves and with our clients or teams. This is especially true if we're dealing with complex systems with lots of interrelated objects. More often than not, how we internalize our understanding of a system is *not* how we should present it to users. This is a common mistake I see made across the board, especially when it comes to new startups with new products, internal incubators, or pivot plays in already-established companies.

How it usually goes is as follows: someone—who is ostensibly, through exposure to a market or a problem space, an expert in a certain subject matter—has a grand idea for a product, service, or platform that is going to solve enough problems to be viable in a market. They work with other people who, either through existing knowledge, extensive research, or access to domain expertise, are—or become—ostensibly experts in the subject matter. These people then build up a shared understanding of what they're building, why it's good, who it's for, and how it will be perceived. These assumptions are baked into a significant amount of decisions—design decisions, business decisions, marketing decisions, technological decisions—and before you know it we're getting ready to ship a behemoth of a product that's obtuse, presumptive, and full of friction.

While this endeavor was almost certainly not prompted by a shared, innate desire to build something complex, there's a *relative* complexity that's inherent in the work that our hypothetical plucky upstarts produce. This is because they're smart and they know a lot about what they're building. The problem is, though, that their users *don't*.

When you work in a specific domain on a specific product or in a specific problem space for long enough, you build up expertise. This is unavoidable if you're even remotely competent at what you do. As you and your team build up this expertise, it's incredibly easy to forget just how overwhelming and complex the landscape was when you first got stuck in. Compounding this is the fact that good designers know how to find answers, so when we *do* encounter something complex or obtuse, we're able to navigate ourselves and our team towards knowledge, answers, and context. This gives us a notable amount of institutional knowledge that's *essential* to doing good work.

We must strive, however, to remember those moments where everything is complex and overwhelming, where we have more questions than answers, to preempt moments where our future users will feel similarly. Just because we've had the luxury to learn and internalize these concepts doesn't mean that others will. It's now our job to take our own understanding and expertise and use it to design something that's simpler, usable, and comprehensible for people who haven't had that luxury themselves. This is where we can start building out different layers of abstraction models.

Domain Models

A domain model is a documentation and abstraction layer of a system. Good domain models facilitate discussion, learning, and collaboration between the people who have to work on or design for any given system, and they can consist of many different smaller models, such as flowcharts to understand your systems' throughputs or causal loop diagrams to show cause and effect. If you're doing deep systems work, then concepts such as *cause and effect*, *stock and flow*, and *causal loops* are going to be super important to you but many of them are beyond the scope of this book—and day-to-day product design in general.

Generally, when we're designing, we're looking to build out and present conceptual models of our systems, and there are a few key areas of a domain model that we need to care about and understand to do this effectively. Many of these will fall under a more generic *system map* type of document, as opposed to domain model documents of higher complexity and specificity. Here's what you most need to know when it comes to understanding the domain model of your systems.

What Are the System Objects?

Objects—sometimes called *actors*—are the **nouns** within our system. They're the *things* that we need to create, manage, or otherwise interact with to effectively navigate and manipulate a system. These fundamental components and the data used to describe them are also what make our systems unique.

Let's say we're building a pet-sitting app where people can offer their pet-sitting services and customers can list their pets in need of sitting. Perhaps we match sitters and pets based on certain factors, and each sitter and customer can also be reviewed by the corresponding party. That's a pretty simple product, but it already presents us with a bunch of objects to think about:

- **Pets** are the critters at the heart of the system, the things in need of sitting.

- **Sitters** are the would-be minders of pets and represent a subset of our user base.

119

- **Customers** are the owners of pets and represent the remaining subset of our user base.

- **Reviews** are left by either a sitter or a customer to explain the experience they had with their respective party.

- **Messages** are things that are sent between a sitter and a customer to agree on specifics or provide information.

- **Agreements** are things made between a sitter and a customer that state things like for how long a pet needs to be looked after, the agreed fee, and any other relevant terms.

As we develop new features, we introduce new objects into the system. There's a great approach that you'll explore in part two of this book around keeping a running, living document of the objects and relationships in your system. It's called OOUX—keep an eye out for it!

How Do Objects Relate to One Another?

A system full of orphaned objects that don't relate to one another in any way is … well, not really a system. Understanding how a pet might relate to a customer, or how a sitter might relate to a pet, is essential to understanding the types of interactions you might need to design. Every relationship between objects is likely something that needs to be instigated through an action in your interface.

Keeping it simple, let's say a **customer** can **own** many **pets**. There's a relationship of "owner" and "owned by" formed between a customer and a pet. It should hopefully be pretty clear that at some point we're going to need to design a way for a pet to be assigned to a customer, or more likely for a customer to create a pet within the system.

A lot of valuable creative ideas come from simply laying down all your objects and asking *how might X relate to Y*. It can be tempting, when documenting a system, to think that you're documenting something that *already exists*, that you're limited to a purely documentarian role and must strive to communicate existing, obvious relationships. However, there's ample room for divergent thought and creativity during the building out of a domain model. Nowhere is this more evident than when you sit with a group of collaborators and stakeholders and ask them to spend time thinking how Object A can relate to Object B in creative or interesting ways. Get the obvious stuff out the way first— of course **messages** can be **sent** to and from a **customer** and a **sitter**, and of course a **pet** can be **assigned** to a **sitter** as a result of an accepted **agreement**—and then make some time to think laterally and creatively. What if a **pet** could send a **message** to a **customer** or a **sitter**? Sounds dumb as shit, right? But maybe we encourage customers to upload a quick video of their pet to help the sitter understand their needs and temperament before they accept the job. Or what if a sitter was given a space to upload videos of the pet they're looking after for customers to check out while they're away, giving them a little glimpse into how things are going? I know that when I leave my dog with a sitter or a friend, I'm *that guy* who asks for videos every eleven seconds. I'm sure I'm not the only one!

These ideas might be cheesy or unviable but do this enough and in the right environment and I promise you'll be surprised by how many creative ways you and your team can find to create relationships between objects in your system. Defining new relationships in this way can lead to entire feature sets worth of innovation.

How Can the System Fail?

If something goes wrong within the system, causing parts of it to behave erratically or break entirely, are you able to understand the impact of this throughout the model? For example, if an API request spawned from your UI hits a downed server and returns a 404 error, what can break? If this is the request to authenticate a user, then they maybe can't log in or use the product at all; if it's a more esoteric request, for example failing to get a deeply-nested array of paginated results for a specific search index, then can the other objects or areas of the system cope with this missing information?

Understanding at a conceptual level how constituent system parts can cause or respond to errors, downtime, or other system-level failings is essential to being able to present an interface. If you can't preempt impactful problem states, then you need to do the work to learn them. Oftentimes this involves speaking to people responsible for the technical implementation of the system—your backend or platform engineers, your frontend engineers, system administrators, network engineers, and every other niche engineer role that makes people sound very clever. In fact, engineers who are able to explain the technical qualities of a system area in conceptual ways are worth their weight in gold. Sit down with the person who has to code this thing up and ask them *how can this blow up?* and I guarantee you'll learn something new; you'll also break down a knowledge silo.

Remember, too, that systems don't just fail at a technical level. It's easy to get lost in systems thinking language and jargon and forget that this system does not exist in a vacuum with no real-world impact. A system being used or manipulated to cause harm is a failed state. Twitter being used as a tool for weird trolls to harass other humans is as much a problem state as it being over capacity or some strange rate limit being reached.

Who Is Going to Be Impacted by This System?

Understanding the people who can benefit, suffer, or otherwise be impacted by the successes or failures of our system is an unavoidable responsibility. It's far too common to see folks rushing to build out products with a blinkered, overly-optimistic view of the potential impact they can have. People believe in their ideas; otherwise why would they build them? The problem is, people struggle to acknowledge that their ideas are *bad* or at least *potentially harmful*, and this blinkered, stubborn mindset can lead to pretty substantial failings.

Airbnb is a pretty apt example of this. Whether through over-optimism, willful ignorance, or malicious intent, Airbnb has contributed to untold, worldwide housing issues and raised questions about rental markets and holiday rentals as a whole. The plucky startup that espoused values such as sharing the joy of your home with strangers, uniting people around travel, and the cultural goldmine leaving your front step can expose us to is, at the time of writing this book, facing probing—and extremely valid— questioning about its contribution to housing crises, property-hoarding, gentrification, and the untempered growth of rentier capitalism and the innumerable deplorable acts allowed by such.

Twitter, too, is another great example of this kind of ignorance to impact. The social media site that promoted brevity and belonging has found itself at the epicenter of major world events far too many times to count. Since its inception, Twitter has been a hotbed of bad takes, bigoted espousing, and overt racism. In 2016, you couldn't move for actual Nazis on their platform. Full-blown, unapologetic neo-fascists emboldened by emerging, extreme populism banded together on a "free speech" platform that couldn't reconcile its own blinkered ideals against protecting the vast majority of the population that weren't fetishizing genocide and just wanted to share dog photos and Shrek memes.

Both Airbnb and Twitter have profited from their harmful use cases. Their founders are rich. Their executive employees are rich. Their services are used, generate revenue, pay salaries, fund expensive lobbies, cover lawsuits, and generate profit for advertisers. There has, as of yet, been very little in the way of a reckoning that couldn't be navigated by slick PR campaigns or puff pieces in centrist journals. Yet, many have suffered because of these systems being used for harm. People are being priced out of owning property in their hometowns because landlords are hoovering them up to rent them out. Vulnerable and marginalized people are being exposed daily to rhetoric that suggests their existence is invalid, under the guise of "free speech" on a platform that's so devoted to upholding an infuriatingly lopsided and ostentatious interpretation of the concept.

I'm not suggesting that preemptively interrogating how a system can be used for harm would have *stopped* these examples from happening, but it at least removes the convenient *we were just trying to make the world better* excuse that gets trotted out in well-polished statements to sympathetic press outlets every time a Silicon Valley darling is used to ruin lives and further perpetuate inequality. Technology moves faster than regulation, and as we've seen with Airbnb and Twitter—as well as countless other so-called innovative tech platforms—it's often too little too late when some kind of tempering or regulation does occur.

By questioning how our systems can fail, and who might be impacted *when* they do, we're able to preemptively implement features or terms that can protect or mitigate these eventualities. We might be killing some vibes or hurting some egos along the way, but this is essential work and *someone* needs to do it. I'll cover the *how* of this in part two of this book, but for now, simply acknowledging that even the most benign-seeming system can be used to cause harm is a start.

Mental Models

Throughout this book you've built up a—hopefully—pretty solid understanding of mental models. The most important aspect to consider here is that mental models dictate what we believe to be possible when we use a product or service. Let's build on that a little with some of the concepts from earlier in this chapter. Firstly, you'll likely remember that it's quite difficult to separate mental models from schemas at a conceptual level. They're both "working models" that we interrogate and update based on past experience, and they're both integral to understanding our world. I won't bore you with the differences again—just know that I'm talking about working models of a *system* when I discuss mental models—but a lot of what you learned about schemas can directly apply to mental models.

Firstly, we'll often see Bayesian inference at work when it comes to the mental models that our users hold. Their expectations will be largely informed by their past experiences with other products or services, or by the real-world interactions and possibilities that we bring into our designs through metaphor. If you think back to Chapter 3, you looked at the razor tool used for slicing video clips in DaVinci Resolve. Past exposure to the practice—or even just a broad awareness of the fact—of slicing real film is what makes this an intuitive metaphor for many, as opposed to mindless esoteric iconography. This is also part of why the oft-quoted Jakob's Law—*Users spend most of their time on other sites. This means that users prefer your site to work the same way as all the other sites they already know.*—is so prevalent. Taken to its extreme it can be seen as promoting homogeneity (I'll discuss how to mitigate this a little later in this chapter!) but I've always seen it more akin to an ode to convention in UI design.

Just as schematic violation causes surprising moments, so too does mental model violation. Mental models are instrumental in the forming of expectations, and if we subvert them, we're almost definitely going to surprise people along the way. While there are numerous valid reasons to subvert expectations and go against the grain with our designs, it's important to understand the impact doing so can have and to make informed and responsible decisions. Doing something because it's novel, attention-grabbing, but ultimately of no value is a surefire way to stoke disharmony and frustrate people who just want to get shit done. With all that in mind, let's first take a look at how we can *meet* expectations, before we run off and throw it all out the window in the name of fun.

Communicate System State

I'm conscious that this piece of advice has found its way into every single chapter you've read so far. And—spoiler alert—it'll crop up a bunch more times before you're done with this book. However, there's a good reason for this: system state is the fulcrum of modern product design. More and more often we're designing interaction layers on top of extremely complex systems, the constituent parts of which can be manipulated and interacted with in myriad different ways. In modern interfaces, things happen in-situation. Long gone are the days of filling in web forms and being taken to a "success" or "error" page upon completion. Now, almost every interaction either causes optimistic updates to your system state or fires off an API request to perform an action or fetch data. Whatever way we code it, inline, pseudo–real-time updates are the norm. Couple this with the fact that we're designing on top of increasingly complex, multifaceted systems, and the importance of effectively communicating the state of said systems cannot be overstated.

Is a certain element non-interactive while data is being fetched or persisted via a back-end or API? *Use disabled and loading states.* Is some part of the system down or broken? *Design appropriate error states.* Is a key part of the system missing user-manageable data? *Give them a nice empty state with a prompt to start filling things up.*

Effectively communicating system state is about being thorough, not cutting corners, and not using edge cases as an excuse to do incomplete design work. It's as much an art of design discipline as it is a mantra for good, stateful, front-end UI. Ensuring that interactive elements are both communicated as such and responding expectedly to interaction is still one of the most overlooked aspects of UI design. Yet the seemingly minute details of element interactivity are cumulative, to the point where an interaction or interface is only as good as its worst-designed element. Correctly implying interactivity and interactive state is the very core of seamless design.

Be Graceful in Error Handling

More complex systems and more complex interactions mean more ways for things to screw up, and things *will* screw up. One of the most common user-hostile patterns you'll encounter in product design is the Crappy Error Message™. The Crappy Error Message™ is a common and recurring blight on design and can take many forms. Sometimes it's an overly technical description of what went wrong, often replete with the HTTP error code (in the case of web-based interfaces) that makes the whole thing feel intimidating and confusing. Other times it's just poor wording that frames the error as though it's the users fault. Now, we know that sometimes, it really is, but here's a little secret: computers don't have feelings. You can blame them for *everything* and they'll still do their thing with 0s and 1s just fine. It's a nice, convenient way to avoid errors that imply the user is somehow at fault.

The final common factor of the Crappy Error Message™ is the complete absence of a potential solution. Humans are problem-solvers. It's intrinsically rewarding to find something in a poor state and perform lateral thinking to bring it back to a correct or harmonious state, but error messages don't need to be murder mystery novels. Tell people what they can try to make the error go away. Chances are, if you've got the "how can the system fail" of your system model documented, there's at least one suggestion you can offer for any kind of major error.

So, to flip the Crappy Error Message™ characteristics on their head, what do we need to do to present a *good* error message? Let's take it step by step (or cheat and look at Figure 4-1).

1. **Explain the issue in as plain a way as possible**. Don't use overly complex jargon. Make your wording appropriate for your user base and their expectations.

2. **Take the blame, even if it's the users' fault**. You don't have to be all *oh my gosh; ever so sorry* about it, but a simple *looks like something went wrong* rather than *you've really messed this up here pal* goes a long way. Don't leave people feeling blamed or shamed, and when in doubt, blame the computers.

3. **Offer steps to resolve the issue and make those steps seamless**. No one wants to be left hanging because of an error message. Sometimes the best you can do is *reload this page*, or even *contact support if this happens again*. If you can offer a more specific step, such as *make sure there are no syntax errors in your .yaml file*, then even better. If you *do* have to settle for the *contact support* fallback, then at least make sure you auto-fill what information you already have about the error so your user doesn't have to comb through logs or keep a load of information in their working memory just to ask you a question.

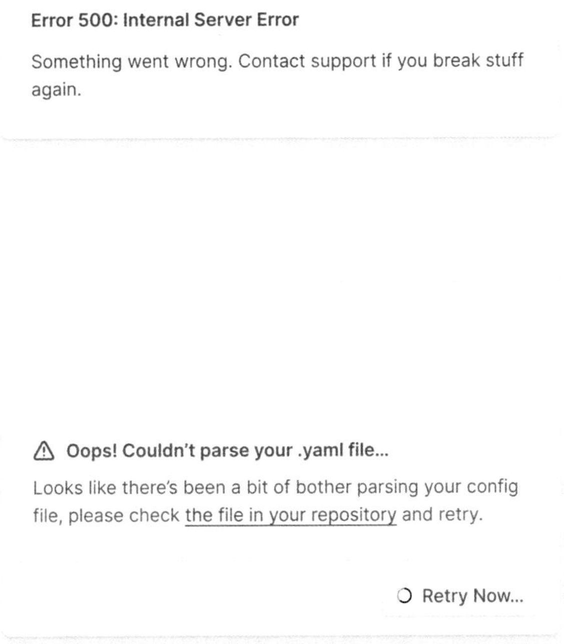

Error 500: Internal Server Error

Something went wrong. Contact support if you break stuff
again.

⚠ Oops! Couldn't parse your .yaml file...

Looks like there's been a bit of bother parsing your config
file, please check the file in your repository and retry.

○ Retry Now...

Figure 4-1. *Two error messages, with a Crappy Error Message™ on the top and a well-crafted error message on the bottom*

Hopefully the comparison in Figure 4-1 goes to show the stark differences in approachability and utility between good and crappy error messages.

Now, this might sound incredibly simple—and it really is bread-and-butter stuff for product designers—but it's still surprising to me just how bad some interfaces are when it comes to error management. People need to feel comfortable experimenting and interacting with your interface so they can start to build up their mental models. If they know that every time something breaks, they're going to be left confused, blamed, and at a dead end, then you're giving them reason to be reticent. These users churn, avoid using your product, and generally have a bad time. Conversely, if someone knows that things *can* break, and when they do they'll be able to understand the issue and try to remedy it themselves, they're often much more tolerant of failed states, much more willing to experiment, and far more likely to stick around and find value in your product.

Use Progressive Disclosure

Complex systems usually mean complex information architectures. If you try to communicate every possible piece of data or potential interaction in one go, people are going to be overwhelmed and cognitively burdened. This is where *progressive disclosure* comes into play.

Progressive disclosure is the act of abstracting longer or more complex data behind simpler interactive elements. This can be as simple as offering a stepped sign-up flow where key information is asked for up front, and then things like customizing your profile or configuring your notification settings are deferred to later steps; or something more complex, such as hiding advanced features until a user has performed a few basic ones. Progressive disclosure allows you to present key information up front, providing abstractions or summaries in lieu of complex, dense data sets or lists.

A good example of this is everyone's favorite student design project: the humble weather app.

Despite apparently being everyone's favorite way to try out a new icon set or play with the newest and bestest visual trends, well-designed weather apps do progressive disclosure really well. When you first open a weather app, you'll likely be presented with a very basic, top-level weather summary for the day: the current climate, current temperature, the forecasted highest temperature, forecasted lowest temperature, and chance of rain for the day. This is a great summary for people who just care what the immediate weather holds in store for them, but depending on your needs you might want to go a little deeper. Let's take a couple of second-level screens into consideration. The first is an hourly forecast for the rest of the day. This usually presents the user with a timeline or other navigation device to browse and check the forecast at various intervals throughout the day. This is great if you've got dinner plans and are wondering if you need to bring a jacket. The second is a weekly forecast starting from a specific date. Similar to the hourly forecast, this might present the user with a timeline of some kind, instead split into days rather than hours. Perhaps we'll show folks the daily summary for each day of the week they're checking and allow further drilling down to explore the daily forecast for any selected date. This is great if you're planning a holiday or a gathering and want to pick the days with the best weather.

Many weather apps will allow people to go deeper still, presenting meteorological data for all the weather fans (I'm sure they exist—hi Dan!) out there, or maybe even suggesting potential days for outdoor activities or allowing for advanced and precise filtering. Unless you're designing a weather app for meteorologists, though, it's *totally fine* to "bury" this information behind—often multiple—interaction or abstraction layers.

By highlighting key features or the most important information of your interface up front and abstracting the more advanced stuff behind interaction or navigation layers, you can slowly introduce people to your more advanced features over time. This has the double benefit of making your most important, higher-level features or data more available and comprehensible, while presenting a simpler, more digestible interface to your users. As I've touched on, mental models are *supposed* to be built over time, and often the best way to accommodate this is to hide away some of your system's complexity, resisting the urge to throw everything at people all at once. This might sound a little scary, especially if some of your most complex features are actually some of your *best* ones, but people can't learn everything in an instant, and enriching an already-solid mental model with extra layers of value over time is often a much more successful approach than trying to throw all your clever, complex features front and center, before people have even had the chance to poke around the basics.

Double-Edged Surprise

So, you know that surprise happens when your expectations are subverted in some way, and that whether a particular surprise is viewed as a positive or negative experience can vary vastly depending on the individual.

Convention and Unexpected Interactions

You've already explored conventions pretty thoroughly throughout this book, but their impact on expectation-setting cannot be overstated. Seeing something that looks like a button, clicking it, and witnessing *nothing happen* is textbook schematic violation. We spend an exorbitant portion of our lives clicking rectangles on a screen to make things happen. It's impossible to *not* build up expectations that interface elements with specific qualities are (or should be) interactive. When we encounter a scenario where those expectations aren't met, it can be incredibly frustrating. You might even provoke *rage clicking*, a wonderfully apt moniker for the act of constantly clicking a single element in the sheer, desperate hope that it'll do the thing you want it to do. The reverse of this situation can be true, too. Elements that *are* interactive but aren't sufficiently signified as such can cause untold confusion.

But can there be any *good* in subverting convention? Is there a scenario where having someone expect a certain pattern or interaction and presenting them with something that defies those expectations can result in a *good* surprise?

I argue that the areas where expectation and convention is ripe for disruption are the visual design and the *personality* of our products. For better or worse, the landscape of modern digital products is one of homogeneity. There's an industry trend of favoring flatter, unambitious visual design languages and more spartan, milquetoast tones of voice. Characterful interactions, "just for fun" features, and novel visual design can all subvert the expectations that are naturally built from interacting with these more spartan visual environments. It's possible to follow most important or immutable UI conventions while still being unique and providing moments of fun and spontaneity in your work.

FigJam—Figma's infinite-canvas, whiteboard style tool—is a great example of this. It's full of random interactions and features that might, at least at a descriptive level, feel egregious, even pointless. What FigJam does well, though, is inject these fun tidbits and easter eggs into a well-designed, fast and snappy, appropriately conventional UI. One feature that really exemplifies this well is the timer functionality, seen in Figure 4-2.

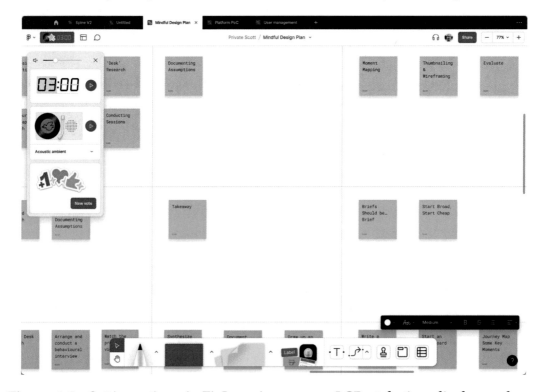

Figure 4-2. *Setting a timer in FigJam gives you an LCD-style time display and a tiny record player to queue up some "hold" music. It's adorable*

This is one of my favorite design details I've ever encountered, so let's unpack it. Firstly, the clock that shows the timer is styled like an LCD alarm clock. In an interface that's relatively flat and unassuming, this is a wonderful, more human touch. Secondly, and probably most controversially, *there's a tiny little record player that lets you play music for you and your participants while the timer counts down.* We've spent a very, very long time being told to avoid audio in our interfaces. It's really quite rare to see an interface on the web make use of sound design or music. Now, this isn't without good reason; most of the time we don't want to distract people with pings and dings from a random browser tab, and a huge swathe of sites and apps that do use audio use it excruciatingly poorly. However, in FigJam's case, there's a few contextualizing factors that make this a really fun addition to the product.

Firstly, think of the environment where FigJam will mostly be used. It's an infinite canvas that you lay digital Post-Its on. We're talking workshops, collaborative brainstorming, and other such low-fidelity, group-based scribble sessions. If you're setting a timer in a tool like this, it's usually as a means of facilitating "active time" during a workshop, where you give your participants a chance to drop Post-Its and ideas instead of listening to a facilitator prattle on for an hour. In these cases, folks using the product are likely gathered in a synchronous call of some kind, so it's not likely they've got their own music blasting or a podcast on in the background (although I wouldn't rule it out!). Setting some background music that everyone gets to hear while they go about dropping their ideas is fun. Not everyone wants this—and individuals can turn it off at any time—but by having it on by default, FigJam subverts expectations and provides a surprise that many (but not all) folks may find novel and endearing.

It's this combination of a pretty unconventional feature—auto-playing background music in a product that's definitely *not* a music player—and the characterful presentation—using a mini record player instead of a more traditional, Spotify-style audio player—that make this such a great example of fun in UI design. It's also a pretty creative and, to an extent, *brave* approach to feature design. If your PM comes to you and says *Hey, we need a timer feature, we need to ship it by end of quarter; can we get some designs?* I'm willing to bet *Yes, of course; here's a tiny little adorable record player that plays ambient acoustic music when you start the timer* isn't going to be the common response. It says a lot about the culture and fun factor of FigJam that this kind of work makes it into a live product that people happily pay for.

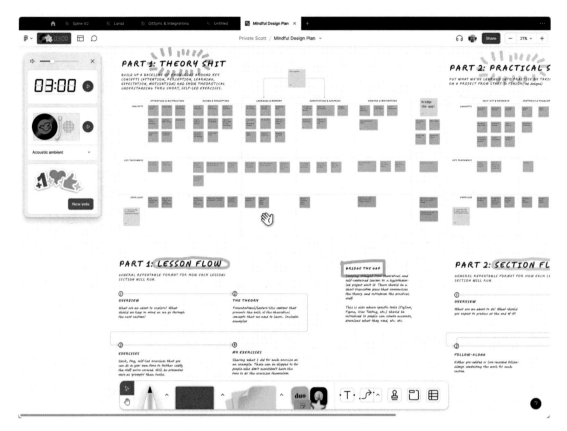

Figure 4-3. *A hand above the user's cursor position waiting for a digital high-five*

FigJam is in fact full of all these small, fun interactions. It's not like they just picked one area of the app and said "this is the fun bit"—fun feels baked into the fabric of the product. Wiggle your cursor in FigJam and you'll see a cartoon hand (Figure 4-3) right above it. Pretty strange (and very hard to capture in the static pages of a book) until you do so at the same time as another collaborator and perform a high-five in the middle of your canvas. Or take the stamp tool (Figure 4-4), a feature that allows you to "mark" any object or area of the canvas with a stamp of your choosing. If you instead select an emoji in this tool, clicking and holding on the canvas releases a wave of that emoji that follows your cursor and is visible to all collaborators (Figure 4-5).

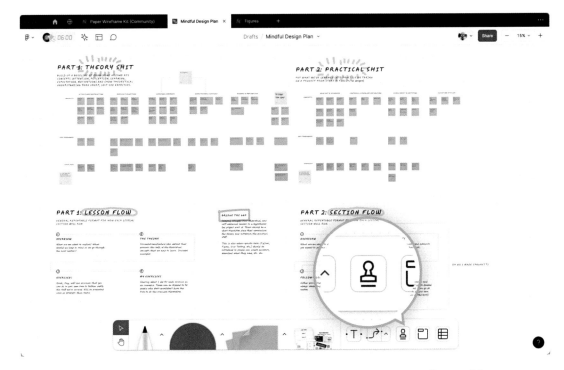

Figure 4-4. *Figma's stamp tool, allowing users to stamp or mark up objects or areas of a canvas with a specific icon or emoji*

Figure 4-5. *"Stamping" an emoji on the canvas causes a wave of emojis to emit from the cursor position*

This is a far cry from how we generally expect interfaces to behave. There's nothing about *digital whiteboard* that screams *being able to high-five someone else's cursor*, and there's nothing about diagramming and workshopping tools that states they *need* to be fun and characterful. However, in doing so, and committing to fun and whimsy *where it makes sense,* FigJam sets itself apart from its competitors. The digital whiteboarding space is hardly a one-product race, and there are fantastic tools that work exceptionally well in their own right. FigJam's whimsical, fun, and delightful (yes, I said it) approach to interaction design, coupled with the fact that it's a robust, performant, and well-designed product overall, really do give it an edge in a saturated market.

Now, not everything we build needs to be injected with fun or character. Sometimes the stoic, spartan approach is best. However, I'm of the humble opinion that far too many products and services are suffering from a chronic lack of character. FigJam isn't some experimental, social-first platform. It's a business tool used by career professionals to communicate with stakeholders and their teams. It would be extremely easy for them to veto these random ideas under the guise that *serious people* need *serious tools* to do their *serious job*. But think about your own colleagues, clients, or teammates. Unless you're unlucky enough to work at Meta or McKinsey, you're probably not surrounded by carbon-copy *Serious Tech People*. Work is allowed to be fun, and work tools are allowed to spark some sense of frivolity and enjoyment while still serving their primary purpose.

Summary

In this chapter, you explored how expectations are set and made through predictive coding and the building of schemas and mental models. You also explored how these expectations can be subverted to induce surprise through novelty, prediction error, and schematic violation.

You looked to how music and movies play with expectations to create novel listening and viewing experiences, while understanding that there's a wide spectrum of schematic violation, and that different people seek out different levels of violation depending on their preferences and contexts.

You explored schemas, focusing on how schemas are formed and challenged over time, and how previous interactions you have can shape and inform your future expectations. You also saw that people are willing to consider certain objects or stimuli as *more* or *less* a member of a specific category, often—as explained through Prototype Theory—treating certain members as prototypical of a specific group or category.

You looked at how important it is to build out different abstraction models of the systems on top of which you need to design, focusing on understanding domain models so you can effectively design on top of your system. You looked at how important it is to focus on the objects and relationships in your system, how it can fail, and who your system can impact. You also explored how mental models can impact expectations, and what you need to do to ensure that people can build solid, predictable models of your interfaces; this includes always communicating system state, effectively communicating error states, and leveraging progressive disclosure to present value over time.

Finally, you looked at how subverting expectations to create positive surprise can be a viable and enjoyable approach to applying this knowledge in a different light. You looked at how FigJam, with its many surprisingly fun and irreverent details, presents an experience beyond the usual, expected homogeneity we're all too used to seeing in modern product design.

If you take one thing away from this chapter, make sure you're aware of the importance mental models have when it comes to expectation-setting. Test extensively and talk to your users to learn about what they expect from your (and your competitors') products. Start with a foundation of understanding, and adhering to, these expectations, and then look for chances to subvert them in fun, creative, or enriching ways.

CHAPTER 5

Reward and Motivation

Dress the literature up how you like, add in as many caveats and as many disclaimer paragraphs as you feel necessary—there is no escaping the technology industry's fetishization of addictive products. Everything from social media attention-grabbing to egregious growth hacks to gamified products that have no business being so make use of obnoxiously derivative implementations of so-called *reward science*.

While many books in the fuzzy category of design psychology attempt to toe the line, remain neutral in the presentation of evidence and theory, and eschew the moralistic debate in favor of some mangled notion of neoliberalism, this book does not. While there is certainly some validity to the science of compulsion and conditioning that has been persistently banded about—usually under much more palatable monikers like *persuasive design* or *behavioral design*—the application of such to modern, systemic product design ranges from ostentatious through to downright depressing and dangerous.

Firstly, I want to make clear the fact that there exists far more utility in our understanding of the mind. That our understanding of reward is but one *part* of an important *whole*. Secondly—and in the hope that the previous chapters have done enough to convey the ethical underpinnings of this book so far—that we hope to understand the mind and its functions primarily to *serve* them and to never, ever do harm. I want to be explicit with this, because, at the time of writing this book, there exists a very real, very widespread misuse of the teachings of psychology, namely in the pursuit of profit and persuasive manipulation.

Finally, and I promise we'll actually start talking about rewards and happy times soon, I'll politely ask that you discard as many of your preexisting ideas or assumptions around the whole *dopamine thing* going into this chapter. And, while you're at the idea bin, just throw in any kind of lingering Maslow's hierarchy of needs triangle weirdness you have knocking around there too. Given how often these overhyped (in the case of dopamine) or inaccurate (in the case of need-based pyramids) concepts come up, get mistranslated, and finally get memed around social media and infotainment web sites, it's quite likely we've all got some long-held misconceptions about needs, motivations, and rewards. Don't worry; we'll top all that up next.

© Scott Riley 2024
S. Riley, *Mindful Design*, Design Thinking, https://doi.org/10.1007/979-8-8688-0143-3_5

The Origin of Wanting

The science of motivation is genuinely fascinating, but within it lies very little consensus, many a controversial theory, and a whole Pandora's box of debate. A rather simplified definition of motivation is to view it as the mind's mechanism for *wanting*: to establish or display a desire to perform (or indeed avoid) a set of activities based on our attachment to their previously experienced outcome. Essentially, we can see this as a combination of various processes that encourage us to seek positive outcomes and avoid negative ones. From an evolutionary perspective, motivation can manifest as a drive to perform our biological needs. If we weren't motivated to eat, would we? The answer to this, apparently, is no. Rats and mice that have been rendered unable to produce dopamine (the primary driver of reward-seeking behaviors) simply do not seek food. Deprived of their source of motivation, they show no need or desire, and they simply lie down and starve.

Reward-Seeking Behavior

The most common description of reward-seeking behavior comes from the radical behaviorist B.F. Skinner's findings on what he dubbed *operant conditioning*. Operant conditioning, an expansion on the Pavlovian ideas that came to be known as classical conditioning, essentially gives us insight into the behavioral underpinnings of reward-seeking behavior and comes from Skinner's work with his now infamous Skinner boxes.

A Skinner box, or an *operant conditioning chamber*, is a structure that allows scientists to test the association between reward, stimuli, and action in animals. The classic Skinner box example comes from Skinner's experiments on rats, where a rat was placed in a box that contained a lever. When this lever was touched, food was released. The rats were left to discover this relationship by themselves and, once the pattern of action and reward was associated, they were observed to head straight for the lever to receive their reward on subsequent trips to the chambers. Further examples of Skinner boxes introduced electric floors, lights, and screens (Figure 5-1) to test the role of punishment and stimuli in association with reward. However, the most significant change to the experiment conditions came in the form of *reward variance*.

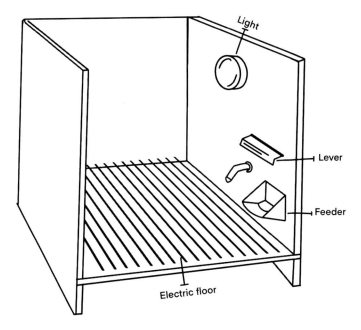

Figure 5-1. *A diagram for a Skinner Box showing a light, a response lever, an automated feeder, and electric floors to provide shocks. All awaiting a rather unfortunate rat.*

By introducing an element of variance as to when, or whether, a reward would be distributed, the behaviorist theories of reward-motivation were able to account for chance and variance in the administration of rewards. This resulted in four commonly referenced forms of reward scheduling:

- **Fixed interval** scheduling involves administering rewards to a fixed, time-based schedule—for example, giving a reward every two minutes without variance.

- **Fixed ratio** scheduling involves administering a reward after a set number of actions, say, on every fifth press of a lever.

- **Variable interval** scheduling means rewards are spaced apart by time (not the number of actions) but with no set or predictable time between each reward.

- **Variable ratio** scheduling is the process of spacing rewards apart based on a varying number of actions. For example, pressing a lever three times may net the first reward, the second might require nine presses, the third just two. Variable ratio scheduling's apparent ability to tap into our compulsive behavior is something that makes casinos, as well as social media apps, thrive in our society. And this is where we get to dopamine's role in the whole sordid affair.

In simple terms, dopamine is released during the *anticipation* stage of the reward cycle (not at the enjoyment stage!). With the dopamine-deprived rats you met earlier in this chapter, their brains' inability to synthesize the chemical meant that they did not perform this so-called reward-seeking behavior. An interesting result of the study of these same dopamine-free animals shows that, when they're actually presented with rewarding stimuli (sugar water inserted directly into a mouse's mouth, for example), they still react with a hedonic "liking" response. This discovery is one of many reasons why dopamine's misreported role as a "pleasure chemical" is challenged. While it *is* responsible for motivational behaviors, it appears to have no say in the hedonic nature of an experience.

Further studies into dopamine's role in reward-motivated behavior have shown that when *chance* is introduced (i.e., through adopting a variable ratio/variable time reward schedule), dopamine synthesis in the mesolimbic pathway is increased. This, arguably, gives us the chemical blueprint for maximizing compulsive behavior: establish an action/reward association and then vary the schedule to which the reward is administered to introduce chance. I'd also be remiss if I didn't point out that Skinner's were undeniably cruel experiments that paved the way for wretched implementations of manipulation.

The classic example of this implementation can be found in the design of the American darling, the slot machine. The accepted reasoning behind the slot machine's addictive nature is that, essentially, it is a human-operable Skinner box. The slot machine offers the association with reward (I can win money!), the ease of action (I put my own money in and pull a lever—just like a Skinner rat!), and the super-wonderful variable ratio scheduling of rewards (I might not win on this spin, but who knows what spin will pay out?!). The slot machine is, to be frank, one of the most depressing inventions I think the world has ever produced that isn't a weapon of some kind. Everything about it is designed to compel human beings to give away as much money as absolutely possible. A slot machine is designed to entice and addict. Worse still, it offers the perfect analogy for how, at this time of writing, technology companies capitalize on supposedly reward-focused behaviors.

The Pocket Slot Machine

Tristan Harris, a former design ethicist at Google, equates the omnipresence of social media apps on people's phones to "putting a slot machine in a billion pockets" (Harris, 2016). As explored above, slot machines work based on intermittent ratio rewards: insert cash, pull handle, watch reels spin, hope for a reward. Harris believes that acts such as checking our phone, refreshing our e-mail inbox, and refreshing social media applications in search of notifications is the technological equivalent of this behavior. Take out phone, pull on screen, watch a loader spin, hope for content. The parallels are palpable.

The majority of tech's relationship with reward-motivating behavior is wrapped up in this very shallow, arguably problematic relationship with behaviorism and compulsion. Relatively new practices such as persuasive design (there exists, believe it or not, a persuasive design laboratory in Stanford University) and behavioral design have reignited discussions around classical and operant conditioning. Crucially, these discussions are notably light on ethics and notably high on unfounded optimism. This act of psych necromancy presents old ideas in fresh contexts. In the rapidly prototyped world of Silicon Valley business practice, it represents a dangerous paradigm where compulsion and addiction are dressed up as "nudging" and "habit-forming." The controversial practices of conditioning and manipulation are touted as wins for an industry already demonstrably devoid of morals, unions, and anything close to resembling the Hippocratic Oath.

The gambling industry is regulated so heavily because it quite measurably costs people money and systematically ruins lives. The irresponsible application of such a thin slice of psychology is proven to prey on the vulnerable and the cognitively burdened. This regulation exists primarily due to the ease with which one can visualize the associated losses. Money put into a slot machine comes from the pockets of gamblers. The very notion that casinos are profitable shows this. Simple economics demonstrates that by capitalizing on our hardwired nature to seek reward, a business profits while a human loses. What is more worrying about our *digital* slot machines is twofold.

First, the loss is currently impossible to measure or visualize—it manifests itself as directed attention to a specific application, as stolen moments, as distractions from important tasks. It's a lot easier to watch a bucket full of quarters disappear before your eyes than it is to quantify the glucose expenditure of attentional misdirection, or the time and mental energy required to re-enter a state of deep working, deliberate practice, or flow.

Second, the reward these applications posit is often far more powerful than money.

It's been shown that humans do not typically find money intrinsically rewarding or desirable. Instead, we understand and preconceive the enjoyable nature of the things money allows us to purchase or pay to experience. What *is* inherently rewarding is an eclectic cocktail of satiety and desire for knowledge, interaction, and mastery, including social validation, information consumption, and learning progression. Rather unintuitively, the rewards offered to us by social media, e-mail, and infotainment web sites represent bite-sized chunks of many of our most compelling desires, whereas the intoxicating allure of slot machines provides money—at best an abstracted facsimile of a reward.

The intensity of our seeking behavior can be broadly viewed as a function of ease of action, perceived potential loss, and motivational salience. Essentially, if we place enough perceived importance on a pleasurable result, our incentive salience—how intensively we focus on achieving a result—can be high enough to encourage us to seek a reward, even in the presence of potential loss. Using Facebook as an example, someone "liking" a post of ours, or commenting directly on it, might be of relatively low salience in comparison to many things in life. However, the work required to reach this is extremely simple. Essentially, we make a post and we wait. Once our post is made, our rewards start to roll in. We might get one or two likes straight away from our ardent friends. (Facebook allows you to receive notifications when a "close" friend posts.) Maybe over the course of the next few minutes, we get three or four more likes, one or two comments, and a "share" from people who are browsing their feed at the time you posted. This initial buzz of social recognition and involvement is often enjoyable, but rarely enjoyable enough to keep us satisfied beyond the first second or two of receiving that notification. Essentially, the reward is just not rewarding enough—we need more.

If I asked you now to predict how many likes, comments, or shares (or likes and retweets on Twitter) a basic, banal status update would get you (say if you posted on Facebook, Instagram, or Twitter about how much you're thoroughly enjoying this book), what would your answer be? I believe most active social media users have a rough idea of the engagement their posts generally receive. Every now and then, though, you might post something that breaks that mold and *goes viral*—the hallowed ground of the social media meme life. This *chance* of going viral could be motivation enough to keep posting and posting. What we see here is almost an onion-skin-like approach to social rewards. There's *usually* a baseline amount of interaction that fulfills a very small, constant level of reward—the typical like/comment/share amounts you're used to. Then there's the chance factor of your post reaching a much wider audience than you usually do, sending a flood of interest and engagement your way. Now you have the same varying schedule of likes and comments and shares but at a *much faster* rate. The sad thing about all of this, however, is that social media relies on these rewards never being salient enough for the process of *liking* to distract you from the process of *seeking*. The entire ecosystem of products such as Instagram and Twitter have traditionally revolved around the reinforcement of seeking behavior through expertly tweaked micro doses of enjoyment.

In many areas of our lives, our seeking behavior leads to a satiating result. We're able to enjoy our result and feel content. This can absolutely apply to our online or digital lives too. Messaging apps let us have long, in-depth, and rewarding conversations with friends across the world; sites like Wikipedia let us consume and *create* democratized, distributed knowledge; and countless apps for musicians, artists, and writers exist to foster and inspire our creativity. However, contentment and satiety rarely allow for fast, conditioned feedback loops—something which social media sites rely on.

Most of those tasks I mentioned involve a pretty drawn-out time investment, and their rewards are often savored over a matter of minutes, hours, days—hell, sometimes *lifetimes*. Our *post, like, refresh, and reciprocate* conditioning to social media rarely, if ever, allows for this. Facebook, Instagram, and Twitter rely on *shallow* rewards— just enough to make you feel like the initial posting or the resulting semi-consistent checking of your phone is worth it. We're not *supposed* to enjoy these abstractions of social interaction much, because that enjoyment and reflection time is better spent— apparently—browsing your timeline so you can be advertised to. This is the tight, tailored *dopamine loop* of social media—the carefully designed balance of reward salience; conditioned, low-impact response; and variable scheduling.

Habit-Forming Bullshit

There is a compelling argument for the application of this knowledge in the formation of good habits—something that the proponents and practitioners of this approach to design are quick to point out. However, this simply has not been the popular manifestation of this branch of behaviorism in tech. It is the manifestation of compulsion and addiction. Calling it habit-forming or persuasive design—or whatever new, diminutive name someone comes up with next—is currently just a cute moniker for a glorified compulsion fetish. Similar to priming and subliminal messaging in advertising, this attack on our biases and mental processes can lead to damaging behavior in the name of nothing but maximized profits. As long as Silicon Valley and the carousel of products it produces remains unregulated, the responsibility for the mental health and the eradication of nefarious manipulation in the name of growth, profit, and funding fall on the leaders and creators within the industry. At the time of writing, the neglectful pursuit of profit continues apace.

Add this all together and the current landscape is inarguably bleak for those of us who do not wish to be (or pander to) venture capitalists, profiteering CEOs, or willing proliferators of addictive experiences. We have popular branches of design that apply the same teachings as casinos to their design thinking, operating in an attention economy where eyes on a screen and misdirected attention translate abstractly into profit. They create and iterate on applications that provide *just enough* chunks of intoxicating content in an attempt to keep us in a reward-seeking loop—all with the backdrop of an industry that fetishizes unfettered growth above all. This is the culmination of what appears to be the tech industry's best efforts in bringing brain science into design—a manipulative application of century-old findings from a school of psychology that has been teetering on extinction for decades. And there's a lab for it. In Stanford.

But we want people to feel good when they use our stuff! This is something I hear a whole lot when I speak on this subject—and it's only half wrong. Oftentimes the application of compulsion in design and technology is not done by profiteering vampires and is done by well-meaning folks who have bought into the hype around mindless techno-behaviorism. They're the people trying to *gamify* accounting software or turning onboarding experiences into a glorified to-do list in some ostentatious growth-led project.

People use our stuff for a reason. They have goals they want to achieve every time they load up something we've designed and built for them. Throughout this book I've asked you to be mindful of the *real-world impact* of the things you design and build—and no more is this evident than in how we perceive goals or rewards in the products we built. Soon, you'll explore how the gamified badges and medals and in-app trophies aren't *rewards* at all. You'll look at the *real* motivations folks bring to our products and why we're falling way, way short of acknowledging or encouraging the behaviors that actually lead to that, but first, I need to touch on the most important theory you'll find in this book: the *self-determination theory*.

Humanistic Motivation

Humanistic psychology emerged out of, in part, a rejection of the behaviorist school of psychology I've discussed throughout this chapter. Humanism is centered around notions of self-exploration, existentialism, and self-determination. Similar to proponents of the Gestalt School, humanists believed in seeing a person as a whole, greater than and uniquely different from the sum of their parts. This application of holism to the subjects of mind, consciousness, and our notions of *self* represented a radical shift from the deterministic, "mind-as-a-closed-box" philosophies of behaviorism.

The principles of humanistic psychology give us a perspective from which to view motivation that is refreshingly antithetical to the reductionist ideas this industry has crudely aped from legacy behaviorism. While the humanistic perspective has a rather narrow reach in interpreting the mind—its focus on qualitative and mandated non-scientific methods of study have seen it applied only to a small subset of the discipline—one of the areas it has had a notable influence on is motivation.

One of the most infamous artifacts of the humanist approach to motivation is Maslow's hierarchy of needs. Maslow's hierarchy focused on the idea that humans have a universal set of needs, the most-evolved model being, in order, as follows: physiological needs (water, food, etc.), safety needs (law, order, protection from the elements, etc.), love and belongingness (affection, intimacy, friendship, etc.), esteem (status, mastery, dignity, etc.), cognitive (curiosity, knowledge, etc.), aesthetic (beauty, form, etc.), self-actualization (personal growth and self-fulfillment), and transcendence.

Maslow's hierarchy has been criticized from many angles. As a humanistic study, it relied on non-scientific means and suffers the same criticism as all humanism. Furthermore, Maslow's dataset was infamously non-diverse, focusing almost completely on privileged white men such as Einstein and Beethoven. Add in the fact that we can plainly and routinely discredit the notion that these needs are hierarchical (for example, those who live in extreme poverty and in exposure to the elements are observably capable of expressing and being motivated by love), and Maslow's hierarchy is quite clearly not fit for means as a motivational theory. However, the importance of this theory as part of a humanistic perspective should not be overlooked—especially its role in bringing the notion of *self* into the discussion around needs, desires, and motivation.

The Self-Determination Theory

The Self-Determination Theory (SDT) is a relatively modern theory of social psychology that presents an extremely elegant model of intrinsic motivation. Seemingly a spiritual successor to the humanistic theories of self-actualization, SDT suggests that humans universally possess three main psychological needs in order to feel a sense of mental well-being.

- **Competence** refers to our need to attain and display mastery, especially as a means of controlling situations and outcomes. When we display competence through an activity, we find ourselves intrinsically motivated to perform that activity. In cases where competence can be seen as a motivating factor, creating environments that are conducive to developing and demonstrating mastery is crucial.

- **Relatedness** is our innate desire to interact with, feel connected to, and care for others.

- **Autonomy** is our intrinsic need to remain in control of our own lives, to feel a sense of causality, and to act within the expectations of our self-identity.

In the early experiments that led to the formation of SDT, a crucial observation on the role of extrinsic motivation in intrinsically rewarding tasks was made. When testing the results of introducing two different types of extrinsic rewards (money and praise), Deci (1971) found that, when performing tasks that subjects found intrinsically enjoyable, subjects who were given money were less likely to perform the tasks of their own volition at a later point after monetary reward was removed. Subjects rewarded with positive communication in the form of verbal praise, however, showed an increased likelihood to perform the task. These results were verified in a later study (Pritchard, Campbell, and Campbell, 1979) where again monetary rewards were shown to reduce intrinsic motivation to perform a task.

These findings suggest a concept that should be of the utmost importance to us when we consider motivation in our work: poorly chosen extrinsic rewards are *worse* than no reward at all for tasks that are intrinsically motivating, and the most effective extrinsic rewards are positive reinforcements.

The self-determination theory allows us to completely reframe our concept of motivation and goal-centered design. How would you approach a design problem knowing that, rather than some bullshit in-app trinkets or badges, someone's main goal was to *find belonging*? Or if your productivity tool was centered around *competence* and *autonomy*?

Self-Determination by Design

There are myriad factors that make the self-determination theory not only applicable but fundamental to healthy, rewarding product design. Humanistic psychology and design play very well together. A focus on qualitative and more introspective evaluation, ethnographic observations, and a desire to understand the behavior of real humans in real situations should speak deeply to anyone who has a love for design research (that's all of us, *right?*)

Competence and Mastery

Peel back the veneer of any *gamified* experience (you know the kind: in-app rewards, pointless badges for superficial, so-called "achievements") and you'll almost exclusively come to see a shallow implementation of the much-maligned legacy behaviorism I've spent a good chunk of this chapter rightfully berating—at best, a misguided attempt to encourage or nudge folks to perform useful or valuable actions; at worst, a transparent *growth hack* that serves no meaningful purpose beyond manipulation, nudging internal KPIs and other product success metrics in the right direction.

As I broached earlier in this chapter, manufactured rewards range somewhere between impossible and improbable, with their impact ranging somewhere between nonexistent and negligible. So where does this seemingly incessant pursuit of engagement through gamification come from?

Our industry is, for better and worse, built in part on *trends*. For example, as of the writing of this book, the current trend in Software-as-a-Service web design seems to be dark websites with lots of purple and glowing gradients (Figure 5-2). This style, spearheaded by the talented folks at Linear, kicked up a visual trend that spawned countless rip-offs and unimaginative derivative creations. In this industry, if something works well, there's a queue of designers, engineers, and founders ready to copy it without exploring what makes it good and—most importantly—applicable to the context of the original.

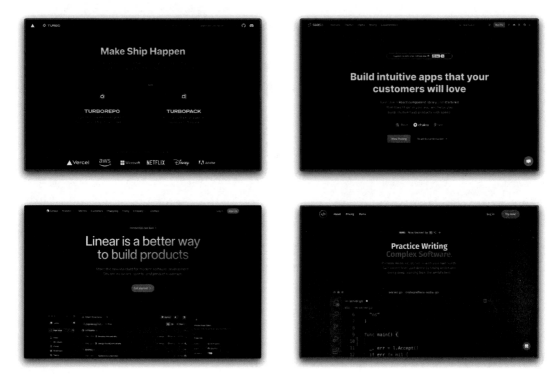

Figure 5-2. *Visual similarities between various web sites, exemplifying the current (as of 2023 at least) trend found in SaaS websites*

This is nothing new, and trends come and go. A superficial and hardly comprehensive look back through the trends of our industry sees us work backwards from the current trend of soft shadows and pastel accents, back through to the starker *flat design* trend and the modern brutalist/Bauhaus spin countering the more corporate minimal interfaces it brought, stopping off for a mercifully quick wood texture acid trip at the best-forgotten skeuomorphism phase, back through the shiny surfaces of Web 2.0, and eventually to the weird and wonderful early days of modern web design, where everything was new and grunge brushes were still cool.

And that's just the visual trends. While they're the most notable, and noticeable, trends we encounter in the industry, we also see trends in things like features, interaction patterns, and even entire product genres. One such trend was the incessant gamification of apps and sites that just did not need it to succeed. Products such as Foursquare (specifically the location-based exploration side that was later branched out into the standalone Swarm app), Duolingo (the popular language learning app that awards EXP and badges as rewards for language-learning feats), and Fitocracy (a fitness social network that gave EXP and levels for conducting workouts) all paved the way with actually useful and—at least somewhat—tasteful and relevant gamification in product design.

Foursquare gamified exploration and visiting new locations by giving various in-app rewards when users visited (ensuring they *check in* on the app, sharing their location to their friends in a prototypical example of location-centric social media) a certain number of locations, or a certain location a number of times, culminating in the most prestigious of all: *mayorship*. Becoming the *mayor* of a popular location in Foursquare was a *big deal* for a not-insignificant portion of the population. Through consistent check-ins, recurring visits, and unwavering self-belief, you too could be the mayor of your local Burger King.

While Foursquare's location-based social networking was somewhat autotelic— the app and challenges within could be seen as a game unto itself—Duolingo takes a different tack: reframing the act of learning (in Duolingo's case, learning new languages) as a game unto itself. Duolingo's approach to this kind of gamification provides a compelling and thorough reference point to explore, but first, let's explore some of the core autotelic mechanics behind video games.

Gaming's Intrinsic Motivators

Video games are, inherently, *fun* things to engage with. They often have engaging stories, offer engrossing escapism, and provide challenges that play to our desire to gain and exhibit mastery. In the environment of video games, the *reward economy* is traditionally discussed as a dynamic that encourages progression through a game. Role-playing games (RPGs) do this exceptionally well. Generally, RPGs have various statistics that represent the skills of a specific character. Perhaps strength determines how much damage your little anime man can do with his oversized sword, or speed determines how quickly a turn can occur during battle. Figure 5-3 shows the classic RPG Chrono Trigger's rather simple stat list.

Figure 5-3. Chrono Trigger's character stats determine the utility and effectiveness of various characters in various situations

Here we're exposed to some of the raw numbers used in the game's calculations for damage dealing (how hard you hit enemies) and reduction (how well you "soak up" damage from an enemy). While these stats start off at a specific number, they can be increased through *leveling up,* which involves battling (the game analogue to the "work" part of our reward flow) enemies and gaining experience points (EXP, one example of in-game rewards). After gaining a certain amount of EXP, a character levels up (Figure 5-4) and their stats are increased. Moreover, as a character levels up, there's a *chance* that they can learn a skill, which can be used in battle. Generally these skill-learning moments are kept as a surprise.

Figure 5-4. *Leveling up in Chrono Trigger*

There's a lot going on here, so let's break this down. Once we have established that battling enemies can give us EXP, we have our first reward association. Yet, EXP is a pretty abstract reward. Pretty soon we'd start getting tired of it, first, because it's a known reward—literally every battle won garners EXP—and, second, because it's really just a kind of *sub-reward* of the real goal of leveling up. In this sense, we can see EXP as a fixed-ratio (it happens every time you win a battle) reward of low saliency (it's hardly life-changing).

After enough EXP, our leveling up moment happens—the *real* reward! Except this is still an abstraction; what we're really chasing is the stat boost and the *maybe, hopefully, please* moment of learning a new skill. In this regard, leveling up can be seen as a variable-ratio reward (the amount of EXP required to get from Level 1 to Level 2 is different from that required for going to 2 to 3) of relatively low salience (it's still an abstraction). The stat increases are a byproduct of leveling up, so we *know* every level up will give us a stat increase—we just don't know *what* stats or by *how much*. In this case, the reward itself is variable, while the schedule is not. We might say this is a fixed-ratio *variable quantity* reward of medium salience. Finally, the new skill learning (Figure 5-5) is a classic example of variable-ratio rewards.

Figure 5-5. *Skills in Chrono Trigger*

New skills allow us to approach battles in a new way, to dispatch previous enemies with ease, and to implement their usage into our strategies for tougher enemies. We could stop there and say our new skills represent the upper limit of our rewards—they're variable ratio rewards of high salience. Except, the *real* rewards from video games don't actually exist within the games themselves but in the mind and world of the gamer. Just as the monetary reward of a slot machine represents an abstraction in that it allows us to purchase the things we enjoy, all this in-game goodness is an abstraction of the reasons *why* we play games in the first place. Getting stronger and progressing through a game lets us know that we're further down that path toward mastery. It lets us express our creativity in the form of opening up more unique strategies for battles and enables self-expression through the choices we can make. These are the real rewards of video games, and they represent a rather interesting context in which to discuss reward-motivated behavior.

One of the primary notions to take away from this approach to rewards is that even though the more salient in-game rewards might feel like real-world rewards (and, to an extent, they are), they serve a very different primary purpose: they are a feedback mechanism.

When you provide someone with an idea of how much they've progressed through a game, you're giving them a heuristic for their mastery. Someone can take a look at their character stats and instantly get at least a rough idea of how far along that journey they are. They can view the skills they've amassed over the course of their play through and formulate strategies, or they get a broad idea of how their own preferences and skills can combine with the in-game skills of their characters in unique and fun ways. In-game rewards become milestones along an individual's path through a video game—mementoes of their journey so far.

Rewards as Feedback

We can learn a lot from this aspect of video game design. By understanding the true goals of their audience, video game designers take a holistic approach to their implementation of rewards. As you explored in Chapter 3, it's very easy to fall into the trap of confusing features or interactions with goals. Great game designers understand that *getting to level 99* is not necessarily a goal—it's an abstraction for something along the lines of *achieve and exhibit mastery of this game's systems*. Similarly, *learn the Omnislash skill* isn't necessarily the goal for skill acquisition. It's something like *learn an important skill that allows me to be more creative in my strategies*. The in-game rewards are always secondary and very often play the role of progress indicators rather than acting specifically or solely as manufactured rewards.

This takes me to an oft-repeated point from this chapter. The idea that you can, or should, attempt to manufacture rewards in an application is flawed, since it assumes that any manufactured reward will somehow be salient enough for someone to desire in the first place. Similarly, forgetting about the *real-world* goals people bring into any conversation with your interface is a surefire path to shallow implementation of rewards.

Let's get back to Duolingo then.

Duolingo is *gamified* in the sense that its mechanics are lifted directly from the rewards-based practices popularized by video games. When you first start learning a language in Duolingo (Figure 5-6), you're taken through a starter lesson, from which you can earn some EXP, contributing to your *Daily Quests* experience.

Figure 5-6. *Completing a starter lesson in Duolingo*

You're also given a clear path to mastery for your chosen language in the form of a vertical skills list. The Daily Goal section gives you a tangible reference point for the shorter feedback loop of daily learning, and the day streak gives you a reference point for how many days you've logged in and practiced. Now, to caveat this, the trend of daily streaks in digital products is quite often a poor manifestation of the behavior manipulation I've spent a good portion of this chapter attempting to discourage. I don't wish to gloss over the fact that I'm not personally convinced this is a positive implementation of the feature—or that a positive implementation of it even exists. Duolingo's approach is far from perfect.

Aside from the dubious "streak" red flag, however, the most interesting aspect of this interface is how it manages to be reward-centric without confusing in-app milestones with explicit rewards. Duolingo's designers understand that *increase my Duolingo level for Japanese* is not someone's real-world goal. It's far more likely to be *learn the basics of Hiragana* or, pushing things a bit further, *learn enough Japanese to survive in Tokyo for a month*. Gems, levels, and EXP are *not* the rewards Duolingo provides. The real world mastery of a brand new language and the subsequent travel, cultural, or otherwise enriching opportunities opened by such are the true rewards of this learning experience. Gems are the rather arbitrary abstraction for our progression toward mastery, and our daily EXP counter plays the role of allowing us to see our progress toward our daily goals (Figure 5-7). The daily streak is there, I assume, to make us feel anxious and compelled to return or to have us watch in dismay as it resets to 0 after daring to take a break from intensive language learning.

Figure 5-7. *Duolingo's dashboard showing current progress and a clear progression path towards language learning*

Rather curiously, the part of Duolingo's interface that one might most associate with "typical" implementations of reward flows represents one of its most intrinsically irrelevant features. The Achievements section riffs on the common gaming approach of rewarding very specific in-game behaviors with achievements or trophies. These trophies are generally attached to a gamer's social profile and represent a kind of status indicator in the social realm of gaming (Figure 5-8).

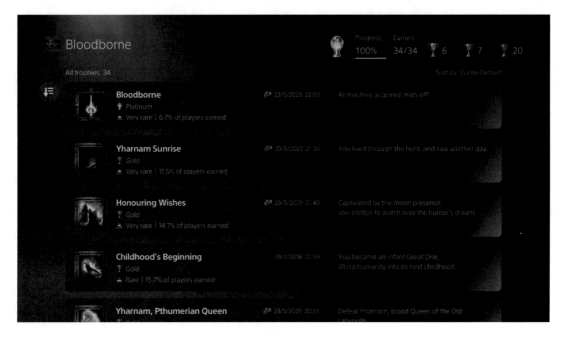

Figure 5-8. *A trophy overview on Sony's PS5 console*

That's not to say achievements unto themselves cannot be tied to intrinsic rewards. Trophies and achievements are often tiered, with the *Platinum Trophy* being the primary indicator of mastery for many video games. However, they are often attached to arbitrary actions that many gamers feel like they need to "grind" (repeat the same task over and over again for reasons beyond enjoyment) to achieve. Many of Duolingo's achievements are also somewhat arbitrary and superficial, such as the "Friendly" achievement asking the user to follow three other users.

This kind of achievement, alongside a few more seemingly arbitrary ones (the *Nocturnal* experience asking users to "complete three lessons after 10 p.m.," for example) seems to be positioned to change or manipulate behaviors for reasons that are, at best, overly abstracted from real-life goals. Learners are motivated by, we can assume, some salient factor that drives them to do the work required to master a new language. It could be argued that there's a benefit, either through collaboration or competition, to building up a network on Duolingo—for example, wanting to beat your friend to the next level of learning—but for many people, this is completely irrelevant.

The idea of attempting to compel someone to practice at a set hour feels even more arbitrary. Again, this isn't necessarily lacking in justification. Perhaps the idea is that implementing your daily language practice into your routine is an effective habit to form—but why 10 p.m.? And why is this a goal that's incentivized to us right off the bat? For a product that has—for many years—executed an extremely well-done gamification strategy, the achievements within Duolingo are disappointingly disjointed and occasionally veering towards the unhinged. Pull back the veneer of gamification and the more transparent attention-grabs and growth hacks reveal themselves with minimal effort. Progress and achievements as markers of mastery towards something as rewarding and important as learning a whole new language are *extremely* well implemented in various parts of Duolingo, and then they have these *nudgey*, transparent, almost desperate grabs for engagement and (shudder with me now) *stickiness*. I'm not angry, just disappointed.

Looking at the behaviors Duolingo tries to encourage with these shallow rewards tells us an interesting story on how Duolingo likely makes money. It stands to reason that daily, continued use of the Duolingo service is important, which is standard for any product that generates ad-based revenue. Consequently, one can assume that the daily streak and the "practice after 10 p.m." achievement are attempts at encouraging this. Friend-following likely involves us having to first invite friends, which plays into our desire for social belonging and social status—but also gets more potential eyes on Duolingo's adverts and upsells. *Viral loops* are a hell of a drug to product folks.

Not Everything Needs a Badge

Showing competence, progress, and mastery doesn't somehow mandate a gamified experience. As with many of the other embellishments you've encountered in this book, the cognitive overhead of all *the game stuff* is not to be underestimated. Having badges and experience points and levels and weird green owls thrust upon you at every turn can be exhausting for even the most tolerant of learners, and we must be wary of the requisite effort we're asking of people when it comes to adapting to the rules and specificities of a gamified or otherwise embellished system.

Fundamentally, what we're looking to do is to celebrate the wins, without creating something obnoxious, egregious, or outsized in comparison to the salience of the reward or impact.

Mindful Design Principle: Celebrate Goals   For any action that can be sufficiently seen as achieving a real-world goal or satisfying an intrinsic motivation of a user, consider marking the moment with a sufficiently celebratory element.

This type of celebration can take many forms. Sometimes a well-made success message is all it takes. Other times, especially with creative tools, taking a step back and seeing our creation in the best light is often enough. An example of a more low-key "celebrate the good stuff" approach can be seen in Unsplash's dashboard (Figure 5-9).

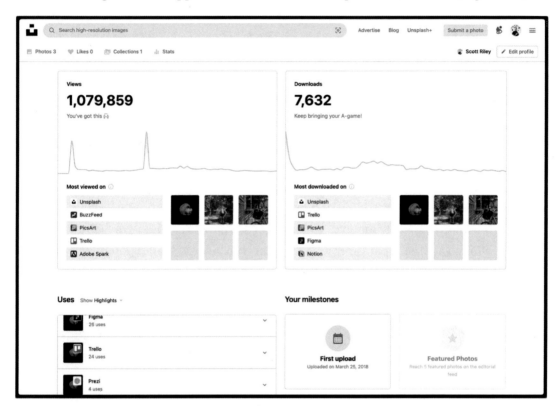

Figure 5-9. *Unsplash's dashboard*

This is a very simple, straightforward dashboard, giving us some basic insights into how many times our photos have been viewed and downloaded. The goal of an *uploader* in Unsplash might be something like *share my work with the world* or even just *get better at hobbyist photography*. In this case, other people using our work can be seen as a potentially validating, intrinsically rewarding experience. Unsplash goes a little further with this, providing us with "milestones"—such as acknowledging your first upload or hitting one million views—and dates we achieved them.

Now, this isn't some intensely gamified experience, nor is it a particularly amazing example of highlighting progress, but it achieves a tiny slice of what we see more broadly executed in apps like Duolingo: celebrating achievements and marking key moments along the path towards mastery.

In fact, timelines are powerful tools when it comes to progression towards mastery. By arranging various accomplishments or achievements along a timeline, we're able to reflect on the stepping stones of our journey from where we first started to where we are now.

Another quite specific example of more low-key celebration can be found in Slack's empty state for their Later tab, shown in Figure 5-10.

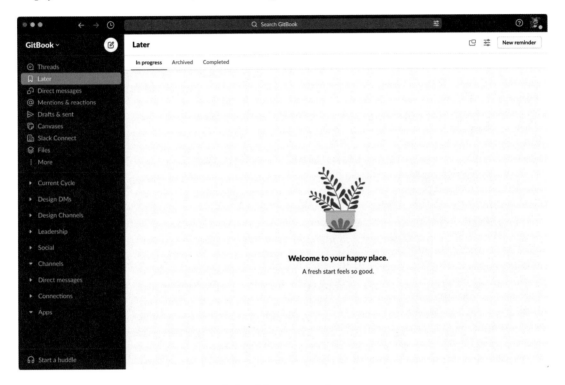

Figure 5-10. *The empty state of Slack's Later tab*

Slack's Later feature allows users to build a kind of message-first to-do list, linking specific messages (let's say, a request to make a logo bigger) to a kind of in-app, super basic workflow tool. Items in Later can either be in progress, archived, or complete. Get through all your in-progress items and you're presented with a calm empty state with some nice acknowledging copy welcoming you to your "happy place" and positing that "a fresh start feels so good" (this is frankly exceptional UX writing) and giving you a moment to bask in your *get-stuff-doneness*.

The empty state of a to-do list is the prototypical place to place this kind of low-key "muted celebration" of user success. While we don't likely know the specifics of someone's to-do items—unless we're building an extremely niche productivity tool—we can reasonably assume that checking stuff off equates to them getting stuff done in the real world. While the real-world goal is "get things done," the in-app abstraction of that achievement is an empty to-do list. We see this reflected, too, in email apps all the time. The pursuit of *Inbox Zero* is an Herculean one, and we can all be forgiven a moment of quiet, fleeting reflection as we gaze upon the nice little illustration and congratulatory copy of an empty state.

However, one question I have that's seemingly much less explored when it comes to to-do apps or productivity, is what happens to all the *completed stuff?* While the out-of-sight, out-of-mind nature of tasks you've already done is fantastic for your day-to-day progress, giving you focus on what needs to be done and blurring the stuff you've already achieved into the background, I can't help but wonder why more productivity tools don't use these completed tasks as ways to highlight achievements and milestones away from the "get stuff done"-focused backlog of tasks. Even something as simple as *look at everything you've achieved this week* can feel great! It's a chance to have a bit of fun and potentially even provide a meaningful moment of reflection. Modern society has a weird fetish for *hustle* and productivity, and moving away from the incessant influx of work items and taking time to embrace the calm and offer reflection can really take the edge off.

Challenge   Find examples of notable actions for popular products or product types that might be worth celebrating and think how you'd do so. As a starting point, my example is **a user hitting their word goal in a writing app**.

Relatedness and Belonging

Designing social applications in a world shaped by Facebook, Twitter, Instagram, and TikTok is *hard.* You only have to look at the abundance of Twitter clones that emerged after Elon Musk tried to get over a divorce by purchasing and tanking the world's leading microblogging platform. Rather than imagining a new paradigm for social interaction, people rushed to build (and flocked to use) copycat products like Bluesky and Threads. At the time of *writing* this book, Twitter has just rebranded to *X,* has gone all-in on asking people to pay for verified status, has declared *cisgender* to be an on-platform slur, and in general has built a platform that exists almost exclusively as an echo chamber for grifters, conspiracy theorists, and right-wing commentators. At the time of *publishing* this book, I'm not even sure it'll still exist.

However, Twitter brought people together like very few platforms before it. The emergence of *following* as opposed to the forced bi-directionality of *friending* previously seen in social networks like MySpace and Facebook, the strict character limit (which you can now pay to bypass, because of course you can) forcing brevity and often irreverence, and the openness of conversations all contributed to a platform where finding *your people* was possible again—a feeling that people who used niche phpBB forums in the past might have felt long lost, at least since the emergence and proliferation of Facebook's "friends and feeds" model. This didn't save Twitter from succumbing to hyper-capitalistic greed, terrible moderation, harmful terms and conditions, and addictive usage patterns, and I would be loath to glorify the product it became, but there was a brief period where Twitter offered a refreshing new paradigm for online social interaction.

And perhaps therein lies the problem with community, connection, and belonging in the age of modern internet products. Social media profits from debate, division, and controversy. The network effects of argument, trolling, and visceral negativity are far more observable and seemingly far more profitable than those of small-scale, contented communities. While it's *possible* to use many of the "universal" social networks right now to find like-minded individuals and unite around shared interests, we're doing so to a backdrop of brands pretending to be human, influencers pretending to be genuine, and bigots pretending to be enlightened. You can't be what you can't see, and the drive towards manufactured, vapid, algorithm-friendly content is a reflection of the values and business needs of the likes of Twitter and Meta. For a technology that's all about connectivity, it really is difficult to design around belonging and relatedness on the Internet. Perhaps it's this dissonance between community and capital? After all, when everything costs money to make, and needs to make money to continue to justify its existence, how communal can you *really* be?

And that's just speaking for the easy stuff. If *literal social networks* suck so bad at presenting people with community-building tools and safe environments in which to exist together, then what hope is there for products where belonging and community are secondary considerations?

Well, in a rather convenient and somewhat meta turn of events, one of the most salient contributors to finding belonging with others lies in building things with other people and sharing in collaborative successes. A shared sense of purpose is a *huge* intrinsic motivator, and working with others to accomplish shared goals encompasses a wide range of discrete motivational concepts.

While I don't want to lean on productivity and workplace tools too much in this chapter, there's an unavoidable—and vastly under-explored—potential for showcasing shared accomplishment and success within these product types. Furthermore, any tools that bring people or teams together to solve problems, get stuff done, or simply just interact with one another can and should be designed with belonging and relatedness at their core.

One of the most important aspects of designing for relatedness and belonging is how inclusive our design work is. Overly-complex language, too-dense of an interface, and patterns or flows that require too much cognitive overhead to parse are the obvious culprits, but it's also extremely easy to bias yourself towards a specific user group or use case and skew your product in subtler ways. While your goal should always be to serve your identified audience, not to try in vain to produce something that's somehow universally appealing, you can go *too far* down this route and create extremely specialized tools that are over-optimized for a small subset of your potential user base. Think about who your users collaborate or engage with on a daily basis. Is there room for them in your product? *Should* there be? If your super fancy developer tool can benefit from having designers or product people on there with them, how different would it look if you expanded to accommodate them?

Understanding how your users and target audience interact with other people in their lives is an incredibly useful reference point, one which should be high on your list of priorities when conducting research, especially if you have the luxury of conducting behavioral studies or other generative, ethnographic research rounds. How someone expects—or might want—to be able to use a product or service with someone else in their life is often integral to the mental model they bring to your product. While it's undoubtedly in part due to simple math (more users = more paid seats = more profit!), there's a very real need powering the emergence of collaboration and sharing in traditionally single-user applications. Shared calendars, shared journals, and collaborative to-do apps are all obvious examples; products like Google Docs, Figma, and Miro have brought real-time collaboration to the forefront of our industry, to the point where multi-person, multi-cursor editing is almost table stakes for many product types; and tools like Slack, Microsoft Teams and Discord all present hubs for teams and communities to exist in together, regardless of physical location.

Oh, and finally, if you're shipping collaborative features, especially if you intend to cater for open or semi-open communities, then you *need* good moderation strategies and you *need* well-trained, well-paid people who are able to enforce said moderation strategies. Anything else is just negligent.

Autonomy and Self-Identity

Really great products, regardless of their problem spaces or key functionality, allow their users to feel a sense of agency. Feeling in control of our actions is fundamental to self-determination and the psychological wellbeing that comes with it and is probably the single most important facet of self-determination we can design around. Agency and autonomy are also somewhat feature- and product-agnostic. This means that, unlike relatedness and belonging, for example—where we're at least somewhat limited to *multiplayer* apps— almost every product can implement principles that allow for autonomy and agency, and benefit symbiotically from the motivation and wellbeing they can instigate.

Of primary concern here is nonlinearity. For too long, the prevailing approach when it comes to complex interaction design has been to produce linear user flows or journey maps, where one stage of an interaction flows into another, which then flows into another into another into another ad nauseam, until some kind of success state is reached. While these are useful abstractions—especially if you consider *Happy Paths*, something you'll explore in the second half of this book—they're often used in far too limiting ways, resulting in linear interfaces that funnel people from interaction to interaction, sacrificing agency for surety. After all, the more choices people have, the less likely they choose the thing that makes us money, right?

So, step one is to throw away your user flows and start thinking about *environments*. If we reject the notion of an interface as an amalgamation of neat, linear flows and push more for open, nonlinear applications, then the idea of a designed environment can be extremely liberating. In the simplest terms possible, an environment is a place where *things can happen*. Just like our immediate physical environment, a digital environment consists of manipulatable objects—that may or may not be related—actors (such as ourselves, other people, pets, those bears who want to eat our face that we keep encountering in this book), rules, and universal forces. Through affordances (in our real world) or signifiers (in our digital world), we can infer action possibility, and through selective attention, we can apply our focus to discrete elements or stimuli when we need to get things done and, most importantly, we can navigate it with intentionality and a notable degree of autonomy.

While translating facsimiles of real-world environments to digital interfaces may appear somewhere between daunting and a fool's errand, we can look to video games to see perfect examples of how this is achieved. In fact, level design—and, more recently, systemic design—in video games revolves around exactly this. Video game worlds are designed with varying levels of autonomy and agency in mind, and you'll often encounter games described in terms of their linearity. Take Naughty Dog's best-selling *The Last Of Us* series as an example: the games are famously story-driven and contain long passages where the gamer is shuffled along a linear path with very little autonomy as gameplay gives way to so-called immersive storytelling.

Contrast this with *open world* games such as From Software's *Elden Ring* or Bethesda's *Skyrim*. Games in this category allow for almost unbounded exploration, opening up an entire world (I mean, the clue is in the name) for the gamer to explore from the get-go. Open world games eschew linearity by design, giving players a sense of freedom and autonomy that linear or level-based video games can rarely live up to.

Somewhere between these extremes we can look at From Software's brutally punishing *Dark Souls* series and their spiritual counterparts *Bloodborne* and *Sekiro: Shadows Die Twice*. These games take a very different, far more balanced approach to linearity. Their stories are told through discrete moments and through encounters and findings in the world directly. While linear moments are scattered around, they're used as tools to create urgency and pacing and to artistic effect. You're thrust into a dystopian, unforgiving world—the creation of which From Software has perfected to an art—and asked to piece things together in whatever way you like.

Let's take Bloodborne as a strangely prescient example of how I think our interface design can evolve. The game's world is structured around discrete areas with their own themes, enemies, bosses and subareas. These constitute a broad, interconnected game world that can be explored and navigated with a great degree of freedom. At the beginning, many areas are closed off, requiring you to defeat a boss (a Super Cool Gamer™ word for a difficult, unique enemy) to gain access.

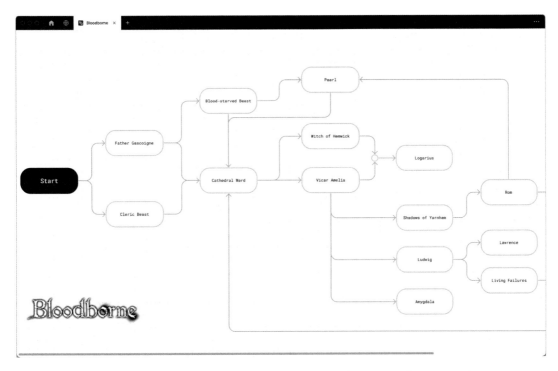

Figure 5-11. *A simplified diagram showing several potential progression routes through From Software's Bloodborne video game*

As you progress through the game however, more and more options open up to you, leaving you to explore and discover on your own accord. Bloodborne's world design is a masterclass in fluctuating linearity and nonlinearity to allow for both agency and author intent. The default state of Bloodborne, after some initial figuring-things-out (or onboarding, if you will) is open, explorative, and nonlinear. At certain points, this openness seamlessly transitions into more linear, focused paths, forcing explicitly required actions on the player to allow for progression. The default, open, explorative state gives us a sense of autonomy and choice in how we navigate the world, while the more linear, focused states maximize our chances of accomplishing a task we set out to do (see Figure 5-11).

This is *almost exactly* how I believe modern interface design should play out: providing open environments full of clear, well-signified options; defaulting to nonlinearity; and seamlessly transitioning to and from more focused, condensed states. This is, at least to me, the logical conclusion of progressive disclosure, essentially amounting to applying the concept to linearity and action possibility, as opposed purely to information density.

While these links to video games might seem tenuous at first—and honestly somewhat ironic since a good chunk of this chapter was spent decrying the attempts to gamify every app in existence—they serve as an aspirational example and salient inspiration for where we can go with modern interface design. Video games often give players a wide range of tools and options—think of an RPG allowing you to pick a class archetype or to level up specific attributes to customize your character's abilities, strengths, and weaknesses—and allow them to solve their problems in ways that appeal to them. While the experience of bashing a goblin's head in with a massive fuck-off axe doesn't exactly equate to dragging a card from "In Progress" to "Done," both are—at least relatively—more enjoyable when we're given some control over how that happens. By eschewing predictability and linearity in the name of agency, autonomy, and self-identity, we can get closer to realizing the intrinsic value of our work. It's up to us to know when to use it.

Mindful Design Principle: Embrace Nonlinearity   Allow for autonomy and agency by creating digital environments and break away from a reliance on linear flows. Seamlessly transition in and out of more linear flows only when user intent for such is clear.

Putting It All Together

Implementing the various facets of self-determination theory into products is a daunting and complex endeavor. Many of the principles fly in the face of proliferated modern practices, and it's quite possible that you're wondering if it's really worth all the effort. Of course I'm going to say *yes, yes it is* but then I've just dedicated an entire chapter of a book to it. Go figure. However, this is ultimately a better, more humanistic, more empathetic way of approaching motivation in design. By flipping the narrative of "nudging" people towards forming habits or focusing on narrow, boring, and constrained predefined paths, we can focus more on presenting open environments where people can be themselves, exhibit and reflect upon progress or mastery, and achieve these things with people with shared goals or interests. All of this ultimately add up to fulfilling and rewarding experiences. Yes, it relies on things *clicking* and yes, it's a much more complex set of variables and emotions to wrangle. But what's the alternative? A digital Skinner box full of compulsion and profiteering? Leave that to the persuasive designers and the growth hackers; there's already enough of them out there.

The goal of self-determination by design is to harness *intrinsic* motivators and limit or exclude extrinsic ones wherever possible. With that comes the required acceptance that—just like how we can't manufacture *delight*—we can't manufacture motivation. Motivation is a complex and fluid concept, a highly contextual amalgamation of needs, desires, mood, cognitive headroom, and salience of previous experiences; it's not just a binary option that we switch on or off, and it's no more a guarantee than someone waking up in a great mood. Our job isn't to try to force any of this, but to *set people up for success*.

Finally, this is another one of those points where we have to accept that our job is complex. While we strive for simplicity and clarity in our understanding of our work, we're dealing with humans. Humans are messy, illogical, fallible, and *real*.

Regardless of how much we might want to try to distill things down into frameworks and repeatable approaches, more often than not we have to roll up our sleeves and learn about the people we're building things for. Self-determination is a starting point, but everyone has a different reason for using the things we build. Everyone has their own story, their own preferences, their own needs, desires, and idiosyncrasies. You're going to encounter conflicting use cases, motivators that seem at odds with each other, and entire user bases that seemingly want competing things from your product. If contradiction is a fail state for your design, then you need to rethink how you approach things.

Summary

This chapter delved into the rather murky waters of reward cognition and motivation. You observed how the tech industry, through concepts such as persuasive design, attempts to utilize the findings of behaviorism to create slot-machine-like experiences. In using variable-ratio rewards, many applications attempt to instigate a dopamine feedback loop of sorts. You learned that dopamine is responsible for reward-seeking behavior and the notion that it is a "pleasure chemical" is deeply flawed.

The Self-Determination Theory (SDT) presents a modern, humanist-influenced theory of intrinsic motivation, suggesting that we inherently require competence, relatedness, and autonomy as basic psychological needs. By providing a well-researched counterpoint to the reductionist, behaviorist approach to motivation, SDT offers us a much more design-friendly framework within which to operate. By creating nonlinear environments and actively eschewing the need to even attempt to control behavior, we can create interfaces that help people satisfy their innate desires for competence, autonomy, agency, and belonging.

The single most important idea in this chapter (and, I believe, this entire book) is that attempting to control behavior—especially through reductionist, behaviorist motivation concepts—is a practice that should be met with the utmost scrutiny. That, as supposedly human-focused designers, we have a responsibility to the people who find themselves using our creations—a responsibility to contribute positively to their lives, to do no harm, and to protect them from practices we believe to be manipulative, especially in the name of sheer profit.

In SDT, we have an alternative theory of motivation that is inherently more compatible with a human-centered approach to design than the reductionist notion that dopamine loops are the golden geese of design psychology. In embracing humans as whole entities, in all our fallibility, we're able to focus our craft on understanding, maintaining, and enhancing our notions of self. To further propagate dangerous behaviorism in the name of profit and habituation is tantamount to accepting that the very basis of our work, creating tools for humanity, is a lie. Profit can exist without addiction and manipulation, and we have the tools, and the science, to prove that.

PART II

The Project

CHAPTER 6

The Setup

Okay, let's take a breather. Depending on how you've navigated your—I'm sure *positively delightful*—time with this book so far, I'm going to hazard a guess that you're in one of three camps. If you're in camp one, you're super motivated by all the lovely theoretical stuff from the first half of the book and are excited to start applying it to your work. Or perhaps you find yourself in camp two, where you've forgotten half the lovely theoretical stuff from the first half of the book and want to refresh with a practical-focused approach. Or maybe you're a proud patron of camp three, where you got bored three paragraphs into Chapter 1 and skipped right to this part because whatever, I'm not your dad.

Regardless, it's high time we got stuck into some practical applications, so here's what we're going to do.

Firstly, we're going to decide on a project. You can follow along with the project I'm building for this book, or you can pick something that's close to your heart that seems fun and motivating to build. Most of us have that *one* project that we know would be amazing if we just carved out the gosh darn time to do it properly. Well, now's your chance.

This will not be a standard design project. You're going to approach it in a fluid, entrepreneurial manner. You're going to do quite a bit more than your standard mid-level product designer at a large-ish company would. You'll be planning and conducting your own generative and descriptive research and synthesizing that into problem definitions and feature canvases. You'll be doing your own system models and looking at how you can use them as the impetus for living design briefs. You'll be looking at key moments and story mapping, and using them to build out backlogs with a sense of priority. You'll be wireframing and prototyping and iterating and conducting evaluative testing and you can even go and build your thing afterwards if you really want to.

You'll notice here that a lot of these activities aren't traditionally seen as "designing." Even now, with modern design being so intertwined with product and systems thinking, we tend to have a very narrow idea of what a designer's responsibilities are and are not when it comes to our day-to-day work. This book, if you haven't clocked by now, is

© Scott Riley 2024
S. Riley, *Mindful Design*, Design Thinking, https://doi.org/10.1007/979-8-8688-0143-3_6

aimed towards product designers. And *product* designers have to do *product* work. This doesn't mean we need to become Agile gurus, or spend all of our days estimating and spec'ing work, or live in Jira and call human beings *resources*, but we *do* need to overlap our design thinking with product thinking. Arranging information on a screen in a way that is conducive to a stated goal is the core of a designer's role, but we're not—at least not in this book—here to be handed a spec, a brief, and a backlog and churn out a UI.

This might seem like an expanded purview for you, and you may be taking on tasks or approaches to work that you've never done before, are not comfortable with, or feel under-skilled or under-prepared to pick up. That's *totally fine*—I can count on one hand the number of designers I've met who have a solid grasp of every (shit, even *most*) layer of the modern product design *stack*. This book isn't going to make you an expert in any of the phases I discuss. If you're not great at visual design right now, you're not going to come out of this with a resounding level of expertise, and if your research skills aren't up to par, you're not going to emerge ready to lead astonishingly impactful research spikes in emerging technologies. The point here, as mentioned, is to get comfortable with *just enough*. Doing the minimal amount of impactful work across a broad range of design phases is a perfectly valid approach to building out ideas and exploring problem spaces. Many fantastic designers—and I—have forged successful careers based not on deep mastery of a single sub-discipline but on an adequate grasp of the full design stack and how each phase can relate to the other. Without opening the particular can of worms that is the generalist vs. specialist debate—it's overdone, boring, and reductive—let me just say it's okay to be bad at something at first. If you're not a confident researcher, you can learn to research. If you're like me and absolutely suck at animation, you can work on it. Lack of skill is fine; negligence is not.

Having said all that, even if you work in a team that has dedicated product folks, or where all your research is conducted by a user research team, or even where the person wireframing isn't always the person doing the production design work, these skills are key to being a well-rounded product designer. Being able to conduct rough and ready research, to articulate your thinking in accessible visual formats, to engage others in workshops and collaborative brainstorming sessions, and to communicate at an appropriate level of fidelity *will* make you a better designer. While I'm not making any claims that following a single project in a single book will somehow be transformative for you across the board, I am confident that taking the concepts from the first part of this book and seeing through a project rooted in the principles and considerations already presented *will* make you at least a tiny bit better as a designer.

Finally, it's important to note that, due to the very one-to-one relationship between author and reader, the following chapters will be structured and discussed as a one-person project. It's prescient here to acknowledge the biases that will inevitably rise from being a—at least in theory—sole practitioner in such a wide-spanning project. Where applicable, I'll take a slight detour towards the end of each major section or deliverable and discuss how and why you would want to involve other people. If you're looking to take some (or all; make my day!) of this into a real-world project with your team, then you should be more than equipped to do so by the end of each chapter. Working with other people on lovely solutions to difficult, impactful problems is a wonderful experience (there's that belonging and shared sense of purpose from the last chapter coming in to play), and diverse teams do better work, so please don't think this is a screed in favor of the Lone Wolf trope that's already so boringly and unabashedly played out in the more "design celebrity"-leaning side of this industry. Learn how to do these cool things, share it with other people, let them find their own way to do these cool things, make cool things together, share the success, and repeat. What a life.

The vast majority of the remainder of this book will be focused on the practical application of what you've learned throughout the previous chapters, but first, let's check off some of the more utilitarian stuff and set the scene for your project.

The Tools

Right. Design tools. There are a lot of them. You don't need to use all of them. Each of them will have their own positives and negatives and a queue of people who have found themselves weirdly devoted to them. If you're an established designer, you will perhaps have a trusty set of tools that you don't want—or can't be bothered—to switch from. Conversely, you might be frustrated with a certain tool, or set of tools, and want to try something new; or you might be completely new to certain areas of design and want to explore what options there are for tooling in that space.

While tooling can absolutely have a major impact on what's possible with our work, I don't want to put too much emphasis on this section. Process, application, mindset, and morals are all far more important than whether you use Figma or Sketch. This section will be broken up by purpose where I'll list some key considerations, the tool(s) I use, and some viable alternatives if you want to go your own way. The key things to understand here are the purposes and *why* a certain tool might be suitable for achieving them; this isn't a list of reviews smushed into the middle of a book.

Before we jump in, some caveats. Firstly, unless disclosed, none of the tools mentioned here have anything to do with funding this book or my career. I get zero benefit from you using them, and I have zero vested interest in the companies who build them. If I list a product or platform here, it's because I use it and find it valuable to my process. Secondly, this industry moves quickly, and there's always a new tool promising to do all the good stuff of your current tool without any of the bad stuff and for half the price. There's a chance that at the time of publishing this book the design tool market will look quite different to how it does now. New startups promising new stuff come and go all the time, and it's impossible to keep up with it all.

Lastly, I won't be diving into any tools that use Artificial Intelligence as a core feature, especially generative AI. AI can supplement a responsible and ethical design practice but it cannot build or sustain one. There might be AI components to the tools you decide to use, and they might be a big help to you and countless other folks, but I'm loath to codify the usage of such a problematic and disruptive technology in this book. At the time of writing, AI is the New Big Thing in tech, and it's being thrown around haphazardly in all kinds of products. Perhaps at the time of publishing the magic dust will have settled and there are real, ethical, and valuable use cases for the technology, but right now it's a minefield of snake oil and impossible promises. If you're excited about the future of AI-powered design, that's fine; I am too, but we're going to put it in a little box and lock it up for now. Sorry. Moving on.

Writing and Documentation

Perhaps a strange jumping-off point given our focus on design tools, but writing words is core to design. Whether you're documenting a problem space, summarizing a research spike, putting a brief together, or simply documenting key concerns and changes throughout a project, you're going to be putting a few key documents together throughout this process.

The main concerns with writing and documentation tooling are simplicity and sharing options. We're not writing books (well I am, right now, but you know what I mean) or hugely complex documents. We're focusing more on one-pagers and brief documents that highlight important findings or decisions, that can be shared easily—preferably automatically—with our team and key stakeholders, and that can evolve as our project progresses.

The Obvious Choice: Google Docs

I've never worked at or with a company that didn't use Google's Workspace tools. Granted I've never worked at or with a Google competitor, but a 100% record over hundreds of freelance and full-time gigs is pretty hard to ignore.

It's not the prettiest tool, it won't win you any street cred, and you have to swallow your pride and use a Google product, but the omnipresence of Google Docs (Figure 6-1) is impossible to ignore.

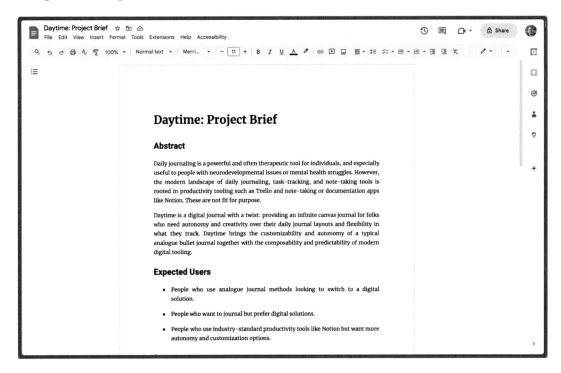

Figure 6-1. *A design brief written in Google Docs*

Also Consider

- **Notion** (`notion.so`) is an incredibly popular writing-focused tool that combines documentation, knowledge-management, and lightweight project management features. Its block-based editor is incredibly intuitive and its nested structuring makes for straightforward content organization. Recommended for smaller teams, people who want to avoid Google's stuff, and anyone who needs a sprinkling of project management and productivity tooling in their day-to-day writing app.

- **Lorist** (`lorist.app`) is a markdown-based writing app designed to get out of your way. It's what I used to write this book! It's also my product (full disclosure: I designed and built it, and it's under the umbrella of Breve Apps, which I own) and I am incredibly biased towards it. Lorist is designed for single-player, focused writing and proofreading. If you need to hunker down and write for longer periods of time, its approach to enabling focused, deeper writing sessions might work for you.

- **Notes**, **Notepad**, **Sublime Text**, and **iA Writer** are all file-based and offline options if you prefer to keep your writing offline and bring it into a shareable format later.

Given its ubiquity, I'll use Google Docs for our example project throughout this book. You might already have a preferred tool; if so, use that! In fact, I rarely use Google Docs these days and usually push for simpler, block-based or markdown-based tools, such as those listed here.

Research Gathering

You should be doing research quickly and often. Research should be a cumulative and evolving practice, and you need tooling that's going to support and enable this. I've split the gathering and synthesis components of research up here as they are pretty discrete disciplines that often (but not always!) require their own specific tools or approaches.

With research gathering, your main concern is recording and preserving the raw data and live observations of your research spikes or phases. Depending on the type of research you expect to conduct, this could involve storing survey responses, raw video recordings, observer notes, and user testing sessions (whether they're moderated or not).

The All-In-One (-Ish) Approach: Maze

Maze (`maze.co`) markets itself as a product insights platform and is heavily focused on research and insight gathering. It allows you to send surveys, recruit participants, conduct interviews, and perform evaluative testing of websites or prototypes.

The DIY-Google Approach: Meet, Docs, Drive, Forms, Sheets

At risk of this whole chapter seeming like some kind of advert for Google's Workspace tools, it's again impossible to ignore the ubiquity of Google Workspace. While not necessarily designed around conducting and synthesizing research, there's enough in Google's various tools to provide a solid option for planning, recruiting, and conducting research.

Meet allows you to video chat with your participants and includes video recording so you don't have to faff around with a separate screen recording tool to preserve your video data.

Docs, as discussed, is a viable option for note-taking and will be fine for things like an initial research brief, scoping your research spikes, and sharing broader qualitative conclusions.

Drive will let you store all of your research in a folder structure and manage access across your team.

Forms allows you to construct simple surveys, whether that's for screening potential participants during a recruitment phase or conducting quick observation or feedback surveys.

Sheets allows you to enter and store your raw data in a spreadsheet and visualize, filter, or display it.

The DIY-Not Google Approach: Video calls, Notion, Dropbox, Typeform, Airtable

A slightly different flavor to the above, and one for the anti-Googlers or those of us who prefer to have our eggs in a sufficiently diverse range of baskets. Your favorite video conferencing software will get you in front of people for interviews and moderated user testing; your writing tool of choice will let you take and store notes for each session; Dropbox (other shared folder tools exist) lets you store everything in a shared folder structure; Typeform lets you send surveys for both recruitment and analysis; and Airtable lets you store results and responses in flexible, queryable table- or spreadsheet-like formats.

Workshops and Synthesis

The most valuable tool we have at our disposal as designers is our low-fidelity "throwing Post-Its around" tool. Whether it's the digital or physical realm, a trusty whiteboard, canvas, or big, massive piece of paper is quite often going to be our go-to brainstorming tool.

In my years of working with and managing designers, I can confidently say that the mistake I see repeated most often is jumping into high fidelity work too quickly. This makes sense; we're often eager to get to "production" work and we're likely very comfortable and efficient in our design tool of choice. It can also feel super productive: going from zero to a finished-looking design quickly feels productive, makes us look good, and oftentimes unfortunately sees us cutting some very important corners, leading to oversights or poor decisions later in our process.

Low-fidelity tooling lets us collaborate with our teams in more democratized ways. Show the average non-designer the Figma interface and they'll likely struggle to intuit how it works (in fact, Figma is such a specific and opinionated tool that many designers probably don't know how half of it works). Put the same people in front of a whiteboard or infinite canvas with a few Post-It notes and markers, however, and there's nothing really to learn. The environment is controlled and specific, limited to broad strokes and stream-of-conscious as opposed to high-fidelity visual and interaction design work.

When looking at workshopping or brainstorming tools, there's a few things you need to consider. Firstly, they should be accessible and intuitive for a broad range of people. You're not looking for hyper-specific tooling for designers or engineers or product people here; you're looking for the basics. If it takes longer than thirty or so seconds to explain the core features of a tool, then it's probably too complex. The simplest option here is a physical whiteboard and a bunch of sticky notes. However, unless your team is colocated and has their physical access needs catered to, it's highly likely that you'll be using some kind of *digital whiteboard* tool. Because you're actively seeking limited feature sets and basic tooling, pretty much any infinite canvas with digital Post-Its will suffice, but if you've been paying attention during part one of this book, my preferred tool should come as no surprise.

Author's Choice: FigJam

Unless you've forgotten (or skipped; it's okay!) the mini love letters to it throughout this book, you might know by now that I adore FigJam (`figma.com/figjam`). It has the basics covered: infinite canvas so you can expand and explore any idea or conversation, digital sticky notes, drawing and writing tools, and flowchart tooling for connecting steps or ideas to one another (Figure 6-2).

Figure 6-2. *A workshop template in FigJam—you'll be making your own one soon!*

Beneath the surface there's some pretty cool stuff to play with too. As a partner to the core Figma design offering, FigJam's integration with Figma is a real boon, allowing us to pull in components from our design systems or access ideas and templates from the huge community of creators who share their work. Features such as discussion threads, timers, and dot-voting all add up to a very viable and well-crafted tool for this kind of work.

Also Consider

- **Miro** (`miro.com`) is another fantastic digital whiteboarding tool, with many of the same features you'll find in FigJam, including infinite canvas, sticky notes, timers, voting, and discussion comments.

- **Pen and paper** is a fantastic tool if you don't expect to need to collaborate in real time with others. Getting offline and away from distractions is always great. Break away from that screen, whip your notebook out, and you've got everything you need.

Sketching and Scribbling

Similar to your workshopping and synthesis work, the tools you'll encounter when you're doodling ideas and wireframing concepts should be limited, designed towards specific, low-fidelity work, and encouraging things like speed of ideas, disposability, and conscious generation.

And that's exactly the kind of behavior you want to encourage when you're generating ideas. Rough-and-ready ideas are inherently disposable; there's much less bias towards something that took two minutes to throw up on a whiteboard compared with something that took two hours to design in a high-fidelity tool. By spending enough time in your low-fidelity phases, you can build up an acceptable level of confidence in your ideas quickly before taking them into the time-consuming process of production work.

When looking at wireframing and brainstorming tools, you'll value very similar qualities as what you look for in your workshopping tools. As a result, it's worth pointing out that it's completely possible to wireframe and generate ideas in tools like FigJam and Miro. While not the primary use case (they're better as workshop tools than they are as information layout tools), it's more than possible to create perfectly passable wireframes in either.

The Old-School Option: Pen and Paper

Unless you need active real-time collaboration, my favorite wireframing tool is a good notebook and a nice fat-nibbed pen. Anything that gets me away from a screen is a winner in my eyes, and the deeper, more focused nature of wireframing and idea generation lends itself well to a disconnected, offline environment.

The Fancy-Pants Option: Figma Plus a Wireframe Kit Library

If you prefer to keep your wireframe work "in the box" or enjoy starting offline and polishing wireframes in a digital tool (as much as a polished wireframe feels like an oxymoron), then installing a wireframe kit as a library in your Figma organization gives you all those components to play with in the less-restrictive realm of FigJam. It takes some initial screwing around, but you get all of the FigJam infinite canvas goodness alongside a more rapid-prototype approach of working with prebuilt components for common interface elements (Figure 6-3).

Figure 6-3. *The wonderful Paper wireframe kit in Figma, made by the fine folks at Method*

It's entirely possible to do fantastic wireframes in production design tools too. However, I have yet to find a way to resist "going deep" and doing silly things like spending four hours picking a font instead of, I don't know, proposing the entire structure for an app before worrying about how it's going to look. If you have more restraint and self-respect than I do, then by all means, jump into Figma or Sketch and get those rectangles moving.

The Focused Option: Balsamiq

Balsamiq (`balsamiq.com`) is designed specifically for wireframing digital products and comes with a whole host of premade components for common interface elements. You'll have a very similar experience with Balsamiq as with the previous approach of using FigJam with a wireframe kit, but it is a much more focused, standalone tool (Figure 6-4). For some, this is exactly what you'll want and the more purpose-built nature of Balsamiq will appeal to you. However, as a standalone tool, for me, there's not enough of a trade-off for me to learn (and pay for!) a completely separate tool when there's such an overlap with tools I already use every day.

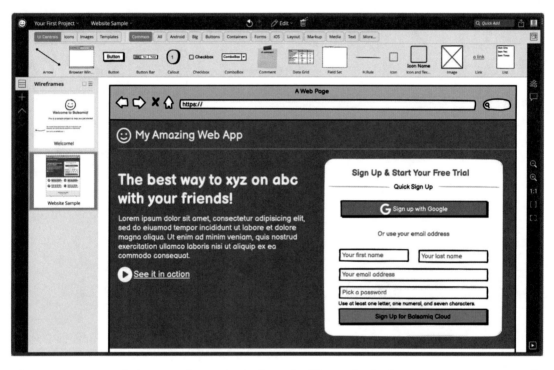

Figure 6-4. *A website wireframe in Balsamiq (from the Balsamiq starter content)*

One thing I'll say about tools like Balsamiq, and wireframing kits in general, is that you need to be careful not to artificially constrain your thinking to what's made available to you. While the components surfaced by these tools are often conventional, widely used, and widely tested, they're not the *only* options for displaying information or interaction on a screen. It's very easy to fall into a design-by-numbers approach without even really realizing it, leaning heavily on what's already packaged with a tool and eschewing the generative and innovative process that wireframing and brainstorming should be.

Remember, the whole point of wireframing at this stage is to generate ideas. You're not really setting yourself up for success if you limit your ideas because of your mental proximity to easily accessible concepts.

Designing and Prototyping

I'm going to keep this one brief. At the time of writing this book, there are two tools so far ahead of the competition when it comes to production design work that it barely bears considering the alternatives.

In one corner, we have Sketch, the first true Photoshop conqueror (shut up, one dude who remembers Adobe Fireworks) and, for a long while, the de facto tool for designing production-quality interfaces.

In the other, we have Figma, emerging initially as a Sketch competitor, only to overtake it as the most widely used interface design tool, becoming an industry standard—and darling—in the process. Murky Adobe acquisition details aside (let's see how well that statement ages, shall we), Figma is an incredibly accomplished product, with an industry-leading team, that continually ships fantastic and important new features.

However, both Figma and Sketch share almost identical benefits and a broadly overlapping list of shortcomings. For me, Figma pips it, but honestly, just pick one and be happy.

The Just-About-Winning Option: Figma

As mentioned, I prefer Figma, and it's what I'll be using for all the interface design work of our project.

Also Consider

- UXPin is a fantastic option for teams who want to design complex prototypes with coded components. It's not as intuitive as Figma or Sketch for "traditional" UI work, but it's worth considering if you have a coded design system all packaged up and ready to go.

- **Code** and **designing in the browser** is always an option, too, at least if you're designing a web-based product. In fact, for solo projects, I probably spend 80% of my time designing in code and 20% in Figma. I'm not going to be doing so for this book because that would frankly be incredibly pretentious of me, but if you like this way of working and enjoy writing code, go wild.

What We'll Be Using

While you're free to use any combination of the above tools as and when your heart desires, here's a quick rundown of the tools we'll be using for the remainder of this book, and what we'll be using them for.

Figma will be our design and prototyping tool of choice.

FigJam will be used for system diagrams, workshops, research synthesis, and brainstorming.

Good old **pen and paper** will be used for thumbnail sketching and early stage wireframing, porting these into **FigJam** for ease of sharing.

Figma will be used here too for higher-fidelity wireframes, as and when we need them.

Google Docs will be our documentation and writing tool of choice.

Maze will be used for research gathering, along with Google's **Meet** and **Docs** for live video interviews, while **Google Drive** will be the "home" for our research raw data. All research will be synthesized in **FigJam**.

If you're ready to get stuck in, then go ahead and sign up for the various services you want to use, bookmark them, grab yourself a nice new notebook and … hold off on getting started while you read a few more paragraphs of exposition. Damn. That was a bit anticlimactic.

The Phases

As sure as I am that you're raring to go and actually have fun making something, you need to understand what the heck you're getting yourself into. Designing a product isn't a crapshoot of "pick a good idea and draw it on a screen and hope for the best;" it's a process of discovery, exploration, execution, and iteration. It's also nonlinear and noncircular (it's more concentrically elliptical but that's far too fancy to remember), and as such you'll be jumping between phases a lot based on feedback, learnings, and good old human nature.

I'll go into enough detail throughout each phase as we encounter it in our project, so let's get the basics out of the way here and explore just what the heck we'll be *doing* for the next four chapters.

Research and Problem Space Definition

Good research is a prerequisite for good product design. While it's certainly possible to create something that looks good, performs well—and even achieves business goals—with no research, this outcome is reserved for the luckiest of designers. Designing without a good enough grasp of the problem space and the people who exist within—and struggle against—the systems we must design around is irresponsible and unethical. There's no excuse, as a serious designer, to work on an under-researched project.

Now, the phrase *under-researched* is doing some heavy lifting here. Ideally you'll be involved in most research initiatives your company or team conduct, but it's far more important that *someone* does this work, at least more so than *who* actually performs it. Many product people will argue that research is a core skill set of a product leader or product owner. This is undeniably true, and product folks who can translate market and problem research into concepts that other team members can understand are worth their weight in gold.

With all that being said, designers should be able to conduct, at a bare minimum, some form of design research. Whether that's exploratory stuff like user or customer interviews or evaluative stuff like user testing, the ability to learn about and observe a cohort of people, understand and empathize with their problems, generate and test hypothetical solutions, and effectively evaluate the efficacy of said solutions is as core to a designer's skillset.

We're going to have the majority of a chapter here to discuss research, but it would be a little too reductive to just throw it in as the first step of a process and leave it at that. Research is at its best when it's a constant. Cumulative research that shapes a shared understanding of the problem space and peoples' lived experiences as well as sanity checking and eventually evaluating potential solutions isn't something that happens as a discrete phase, more so something that is more or less overt—or even blocking— based on our current project's state or circumstances. It can help to think of research as a companion throughout your design process. It's where we turn when we find gaps in our knowledge or when our intuition fails us. You're going to get comfortable with quick, rough-and-ready research spikes as opposed to longer-term, R&D style research initiatives. There's room for both—and more—approaches to building out a body of research, but if you recall the stance from earlier in this chapter, we're looking to move fast and will be embracing the idea of *just enough* throughout this project. Shout out to Erika Hall and her incredible work on *Just Enough Research* for driving that idea home; rest assured I'll be talking a lot more about this fantastic book very shortly.

Solution Gathering and Exploration

As product designers, we're uniquely positioned between observation and execution. While product folks and founders are often extremely well-versed in spotting problems and proposing initially viable solutions, and while engineers and design engineers are adept at bringing interfaces to life in their final destination through production and prototype code, we sit right in the middle of the two—design is the perfect place for documented goals to be explored and tested.

This gives us a pretty expanded purview, provided we're content and able to take on the responsibilities and be accountable for the decisions made during these exploratory phases. Gathering solution ideas and workable hypotheses off the back of well-done research is often the catalyst for a successful product. You go into this phase with vague ideas of what people are struggling with and broad hypotheses of what might do a good enough job of easing those struggles such that people will pay for it with their time or their attention (and quite often both) and come out of it with defined product ideas, features, and scope. Fuzzy stuff goes in, neat stuff comes out. It's design in microcosm.

This phase is so often skipped by inexperienced designers, with temptation to go from observed problem to designed solution with minimal inertia being particularly intoxicating and difficult to overcome. We're so often told that our job is to "solve problems" and we're so often skewed towards working at the high-fidelity, production phase of design that we can rather automatically and rather erroneously conflate the two.

Skip this phase and I can all but guarantee you'll make some great early progress in your designs or wireframes—after all, you've got a problem definition and a big ole basket full of empathy, what more do you need?—only to quite rapidly fall off a cliff when the initial idea hits a complication or feedback derails your project. Aligning on proposed solutions and treating the rest of the design process as a means of exploring and testing said solutions puts you in a much more confident position from which to start the comparatively expensive work of solution design.

Solution gathering is all about evaluating ideas and potential solutions (I mean, the clue's in the name, right?) and how you perceive their potential reward in relation to their comparative risk. Clear goals and a great shared understanding of the problem space are essential here, and the work primarily consists of workshops, brainstorming, and feature canvassing. The goal is to arrive at a feature set and a clear enough brief to facilitate more granular mapping and design work. I'll talk a bunch about managing granularity here: it's super important to stay broad and resist the temptation to go deep.

System Mapping

Once you develop a clear enough understanding of the problems you want to solve and the broad solutions you expect will be viable, you need to start building your understanding of the system you'll be creating, as well as the broader societal or organizational systems that your expected audience will have to navigate.

This section can be seen as a culmination of both research and ideation, and it helps you to rationalize system qualities and observed behaviors at a much more nuanced level. I'm talking about things like documenting mental models and drawing up empathy maps, mapping out happy paths and user journeys, and documenting the system layer of your project with OOUX (more on this soon!) methodologies.

The vast majority of tasks from this phase will generally fall under the *User Experience (UX) Design* umbrella, and if you've worked with (or are!) a good UX designer, you'll likely understand the value and clarity that a solid empathy map or happy path can bring to a project. I'm loath to denigrate or overly distill the work of UX designers, but I really want to call out the strange and arbitrary drawing of lines between this work and the phases before or after it. In many situations, especially at larger companies, having teams or roles devoted to this kind of work *can* make sense, but for our purposes, having a good grasp of more typical UX work is integral. The whole UX/UI moniker has only served to compound confusion here, too. It's design. We have to make something that's functional, user-centric, well-researched, accessible, and aesthetically suitable. We're not going to get there by artificially constraining the types of design work we do or don't perform.

Job title woes aside, this is a great chance to get stuck into some really impactful workshopping. You can and should see all phases of this project as collaborative, but solution gathering and system mapping phases are where it becomes essential to open up your practice to stakeholders and team members. Not only will you be working in low-fidelity workshopping tools—making collaboration and participation straightforward—you'll also actively benefit from a diverse range of inputs and expertise throughout this work.

You'll come out of this phase of your project with a solid idea of how people might approach or understand your product; what mental models they might bring; what existing solutions exist; what people might say, think, feel, and do when using your product; and how the various objects and concepts in your system might depend on or otherwise relate to one another. This will set you in good stead to *finally* start putting rectangles onto a screen.

Information Architecture and Wireframing

With the system all scoped out, your research on point, your empathy for your audience through the roof, and your dreams haunted by sticky notes in perpetuity, you're finally ready to start laying some information out.

This phase is all about turning well-defined solutions into digestible, understandable interface sketches. This is also where things get really quite specific to the individual. When it comes to wireframes, there's a whole spectrum of fidelity to consider. I've seen everything from a thumbnail sketch on the back of a napkin through to a structural prototype so polished it's more "finished" than many people's final designs be labeled a "wireframe" and, honestly, none of them were wrong.

Some of you might also be cursing me for including information architecture and wireframing as a single phase. *How can you wire the frames if you haven't architected the information?* The short answer here is that, while it's absolutely possible to treat these as discrete phases, in faster-paced design projects, they almost always meld together into some bastardized dance between conceptual buckets of information and structural interface facsimiles. Sometimes the IA *is* the wireframe. Sometimes the wireframe *is* the IA. There is no spoon.

While the diversity in *format* of wireframes is striking, the diversity in *purpose* is even more notable. To some, a wireframe is nothing more than an incredibly basic starting point, bridging the gap between IA and production design. To others, wireframes are prototypes to test with users, and within this group you'll find everything from fully-coded, interactive wireframes through to low-fi paper prototypes replete with pop-up book style attachments to mimic interactive elements. People take their wireframes very seriously and can get very attached to the practice.

The reality for us is, thankfully, somewhere in between rushed scribbles and arts-and-crafts for millennials with too many Ugmonk products. Wireframes *are* disposable. You should be able to put wireframes together quickly and sanity check them even more quickly. But they're still the first foray into the concept of a *proposed interface*. That's a big deal and not something that can be rushed. Again I hark back to the idea of *just enough*. The ideal output from this phase is something that gives you the confidence to step into the very time-expensive realm of production design.

Design and Prototyping

Finally it's time to get stuck into some production design! While this is oftentimes the most time-consuming phase of a design project—it's not unreasonable to suggest that you'll spend as much time in your production design tool as you will in all other tools combined—there's really not a huge amount to talk through when introducing this work. You likely know what it involves, and it's patently removed from the rapid, scattergun, low-fi approach that you've adopted until now. This is where the headphones come out, the distractions get cast aside, and the detailed work begins.

However, the sparsity of my priming for this phase of our practice should not in any way detract from its importance. This is our craft. This is where we bestow character, meaning, and emotion to our erstwhile spartan ideas. Production design—or visual design, interaction design, UI design, or whatever the cool kids are calling it these days—is not an afterthought. Nor is it "coloring in" wireframes, the drawing of "pretty pictures," or whatever other derogatory moniker is being used to denigrate or diminish the practice of producing detailed, prototypical design work. As much as certain corners of the design world are quick to decry polished UI work as unrealistic, even unimportant, we ignore it at our peril.

The truth is, almost no one ever got successful off the back of a wireframe. Just as a blueprint for a house is pointless if the house is put together like shit, so too can our previous efforts be rendered ineffective by poor or inappropriate visual or motion design. This is where we earn our stripes—the culmination of our craft.

Having said that, we want to take a balanced approach here. The focus we put on—and effort we subsequently put into—this phase will vary based on numerous factors. If you're entering a saturated market and want to win on quality, you're going to approach

189

things very differently than if you were looking to take an emergent technology to market. Equally important are the expectations and preferences of your target audience. Very few people are out there overtly stating their love for bad UI work, but the truth is that people's experiences and the interfaces to which they're exposed will absolutely dictate their expectations to a degree. You should go into this phase understanding just how much polish your interface needs and, most importantly, where your efforts should be placed.

Should you be prototyping complex interactions or can you get away with more streamlined interaction patterns? Would that time be better spent on highly polished visual elements? Or is the opposite the case, where it makes more sense to be a little more spartan with your static elements and focus on creating highly-polished, seamless interactions and animations? Or are you somehow simultaneously trying to take on Linear, Stripe, and Vercel and need to nail every possible element of your prototype to pixel and microsecond perfection?

The Project

Hopefully you're both prepared and excited to finally get stuck into a project. As mentioned at the beginning of this chapter, you have a few choices to make that will greatly shape the work you do.

Firstly, you want to decide up front what project you want to work on. There are a few options for this:

- You can follow along verbatim to the project I'm developing for this book. This will give you the most seamless experience throughout the book, but it will also feel a little like design-by-numbers in parts and might rob you of some of the transformative moments in a project that spark innovative ideas or reveal problematic decisions. You'll also have a pretty copycat project at the end of it, and nobody likes a copycat. Well, unless you're Instagram. Okay. *Almost* nobody likes a copycat.

- You can create your own interpretation of the same project I'll be developing. Start from the same observed problems and project brief but go in a completely different direction from there. Set a different north star, work to different principles, solve problems for different people. This way, you'll be able to follow along with a project that's in the same ballpark as your own at the beginning but be left to your devices—conducting your own research, performing your own system mapping, and so on—for large portions of the process. This is my recommended approach.

- Finally, you can just go out and build whatever the heck you want. Uber for cats? Ship it. IKEA for sea otters? Absolutely. Spotify for Pokémon cards? Just save me the Psyduck. This approach will render the majority of the remaining chapters of this book more as reference as opposed to a fully-fledged guide, but you'll have a much more engaging and affirming experience if you emerge on the other side with a shippable prototype for something you've always wanted to design or build.

You might also like to approach the actual reading and project work in one of a couple of different ways. Some benefit most from following along with written information as it is presented—that is to say, you work on each phase of the project as and when you encounter it in this book. Alternatively, you can read everything up front, then revisit the critical points as you build out your project or ideas, using a second read-through more as a companion than a guide. Either way is fine. If you're not sure what type of learner (or follow-alonger) you are, I recommend taking the second route; it gives you an idea of what you're letting yourself in for, from start to finish, and you get the benefits of a little refresher when it comes to actually doing the work.

Having said that, I'm a massive hypocrite, because I always go for option one. I like to learn by doing, and I'm an impatient little so-and-so.

Following Along: Finding Materials

The repository for this book contains either links to or copies of the various documents and files you'll see mentioned throughout the following chapters. Each chapter will have its own folder, and the files will be numbered based on the order they appear in each chapter. For example, the project brief I'll be talking through imminently can be found in the `Chapter 6: The Setup` folder under the filename `[01] Project Brief.html`. Shorter text files and design or workshop artifacts will also be included either directly in the chapters' text or as screenshots included as figures throughout each chapter.

When a file is referenced, the folder and filename structure will be displayed as follows: `Chapter Name/[00] File Name` (again with the project brief example: `Chapter 6: The Setup/[01] Project Brief.html`) so you can—hopefully!—find your way around the provided materials as you progress through the book.

If you'd like to download the materials now, head on over to the repository for this book, and either clone it if you're comfortable with Git, or use the Download as ZIP functionality in GitHub to download a compressed archive of all the files that you can then save to your device.

Project Brief

Before I ask you to decide if you'll be building the same—or an adjacent—product as me, you should probably learn what that product actually is. If you've grabbed the files from this book's repository, open up `Chapter 6: The Setup/[01] Project Brief.html` in your browser of choice. A Markdown (.md) version of this file has also been provided for those who prefer the format, with the added bonus of being accessible directly through the GitHub web UI. See Figure 6-5.

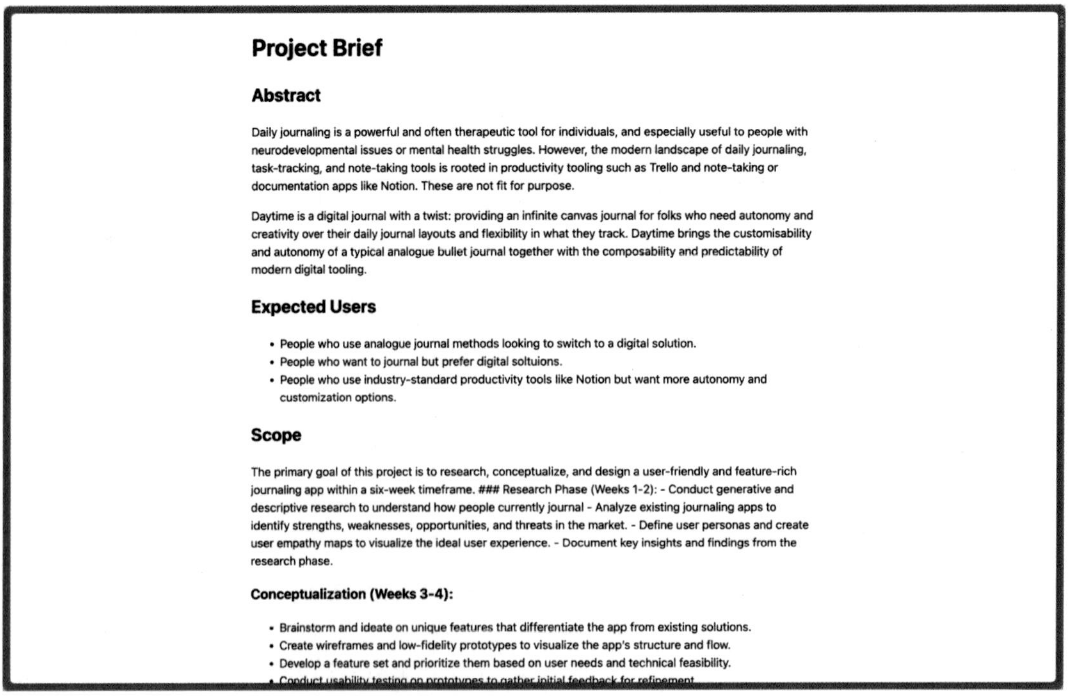

Project Brief

Abstract

Daily journaling is a powerful and often therapeutic tool for individuals, and especially useful to people with neurodevelopmental issues or mental health struggles. However, the modern landscape of daily journaling, task-tracking, and note-taking tools is rooted in productivity tooling such as Trello and note-taking or documentation apps like Notion. These are not fit for purpose.

Daytime is a digital journal with a twist: providing an infinite canvas journal for folks who need autonomy and creativity over their daily journal layouts and flexibility in what they track. Daytime brings the customisability and autonomy of a typical analogue bullet journal together with the composability and predictability of modern digital tooling.

Expected Users

- People who use analogue journal methods looking to switch to a digital solution.
- People who want to journal but prefer digital soltuions.
- People who use industry-standard productivity tools like Notion but want more autonomy and customization options.

Scope

The primary goal of this project is to research, conceptualize, and design a user-friendly and feature-rich journaling app within a six-week timeframe. ### Research Phase (Weeks 1-2): - Conduct generative and descriptive research to understand how people currently journal - Analyze existing journaling apps to identify strengths, weaknesses, opportunities, and threats in the market. - Define user personas and create user empathy maps to visualize the ideal user experience. - Document key insights and findings from the research phase.

Conceptualization (Weeks 3-4):

- Brainstorm and ideate on unique features that differentiate the app from existing solutions.
- Create wireframes and low-fidelity prototypes to visualize the app's structure and flow.
- Develop a feature set and prioritize them based on user needs and technical feasibility.
- Conduct usability testing on prototypes to gather initial feedback for refinement.

Figure 6-5. *A project brief, which you can use to kick-start your own project*

Let's dissect what we're working with here, as it's probably the most make-believe piece you'll encounter in this project. Suspending disbelief for a little while, I want you to pretend that you've been approached by a founder with a grand idea for a world-changing product. For those of you going your own way, this is your chance to wear your CEO (or CPO, or whatever you want to be; it's your weirdly corporate-centric power fantasy after all) hat and do what all good CEOs do: pluck an idea out of thin air and then use money and influence to get other people to put their labor into your ideas! I mean, use your visionary skills to find a gap in the market that only you and a fabulous designer can address.

Not all projects start with a project brief. This one does, because we're in a nice fantasy land and at least *some* parts of this project need to be ideal. The fact is, putting together a good brief is a skill, and a skill that can be incredibly valuable to learn as a designer. One of the first things I do at the start of any project that either does not have a brief, or has one that is bad, incomplete, or otherwise in-actionable, is sit down with the founder or project lead and hash out something serviceable. This is the foundation for the rest of the project and is something that should be referred back to *constantly*. If your barometer for success sucks, you're already on the back foot.

A good project brief will address at least most of the following questions:

- What are we building and why are we building it?
- Who do we think we're building it for?
- What is the scope of the impact of this work?
- How will we know if what we build is successful or not?
- How long do we have to work on this? What are we willing to spend to get this done?
- What risks and challenges can we expect to face?

For now, let's focus on that first section, the project abstract:

> Daily journaling is a powerful and often therapeutic tool for individuals and is especially useful to people with neurodevelopmental issues or mental health struggles. However, the modern landscape of daily journaling, task-tracking, and note-taking tools is rooted in productivity tooling such as Trello and note-taking or documentation apps like Notion. These are not fit for purpose.

> Daytime is a digital journal with a twist: providing an infinite
> canvas journal for folks who need autonomy and creativity over
> their daily journal layouts and flexibility in what they track.
> Daytime brings the customizability and autonomy of a typical
> analogue bullet journal together with the composability and
> predictability of modern digital tooling.

If this sounds like something you'd like to build, then welcome to the club! This is the project that we'll be taking to a finished design at the end of this book, and it will be the focal point for the remainder of our time together on these pages. Let's see what we've got to work with.

Firstly, we have abroad acknowledgment of the utility of this kind of product and a justification for its proposed existence. We know that daily journaling is valuable, and we can at least predict there's a market for this kind of product. This is great, and it gives us a good jumping off point for our research. We also have a very quick read on the current approaches people tend to take: a combination of task management and note-taking tools if they try to journal digitally or a semi-structured physical journal.

Finally, we have a very broad, one-line proposal for what our product should be: bringing the autonomy and flexibility of analogue journaling to the digital world. This is yet another jumping off point for our research: we want to find people who journal and see just what the fuss is all about.

I'll leave you to dive into the specifics of the project brief. There's lots there in terms of what success looks like for our project, examples of how you might see budget or effort split between teams or individuals, and some other bits to give us a good idea of the key considerations of our project. I'm not going to ask you to stick to a timeline or budget, but if you really do want to get masochistic, you can go full product manager on yourself and implement some self-imposed deadlines.

Start a Project Diary

One of my non-negotiables for any project work these days is keeping a project diary. A project diary is an extremely lightweight document that you can keep for your eyes only or share and even make collaborative. I use this to keep track of daily progress, but also *especially* for documenting any key decisions that get made throughout a project.

If someone decides one day that we should scrap a feature, or skip a research phase, or pivot to Spotify for Pokémon cards I want to make a note of that with as much information as possible.

Similarly, if we hit any major milestones or inflection points with the project, I like to note them down to reflect on later. I have encountered literally dozens of situations where a project diary has saved my ass. Sometimes clients forget what decisions they've made or what they've agreed to; sometimes key stakeholders make judgment calls and shirk accountability if things go awry; sometimes I make a shitty decision that I don't think is shitty at the time. When things go sideways, having a decent paper trail can be a big difference-maker. On the positive side, too, it's often quite easy to forget just how much *good work* goes into creating something. On the inevitable rough days, where you're banging your head against a wall, or your colleague is beating themselves up for hitting a stumbling block, it's always great to have a reminder of what you've achieved together.

Start a diary, either in a nice fresh notebook or as a living Google Doc or Notion project. Update it at the end of each working day, making notes of decisions, progress, interesting conversations, and random ideas. At the very worst, you'll have a nice artifact to look back on when everything is settled. At best, it'll save your ass a dozen times over.

Let's Get Researching

This was a dry chapter with *lots* of exposition. I hope that the importance of knowing what you're about to get yourself into is clear and you've made it through excited and motivated to make something fun and impactful!

Take some time to reread the project brief, or better yet, write your own, and we'll get straight into the first phase of our project: the initial research. So dust off that project diary, get up to speed on what you'll be building, and I'll see you a page over for some research fun.

CHAPTER 7

Researching a Problem Space

The start of any exciting project is a whirlwind. There's a special cocktail of chaos, excitement, momentum, and intrigue at work when you have very broad ideas and a hundred different enticing things you could be working on. Balancing the driving force of momentum that comes from feeling like you've identified a winning idea against the reality of the work—and learnings—required to deliver it is *really bloody hard*.

This, in my experience, is often the factor that leads many folks toward skipping, rushing, or under-valuing research. While research should absolutely be continuous and cumulative, it's also the first thing that should be done after the lofty and optimistic project brief. This positions our initial research as something of an inflection point: it's the first task that could prove us wrong. That's pretty scary.

It's also traditionally slow work, at least relatively. When you're bootstrapping something, throwing ideas back and forth, and brainstorming (with yourself or with an equally motivated and mobilized team), your feedback loop can be almost instant. Research, on the other hand, can see that feedback loop extended, sometimes by days, sometimes by *weeks*. Taking a team—or even yourself—away from intoxicatingly rapid ideation through to slower, albeit sensible research when a project is still ostensibly embryonic can often feel like a bit of a buzzkill. Unfortunately, convincing skeptics to calm down and do some research is often an uphill battle.

However, *no research, just vibes* is not a long-term strategy. Taking a breath and taking the time to conduct the right kind of research can set you on your way to a smoother project that your whole team can be confident in.

© Scott Riley 2024
S. Riley, *Mindful Design*, Design Thinking, https://doi.org/10.1007/979-8-8688-0143-3_7

Why We Research

We research to learn. Roll back the clock to your first year or so of education and I'm sure you'll have been taught the basic *questioning words* of your native language: that's *who, what, where, why, when,* and *how* for us boring English natives. In its simplest form, research helps us answer these questions in different contexts across various vectors. Who experiences the problems we want to solve? Why do these problems occur? Where are they when they experience them? When are they most likely to struggle with them? How do they currently navigate them? What can we build to solve them?

There are dozens of research frameworks, baked into further dozens of product and design frameworks, but everything ultimately boils down to answering these basic questions. The more we cover these questions—admittedly, it's the *who* and the *why* that matter most right now—the better we can build and evaluate potential solutions. While there are myriad outcomes that validate this kind of research, we're going to focus on three.

It Builds Confidence and Understanding

Research allows us to learn about people and problem spaces as much as it empowers us to test our hypotheses and evaluate what we've built. Sometimes, simply knowing that people actually experience the problems you want to solve is enough to keep things moving along. Seeing that not only are the problems you want to solve experienced, but that there's a clear desire for a solution to said problems to exist is even more empowering.

A well-conducted research spike gives you all of this and more. Having a foundational understanding of your audience, their experiences, their mental models, and existing competing solutions is a boon, and one that's well worth the investment.

It Saves Money and Effort

In all but the immediate term, research is a time-saver and, ultimately, a cost-saver. While diving into building, shipping, and iterating is tempting, going in dark bakes in assumptions and almost invariably leads to confusion further down the line. Do the right research and do that right research right (say that five times fast), and you're paying a pittance for answers to the most important questions you face at the start of any project.

Are you building the wrong thing? Research will reveal that rather abruptly. While nobody wants to invest time and energy into generating, elucidating, and ultimately briefing an idea only to see it fail due to lack of feasibility or viability, it's *much* more painful to spend months of time and energy before you get to that point. *If* your idea is doomed, it's better to realize this at the first stage than the last. Well-run research has an uncanny ability to lay bare bad ideas.

Conversely, making it past the seminal step of proving viability allows you to take that confidence into more generative and descriptive phases of early-stage research, with the goal of documenting problems and behaviors. Having a grasp of your audience's behaviors, lived experiences, mental models, preferences, and how they use existing tools to navigate their problems are all inputs to a much more efficient and direct design process. Furthermore, many of the observations made at this stage have a compound effect on other business areas. Hearing how potential customers talk about problems and competitors in their own words and in relation to their own goals is integral to any marketing team. Early indicators of shared languages or conceptual structures are huge for information architects and content designers. Even your useless CEO can get involved, using snappy quotes unearthed in research to convince investors to throw more Monopoly money at their AI-powered web3 lunchbox product. Everyone wins.

Whether it's through quickly revealing unviable or infeasible ideas or enabling more focused follow-on phases and more confident design decisions later in a project, good research provides an undeniable return on investment.

It Helps Us Tell a Story

Research provides us with many of the tools we need to build a compelling narrative around the product or project we're building. It lets us sow the seeds of empathy for people at these foundational stages. It shows us and our team glimpses of real people living real lives with real struggles.

While the furore that often follows a seemingly genius idea is motivating and momentum-building, it pales in comparison to the unifying nature of a talented team aware of the real people and real problems that they're empowered to serve and solve respectively.

Never underestimate the power of a good story. While the raw data you gather during research is critical, and while the various ways you synthesize and visualize that data enables you to move to the next phase of your project with confidence, the real outcome of research is the beginnings of a story. Early stage research is exposition. It introduces your characters, sets your scenes, and provides the first fibers of a thread that will run throughout your project.

Just Enough Research

I've made a conscious effort throughout this book of not relying too much on existing industry literature or the unfortunately far-too-common self-help books that have come bursting out the seams of cognitive science and its adjacent fields in recent years. Predominantly this is to avoid falling into the seemingly common trap of writing a glorified reading list when producing a book broad in scope (this is not to say you're reading some kind of far-reaching masterpiece that you should be grateful to hold; more so that we're covering a *lot* and it's not a specialist, niche design book) but I am absolutely making an exception for Erika Hall's incredible *Just Enough Research*.

The idea of *just enough* is integral to any kind of generalist approach I take or advocate for when it comes to design. Unless you're blessed with unbounded timeframes or infinite budget, knowing when you've hit a maximal point of return on your time or money investment is absolutely invaluable. While there is no particular *Just Enough* movement, I'm all in on the idea. *Just enough* works for almost every phase of a project: just enough research (of course), just enough system modeling, just enough wireframing, just enough design, just enough coffee, just enough meetings, just enough existential dread, just enough *everything*.

While I'm going to present my own research philosophy, I would be remiss to not credit Erika Hall's work as the groundbreaking title it is, and one that has profoundly shaped my approach to design research. Go grab the second edition, put this book down, read *Just Enough Research* cover to cover, then come back. I'll wait.

Back? Awesome. Yeah, it is better. I know.

Let's take a look at the approaches to research you'll encounter throughout this chapter.

Behavioral Interviews

The core component of any design research process is the humble behavioral interview. While there's absolutely an art to conducting a great behavioral interview, it's an art that pretty much anyone with a modicum of self-awareness can pick up pretty quickly. In fact, for many folks, the hardest part of conducting a behavioral interview lies in shutting the hell up.

Behavioral interviews are a component of ethnographic study. Ethnography is the art and science of observing. Whether that's large-scale observations of entire societies or small-scale observations of tiny communities, ethnography is all about exploring social relations and observing how people navigate the world around them.

The vast majority of design research is ethnographic at its core. We're not conducting huge quantitative studies. Although we make extensive use of quantitative data at scale, notable data, trends, and anomalies are almost always the *what* that precludes the *why*. Qualitative data is ubiquitous in the world of design and there's rarely a better tool than simply watching and listening to how real people navigate real problems in their real lives.

A good observational interview is conducted more as a fluid series of prompts than a meticulously planned question-and-answer session. You will absolutely prepare questions in advance, but you'll be relying as much—if not more—on your ability to improvise and to spot opportunities to learn.

Task Shadowing

The yin to observation's yang is *immersion*. While observation (with some interviewing sprinkled in) is our primary form of gleaning information about the people in our problem space, immersion gets us deeper into their lived experiences.

One of the most common approaches to immersive ethnography is task shadowing. The goal is simple: researchers (and this could be anyone working on your project, not just the people with "research" in their job title) want to build empathy and deeper environmental understanding by placing themselves directly into the environments in which their participants experience and navigate their problems.

Traditionally, task shadowing and other immersive observation approaches involved going into *the field*—the scientific term for leaving the house and touching grass—and getting amongst your participants wherever they might conduct their business. In the (insufferably dull) world of corporate *Design Thinking*, this often involved going to people's offices, following them on their journey to/from work, or even flying out entire teams to poverty-stricken corners of the world so they can practice empathy and white savior complex at the same time.

Global pandemics have a way of changing that kind of thing.

Nowadays, it's increasingly common—not to mention cheaper and easier—to do some kinds of remote shadowing. People are more used to video calls, they're more used to asynchronous collaboration, and they're more used to going about their business from unique, remote locations. If you're working on a product that you expect will live on a screen, then you're going to really struggle to find a "standard" location where your problems will be experienced and navigated. This means you're more than likely going to need to adapt typical shadowing to work more as a remote session.

Now, the caveat here is that, depending on your problem space, you could be baking bias in right at the start of your process by assuming that not only do your participants know how to use remote communication tools, but they own or have access to devices that can run them and internet connections that can connect them. For our digital journaling app, we're on the safer end of that assumption, but even so, we'll need to ensure we're not discounting vulnerable or underrepresented communities from our research efforts.

Skip the Surveys

While Hall takes an *if you're going to do them, do them properly* approach to surveys in design research, we're going a little more nuclear with our take: we're not doing them at all.

Surveys are a confounding purgatorial hellscape situated somewhere between ethnography and data analysis. They lack the objectivity and scalability of product data and they eschew the observable, in-the-moment, qualitative revelations of behavioral studies. They're worse than useless because they're easy to make, can be sent out to thousands of people, and are often positioned as being far more factual than they actually are.

The only time we'll send a survey is to screen potential research participants.

Let's Get Researching

Now that we know the types of research we want to focus on, we can get stuck into preparing and conducting it.

The first thing we need to do is decide what we actually want to research. Our research endeavors will be limited by various constraints of our project. Budget is likely going to have the biggest impact here; whether that's monetary budget—that is, how much we can spend overall on the project or how much has been set aside per phase—or effort/time budget—that is, how many people for how long will work on this phase of our project. While we have the luxury of working through a project that's a little removed from these constraints (although I'm not going to stop you if you want to put a time constraint on your project if it helps!), every real-world project will be limited by either time or money, and almost always by both.

We should also look at the research skills we have in our team. While ideally we'll have a diverse range of researchers and skill sets, in reality, research responsibilities at smaller companies are almost invariably left to either a designer or a product person, and it's a little unreasonable to expect a full-time product designer to *also* be an adept and versatile researcher. If you know you don't have the skills for long-term field research or large-scale sociological studies, then stick to the basics: talking to people and observing their behaviors.

Desk Research (AKA Just Google It)

While it might often be frowned upon, or at least not regarded as "real" research, the practice of "desk research"—sometimes labeled "secondary research," perhaps reinforcing the reasons for its denigration—can be extremely useful for us lowly designers.

While a lot of the so-called real research we'll be performing aims to collect, codify, and present new data and findings, desk research relies more on finding information that already exists. If you're researching software engineers, taking a look at Stack Overflow's yearly survey results to get an idea of the technology preferences of a subset of software engineers would be your *desk* research. Conducting your own behavioral interviews where you speak directly to a small number of software engineer participants would be your *observational* research.

Desk research lets you start gathering data and insights with almost no inertia. The planning and screening of a more in-depth behavioral study can take a good while to get going, while you can pretty much begin your desk research as quickly as you can type a query into your search engine of choice.

When we're conducting our desk research, we're mostly looking to fill in knowledge gaps about the space we want to design in. How do people talk about the space? What tools and competitors exist already? How are those tools and competitors marketed? What activities and principles exist around the disciplines or hobbies within your space?

This stage can also help when it comes to preparing your early stage ethnographic research, often revealing talking points and early lines of questioning that fit perfectly with your initial semi-structured interviews.

Bring on the Influencers

Love them or loathe them—and there's a lot to loathe, let's be frank—influencers and content creators in general are here to stay. While at first glance our very serious design research might have no use for the budding celebrities that grace our YouTube and TikTok feeds, in reality they might just send us down a rabbit hole that becomes a goldmine of secondary data points for our research.

Almost every hobby or activity has some kind of community of content creators and consumers. There are knitting videos with tens of millions of views on YouTube. People make legitimate and lucrative careers out of recording themselves dying their hair, fixing horseshoes, painting miniatures, and sundry other things, many of which should probably be avoided by anyone with eyes. Every skill, hobby, job, kink, interest, and sport has some corner of the internet where people share their experiences and ideas.

I recommend starting every project with a day or so of desk research. How niche your project is might change your potential data points from millions to thousands, but we live in an age where there's a subreddit devoted to pieces of bread stapled to trees. You can find content relevant to your project's remit.

Spotting the Patterns

Desk research should give you a basic understanding of the field you're about to plunge into designing for. Learning how people perform the various tasks related to your project's purview is the most basic, fundamental outcome of preliminary research. Beyond that, though, you'll very quickly start to notice patterns and conventions within the field or community you're studying.

It's really important to note things down if they start cropping up multiple times. You're looking for things like common metaphors, shared languages, trends and best practices, and anything else that can help you intuit some kind of shared understanding between community members. Some fields and activities are full of best practices and niche terminology so ubiquitous that it becomes a kind of distributed cognition. Hearing drummers talk about being *in the pocket* might seem extraordinarily weird—*Whose pocket? Why are they drumming in it? Surely the acoustics are awful?*—but it's a phrase that is used and seemingly understood by almost every drummer I've spoken to.

Or think about how folks in the mental health and neurodivergent communities talk about having *enough spoons* for a cognitively burdening activity—relating to a concept where we start our days with a bunch of metaphorical spoons, spending a certain number any time we need to perform something burdening, attention-grabbing, or anxiety-inducing. Both my wife and I are neurodivergent and the phrase *I haven't got the spoons for that* is common enough in our home, but in a more general setting results in us receiving some extremely weird looks. This kind of shared language or behavior can be integral when it comes to understanding the conventions and idiosyncrasies of the communities you'll be designing for. Don't overlook it.

Prepping for Research

The best way to prepare for a round of research is to write a research brief. Yes, *another f#&%ing brief.*

Formulating a Research Brief

Just like our project brief, a research brief is a statement of intent. It's not a long document (I guess they're called briefs for a reason) but it's an important one and it is something that you, your team, and your stakeholders should refer back to often.

Your research brief should include the following key points:

- An **abstract** or **background** that contextualizes the research you're going to conduct

- **Goals** or **objectives** of the research round. These should be somewhat broad, but not so vague as to be useless. *Watch people talk about journals* is not a great objective; *understand the various journaling techniques people use to navigate their day* is much better. You should have several objectives.

- A section detailing the **methodology** you plan to employ in order to meet the goals and objectives previously laid out. This should communicate specifics about any interview or evaluative rounds you expect to conduct. Will you be interviewing people? Shadowing their working day? Will you be conducting this remotely? At a specific test location? In the field? How will the sessions be recorded?

- Any **budget** or **timeline** considerations for this particular research phase

You can fold all of your research into a single brief with multiple methodologies, or you can write a shorter brief for each methodology. I prefer the latter; I'll usually write one brief for the behavioral interviews I want to conduct, a separate one for any shadowing work, and so on.

Even if you're working on a solo project, you should still write a research brief. It's just as likely that you will lose track of your goals and objectives or need refreshing on the methodology as it is for any of your rhetorical collaborators.

Take a look at the research brief in the repository in `7 - Research and Problem Space/[1] Research Brief.html` (or the Markdown file of the same name)—there are a few things to highlight before you dive in to formulating your own brief.

You'll notice in the Criteria section that we're specifically looking for participants who self-identify as having some kind of neurodevelopmental or mental health concern. We know from our desk research that many people with anxiety, depression, ADHD, and OCD can reportedly benefit from journaling. While it's important to involve participants diverse in background, race, ethnicity, gender identity, and myriad other demographic qualities, sometimes the most vulnerable members of a community are the least willing or able to participate in research. We should be constantly challenging ourselves and our team to maintain a diverse participant pool, but if that's not codified in a brief or other working agreement, it can be dishearteningly easy to find yourself working with a homogenous participant pool.

Finding Research Candidates

Welcome to the most frustrating part of behavioral research: actually finding people to interview. The act of finding and screening candidates for a research phase is known as *recruitment*. Recruitment is all about maximizing our efforts, mostly around finding a sweet spot between size and relevance in our candidate pool. A candidate pool is simply a list of potential research participants and is usually built up through an initial outreach process.

In a similar vein to our desk research, the more niche our target audience, the more difficulty we can expect to encounter when we try to engage with them. Designing a product for "anyone who uses the London Underground to commute" is going to have a wider potential participant pool than designing one for "genderfluid cage fighters who collect Pokémon cards and have no sense of smell." Whatever our target audience might be, the recruitment phase of a research project is incredibly important. I've done my fair share of "hail Mary" recruitment in the past—casting a wide net and hoping to filter a large pool of candidates at the screening stage—and while it's viable, it's far from optimal.

One of the first pieces of advice you'll get when searching for participants is to "meet people where they are." This concept is fine in theory, but in practice it's an incredibly nuanced statement. Sometimes "where they are" is an open and welcoming forum or public social media group; other times it's a tight-knit community or a safe space for vulnerable people. Different communities are, quite rightly, more or less open to people wandering in and asking for research participants.

The first thing to address: participants must be compensated for their time. If you're building a greenfield product with no existing user base, this compensation will likely be in the form of gift vouchers to online stores. If you're conducting interviews with existing users, then free months, free plan upgrades, or discounted rates for your product might be satisfactory too. Some companies offer swag bags to research participants, sending out company branded t-shirts and notebooks and other ostentatious crap destined for landfill. Don't be like those companies. How much you compensate participants will vary wildly depending on your research budget, candidate scarcity, the time you expect them to spend with you, and the emotional or cognitive impact you might expect them to expend during your interviews. Asking a well-off corporate worker about their daily commute to their office isn't going to be super demanding; spending an hour asking a vulnerable individual on the poverty line about their personal finances could very easily verge on traumatic for them. You should compensate accordingly. $20 for a quick chat is often fine but expect to pay closer to (and often in excess of) $100 for longer or more in-depth sessions. Do not ask participants to attend sessions without compensation of any kind. It's unethical. You're better than that.

The main thing we need to address during this phase of recruitment is how we expect to find participants in the first place. While the screening phase can be a discrete phase of this process (more on that very soon), it's quite often folded into a combined outreach and pre-screen approach, where an application survey containing criteria that helps us deem their suitability as candidates is sent out through predetermined channels to a pool of potential research participants. In simple terms, imagine we want to talk to Pokémon fans who also identify as part of the LGBTQ+ community. We could post a link in a Pokémon subreddit to an application survey that also contains a question from which we can glean whether or not a participant identifies as belonging to the LGBTQ+ community. Any applicants who answer No (or give any other indication they don't identify as such) can be discarded, and any who give an answer which we could reasonably infer as a positive will be saved for later (in notes, a spreadsheet, or other applicant tracking tools) so we can organize potential interviews or shadowing sessions.

Where you go to reach out for participants is going to depend massively on the types of people you want to speak to. If your target audience are working professionals and your product is also a work-focused tool, you might prefer places like LinkedIn or Slack communities. If your product is aimed more towards millennials and is adjacent to the fashion industry, advertising your application form on Instagram might be a more sensible choice. Much like a marketing campaign, we're really looking for maximum return on investment—that is to say, we want to spend as little as possible of both our time and our budget to get the best possible candidates. If you're working with an existing team on an existing product, it's possible—arguably quite likely—that your team has at least a basic market-level understanding of your audience. What social tools they use or the most popular websites they visit might well be a part of that understanding, and you can lean on your marketing colleagues for this kind of information. However, those of us working on a new product aren't out of luck either. Oftentimes a browse through market analysis reports can go some way to shining some light on the behaviors and preferences of our target audience. Chances are, we'll be able to at least have an educated guess as to where we should be posting our outreach.

Screening Participants

So you've planned your outreach properly, you're offering good compensation, and you have a decent idea of where you're going to find your participants. The next step is ensuring you're finding the right candidates from your candidate pool. Here comes that one survey I promised earlier in this chapter.

Crafting a candidate survey is pretty straightforward when you understand that the goal is to find the most appropriate candidates from your pool. You've done the hard work in the **criteria** part of our research brief, and now you just need to ensure that you're recruiting participants that match this criteria. Taking a group of candidates and whittling it down to a subset of the most-applicable potential participants is known as *screening*. The simplest method of screening is to send a survey to your candidate pool.

More sensitive or complicated research spikes might warrant screening interviews, especially if you have nonstandard or very specific criteria for your study, but at that point you're really veering into the kind of specialized research that should be outsourced to research specialists.

When screening candidates, try to use scaled answers as opposed to simple yes/no answers. Binary questions are fine if you expect to include/exclude a candidate purely based on a yes/no answer, but more often than not you'll be looking at degrees on a scale.

So, rather than asking people *do you journal every day?*, we should be asking something like *how often do you journal?* with options such as *every day, once a week*, and so on (Figure 7-1).

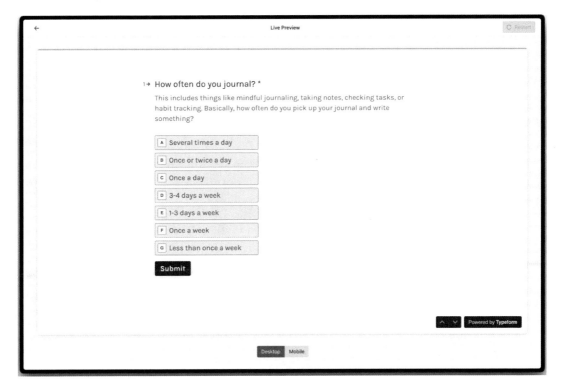

Figure 7-1. *A question with a scaled answer is much more useful than a binary yes/no option*

You can find the full list of screening questions in the repository, under
`7 - Research and Problem Space/[02] Candidate Screener.html`.

While sourcing and screening can be done sequentially as two discrete stages of a recruitment phase, it's often much more economical to pre-screen candidates. This simply involves having your screening survey do double duty as an application form. Again, your recruitment approach can and should differ based on the demands of your research, and you might find it beneficial to have a broad outreach to build a large candidate pool that you later filter with screening surveys or other filtration methods. This will be especially applicable if you plan on running multiple rounds of ethnographic research and want to maximize the breadth of your candidate pool. For larger-scale or more complex research projects, you might even want to have multiple rounds of screening, building out an almost tree-like hierarchy of candidates.

For our purposes—we're looking to conduct a fairly quick research phase with a small number of participants, and we're not building a super complex or niche product—taking the faster approach of pre-screening is worth the trade-off of a potentially limited candidate pool.

Any outreach and screening efforts should be documented in our research brief. Aside from a solid methodology, that's all we really need to have in place before we can get stuck into research. If you're following along with the project, take some time to make a note of where you'll conduct your outreach and links to any survey you plan to use during candidate screening. In the research brief for this project, you can see I've already laid out where we'll be posting our outreach, and the screener questionnaire can be found in the Candidate Screener document associated with this chapter. In short, we're going to post to our networks on Twitter and LinkedIn. Now, let's say this didn't play out super well and we got an unfortunately limited response from our outreach. This is unfortunately common, and relying on limited networks or non-guaranteed reach can quite easily result in limited exposure and, ultimately, inactionable candidate pools. In such circumstances, we either need to rethink our chosen outreach approach or invest more into outreach in general. If the "social blast" approach isn't right for us, we might consider investing in a short ad campaign or even outsourcing our recruitment entirely.

Document your sourcing and screening plan in your research brief and get your outreach campaigns set up. For our purposes, we're going to send links to our screener survey through Twitter and LinkedIn. This puts us in a position where our outreach is ostensibly free, but we're relying on the network effect of these tools to boost our outreach to a wide enough audience to satisfy our candidate pool needs. We'll also make a post in the bulletjournal subreddit (`reddit.com/r/bulletjournal`).

Scripting Interviews

You can find an example interview script in the repository, under 7 - Research and Problem Space/[03] Interview Script.html.

It's important to note that interview scripts will vary drastically between projects. After all, the simple structure and specificity required leave us with more of a guide than a framework or template that we can use in a diverse range of circumstances. One constant, though, is that interview scripts are a guide for the facilitator and a planning tool, *not* something to be performed from. Reading a script verbatim is one of the fastest ways to ruin a behavioral interview.

Instead, focus on positioning your script more like a rough sequence of prompts, put together with the intention of being a guide or a fallback as opposed to a rigid structure or lines to be dictated. For recorded interviews, whether that's recording footage at an in-person session or recording and transcribing a video call for a remote session, make sure to lead the interview with a statement noting that they are being recorded, they can request a copy of the recordings at any time shortly after their session, and that they can ask for recording to be stopped—or indeed, stop the interview entirely—at any point. You should also state how long you will hold on to the recording before it's destroyed. This is the one area where it can pay to read verbatim from a script, as you want to ensure your participants' comfort and safety, as well as getting informed consent before jumping straight into the bulk of your interview.

Ensure that your script includes reminders for any subjects or lines of questioning that might frighten, upset, or otherwise trigger your participant. This is more common that you'd likely expect. Many of us struggle navigating or understanding our place in the world, and there are certain subject matters that can trigger thoughts of anxiety, helplessness, and even trauma in many people. Someone with anxiety who also lives close to the poverty line is going to have a vastly different response when asked about how they manage their personal finances than an affluent, neurotypical individual who has very few financial anxieties. Trauma-informed research is imperative given the times we live in, and you should pay special attention when talking about someone's financial stability, sexual orientation, gender identity, mental wellbeing, family history and employment status. Trauma-informed research is a little out of scope for this book, but I absolutely implore every designer to educate themselves at least in the basics. Understand—and note clearly in your script—areas where a participant may be triggered in some way and make a plan for how you can avoid or diminish exposure. It's your job to ensure participants' psychological safety. Don't mess it up.

Be sure you tailor your script for your particular participant, too. If you've screened your candidates well, you should have a little more information to work with than just the participant's name and bio. If you know that you're chatting with someone who describes their journaling as "very consistent," you might want to ask them how they maintain this consistency; however someone who describes their journaling as "erratic and forgetful" should be asked what's blocking them from being consistent, or what motivates them to journal on the days they do remember. While the goal of the question is the same—to find out what motivates people to journal consistently—the line of discussion is tailored to the participant.

Conducting Interviews

While a good script is important for mapping out a general potential flow through an interview and can provide a useful set of questions to fall back on, the most important skill when conducting ethnographic interviews is the ability to *listen*.

One of the first things I hear when I encourage designers to jump into behavioral interviewing is something along the lines of *I don't have the people or social skills to talk to someone for that long!,* which fundamentally contrasts with the goals of a well-done behavioral interview. Even thinking solely in terms of useful data, we want to maximize observations and insights from our participants. Talking too much is just noise we have to filter out later.

So, in short, get comfortable shutting the hell up. Aside from tempering our love for our own voice, there's a few simple points that will serve us well during our behavioral interviews.

Do a Dry Run

Things go wrong with technology all the time. Video conferencing tools have a wondrous habit of going down seconds before an important call, screen-sharing technology almost always needs configuring, and you and your colleagues need to be explicit about your shared and individual responsibilities.

Having someone from your company, or even a friend or family member, who is not part of your research team play the role of a participant while you and your team conduct the first five minutes or so of interviewing can help iron out technology and people problems. Don't leave testing your setup until 45 seconds before your first participant call only for everything to screw up and eat into your interview time. Trust me; it's not fun.

Use Your Script As a Guide

Very few occurrences tank a research round as effectively as a facilitator reading robotically from a script. As mentioned, a research script should be seen more as a guide, a list of prompts that you can fall back on if your interview goes off track or you're lost for questions.

Give Your participants an Out

Make sure the person you're interviewing knows that they can end the session at any time, without giving a reason and without prejudice. Acknowledge this at the start of the interview and remind your participant.

If you're conducting remote interviews and recording the call, remind the participant before, during, and after the call that they can request copies or deletion of the raw data. If your work falls under GDPR, this is legally imperative, but even if it doesn't, it's ethically sound. Your notes, observations, and synthesis should be more than enough documentation of your research that raw recordings should be more of a bonus than a requirement.

Know Your Roles

If you're collaborating on your research, you should have very explicit roles for your team members. There are two roles that I see as essential to a good research call.

- The **facilitator** is the person who conducts the interview. Their job is to introduce everyone, set the scene, and guide the interview in the direction it needs to go in. The facilitator is the *only* person who interjects or asks questions during the dedicated interview phase. They are accountable for the quality of questioning, timekeeping, participant safety, and the overall interview experience.

- The **observer** is a mostly-silent attendee who is there to observe language, behaviors, and nuances that the facilitator is likely to miss. These are things like repeated phrases that could hint towards the linguistic area of a mental model or repeated behaviors that could speak to some sort of habit or convention. It's important that the observer stays passive during the dedicated interview phase, only asking questions during the free-form Q&A phase.

Depending on the size of your research team and the complexity of your research project, you might need more granular roles, such as an emotion or body language tracker there solely to observe expressions and other emotional cues, a dedicated timekeeper, and even translators or technical support folks for super complex projects.

Too many cooks do indeed spoil the broth, though, and it's always a good idea to limit the number of people involved in your interviews to the bare essentials. Research is quite exciting for lots of folks, and you might find you have to disappoint your colleagues by rejecting their requests to be involved. Marketing, sales, customer success, customer support, and even leadership (when they're actually doing something useful) may all want to be invited to these sessions—after all, they're incredibly valuable learning experiences—but nothing gets participants uncomfortable quite like staring down a table (or a video call screen) full of over-eager faces watching them with bated breath.

Let's Conduct!

For the purpose of our Daytime project we'll be conducting our interviews remotely and using a remote research observation-taking template. The 7 - Research and Problem Space/[04] Behavioural Interview Canvas.html file in this book's repository contains links to both an example board and a blank template which you can use as a starting point. Take some time to copy your script questions over and customize them based on the participant's screener responses if needed. Ensure you and your colleagues have this open during your interview and be prepared to take some time after the interview debriefing with your observer. If you're going solo in this, still take the time to debrief and decompress, and consider having a re-watch of your recording a day or so after conducting your interview to somewhat mimic the experience of a silent observer.

It should be noted that this board contains an area for follow-on questions, too. These are questions that arise during your interview that someone in the call feels relevant to ask. For example, if you're interviewing someone about their journaling habits and they mention it's frustrating to have to copy the same template structure onto a new page at the start of each new day, you might want to ask a number of follow-on questions from that—*Can you tell me more about how you start from a template? What in particular frustrates you about this approach?* Jumping straight into asking these questions can disrupt the flow of an interview, so having a place to note them and dedicated time at the end to ask them is important to consider.

During the interview, ensure you ask open questions—anything that starts with *tell me about a time...* is always good; *do you like Pokémon?* is not. Resist the urge to direct the conversation too much. Spotting an interview that's slowly diverging from its original point isn't too difficult, and you should absolutely redirect things back on track where required, but letting things flow can be surprisingly so. Get comfortable with silence, too. Let your participants think, don't *save* them from awkward pauses, and don't treat every gap in conversation as a requirement for you to jump in and direct things.

After an interview, as mentioned, spend some time debriefing with any observers, note-takers, or other call participants. Jot down any extra observations or notes that come up during this debrief, then simply move on to the next interview or move to a different phase of your research!

Synthesizing Findings

Everything we've done up until now has been a fancy form of data collection. While I'm sure your interviews and any shadowing you conducted revealed behaviors and raised observations that fundamentally shifted your understanding of your problem space, we can't expect others to have the same response to our raw data. Research synthesis is all about taking this raw data and finding—and I'm going to get very scientific now—interesting shit.

Good research synthesis saves your team time by giving them the highlights and key findings that can be garnered from your research. Great synthesis goes beyond that and lets you present a compelling, motivational narrative, spurring a project on and justifying the inertia that some folks on your team might have been anxious about before this research phase. For this phase of our research, we'll be conducting a few workshops designed to help us surface and structure our raw research data into more actionable formats. While we could just as easily write all our findings in one big doc or craft a wonderful Keynote to present to our team, the benefits of involving collaborators during synthesis—as opposed to having them simply be consumers of our reports—are almost countless.

Synthesis is all about collecting and presenting the information required to support future decisions. It's important to not conflate synthesis with solution exploration and to especially avoid allowing our own personal bias to seep in. Chances are, if you're working on a problem, you have some solution ideas floating around your head that you're eager to explore. Here's the thing though, *everyone* working on your project will have these kinds of ideas, and they're not any more or less valid than yours. You've spent the time researching so you can avoid biased or ungrounded ideas, so it's imperative that you eliminate this kind of idea creep from your synthesis.

The first step to this is to make synthesis collaborative. The types of workshops and diagrams you'll be producing as part of this phase rarely require any kind of impressive technical knowledge or expertise. Fundamentally you're just arranging information into various groups or connecting dots through various relationships. Involving at least your whole design team is a good start but consider inviting stakeholders to some synthesis sessions too. I've run dozens of foundational research phases with teams and clients all over the world, and I've never seen a situation where collaborative synthesis didn't improve collaboration throughout the project.

The second step lies simply in being a good facilitator. Leading a research project is as much about being disciplined and pragmatic with your team as it is being a thorough interviewer or a canny observer. Eliminating solution ideas is an impossible task. After all, it's human nature to see a problem and think of ways it can be solved. With that in mind, good facilitation isn't saying *we're all banned from having ideas until we've synthesized our research;* it's more about providing ways for ideas to be parked for later while still pushing your team towards what's important right now. Keeping conversations relevant and on track without stifling others is as much an artform as any other workshop skill, and you should be using this liberally as you progress through your synthesis workshops.

Affinity Maps

An affinity map—or affinity diagram—is a versatile tool that helps us take large pools of discrete data and arrange them based on the relationships or similarities found within. Affinity maps are not unique to design research, nor are they exclusive to a research phase. Part of the utility of affinity maps as a concept is that they can be applied to pretty much any pool of data—we'll be using them predominantly to group our research observations, but the data could just as easily be customer support feedback, product ideas, or competitor feature sets—and produced quickly, at pretty much any time in the project. We'll be sticking to using them solely for our research phase, but they can just as easily be conducted throughout the design and development of a product. The point is, these maps are versatile and multifunctional.

However, this versatility and multifunctionality doesn't come without tradeoffs. Affinity mapping workshops can often result in diagrams that are too vague or too idiosyncratic to be useful. Like any other output of our process, it's important to start affinity mapping with clear goals in mind. Reminding folks of the real purpose of any mapping workshop throughout the session is a good first step towards ensuring you get the most out of the time you put in. With that said, let's plan and conduct an affinity map workshop, starting with documenting our workshop goals.

You can find an already-completed example of an affinity map (rather, a link to a FigJam project) in this book's repository, in the `7 - Research and Problem Space/[05]` `Affinity Map.html` file. Figure 7-2 shows the Goals section that we'll be filling in first.

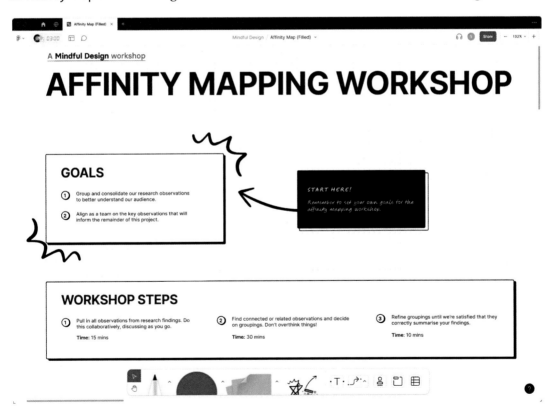

Figure 7-2. An affinity map workshop file zoomed in to show the goals of the workshop

The affinity map file in this book's repository contains another link to a template for an affinity mapping workshop. If you follow that link, you'll be able to duplicate the template in FigJam for your own purposes. If you prefer other tools, it's a pretty simple template. Feel free to recreate it in your tool of choice.

Let's start by acknowledging the goals for our workshop. For ours, we have two key purposes:

- Group and consolidate our research observations to better understand our audience.

- Align as a team on the key observations that will inform the remainder of this project.

Depending on your project, phase, team structure, design/product framework, and even personal preferences you might have different goals for your workshop. Regardless of what your goals are, open your workshop by reminding everyone of them and giving folks a short window of time to ask any clarifying questions. It really is important to have everyone aligned at this point, so don't rush into the fun stuff right away!

Next, we're going to pull *all* of our research observations into the Observations section. This is the "data dump" part of the session and can be done collaboratively during the workshop or preemptively before kicking off. Both approaches have advantages, with the collaborative approach often sparking discussion and the preemptive approach saving time and being async-friendly. Use your best judgment, but in our case, we're going to pull our observations in now. Here's where we make use of our interview notes board from our behavioral interviews. Having everything already in Post-It form means we can just drag them over directly. See Figure 7-3.

Figure 7-3. *Observations filling up during an affinity mapping workshop*

As you fill in your observations area, you'll likely start to notice similar or related notes. Start grouping these notes as you go. It's important right now to not focus too much on being perfect with your groupings. There's no hard and fast rule as to what connects one observation to another; you might start grouping things by sentiment (e.g., *things people like about their current process*) only to realize that this is too broad, instead switching more to organizing around observed behaviors (e.g., *starts with a template*). This is a dynamic workshop and you're not going to finish with the same groups you started with.

Once all your observations are populated and grouped, you have an affinity diagram! This is when it's important to take a step back and see if your groups are actionable enough or if you need to adjust or even regroup entirely. As mentioned, it's very common to re-architect your groupings multiple times throughout an affinity mapping session, so much so that I'd say *not* getting your groupings "wrong" the first time is a red flag. Once you're happy with your rough categories, you can formalize them by creating separate areas for each one and then dragging the relative data over. This will give you something far closer to a final affinity map. See Figure 7-4.

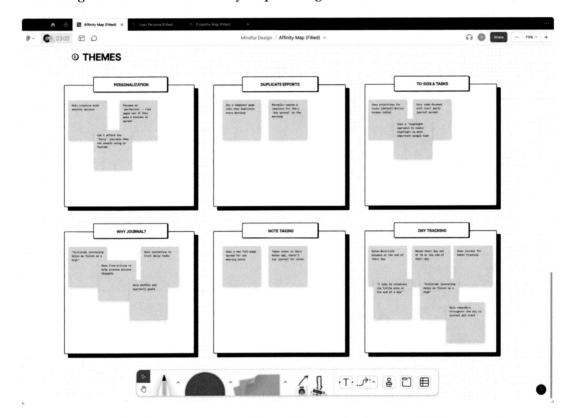

Figure 7-4. *Related post-its grouped into themes during an affinity mapping workshop*

The next step is to prioritize your themes. If you have themes that are relevant to your project's vision or that represent important observations, they might be of a higher priority than tangential observations or more idiosyncratic behaviors. Not all affinity maps need to be prioritized, but it's useful in most scenarios. Getting a consensus on priority can be tricky, so if there aren't any obvious candidates for highest priority, you might need to get a little creative. A simple hand-count vote or some dot voting can quickly unblock a priority stalemate. Excluding that, another option—perhaps the nuclear option depending on your team structure—is to have your main product decision-maker or stakeholder break a tie or even mandate a top priority during the session.

Personas

I have, throughout this book, aimed a few subtle digs at user personas, for various reasons—all of which I feel are relevant and most of which I will discuss. However, I must stress that they stand alone as the single artifact of the research and planning phase that can best present and communicate compassion and empathy throughout a project's lifecycle.

User personas are simple, digestible *archetypes* of human beings. In Chapter 4, I spoke about Prototype Theory—how we form underlying "feature sets" and rules that underpin a category and how the things we perceive in life can be more, or less, applicable members of that category (Rosch, 1988). User personas operate on a similar level; they act as statistical averages for human beings, and they're often used to present collaborators and stakeholders with a semblance of understanding of our audience. A sample user persona is shown in Figure 7-5.

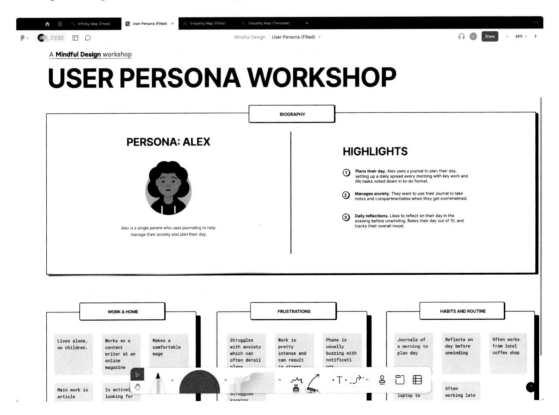

Figure 7-5. *An example user persona from our project*

Now, deep breaths because here are my problems with user personas. First and foremost, they are manufactured empathy, an abstraction of a human being often distilled into a banal and mundane list of life experiences, skills, abilities, and preferences. Human beings do not fit into such a box. All of us have idiosyncrasies, bad days, things we enjoy, secrets, desires, dreams, and ambitions. It's impossible to cram all of this into an entire book, never mind the single PowerPoint slide format that most personas occupy.

Second, personas can suffer greatly from a cascade of bias and assumption, depending on how many people there are between the people who've been observed and the weird, digital protohuman that sits in your research slide deck. It's impossible, when creating these fantastical fictional characters, to avoid project-level, colleague-level, and personal-level biases and assumptions. So we often end up with personas that not only fail to represent even a fraction of the humanity that we're *really* designing for, but that are essentially pre-judged and pre-victimized by the unconscious and systemic biases that live within our teams and ourselves. The overwhelming majority of manifestations of user personas I have witnessed in my career have served both as placation for executives that we feel are too busy, too important, or too removed from the project to display true empathy and as a convenient dictionary of the biases of our teams and companies.

Once we've traded away people's frustrations, eccentricities, and self-expression for nicely formatted human-shaped pigeonholes, these artifacts often become the single point of reference throughout our work until we finally get some working prototypes and ideas in front of real people. This is a dangerous and insidious precedent in an industry that is already insufficient in the empathy department.

Now, why then, if I dislike personas so much, am I treating them with such importance? Simply put, *they work*. Personas' ability to unify a team around a core set of principles and supposed human qualities is unrivaled in the world of design artifacts. We just need to make sure that our personas communicate the correct principles.

Here's my suggestion: every user persona should challenge an ingrained assumption or bias that you feel exists within your team. Maybe that assumption is that only able-bodied people will use your product. Or perhaps the assumption is that only affluent, white millennials care about your solution. Every time someone on your team makes an assumption, write it down and figure out how to break that assumption down in your persona work. Nominate someone on your team—preferably someone who will be involved in early-stage planning—to call you out on your own assumptions and vice versa. Personally, I've had the good fortune to work with amazing and compassionate product owners who make the perfect foil for BS-calling-out—they're usually involved from the very beginning, and the artifacts of our work massively impact their job.

Tools like Cards for Humanity (Figure 7-6) can help with this approach, providing prompts and reality checks when it comes to challenging the over-optimistic thinking and baked-in privilege that are often anathema to inclusive design.

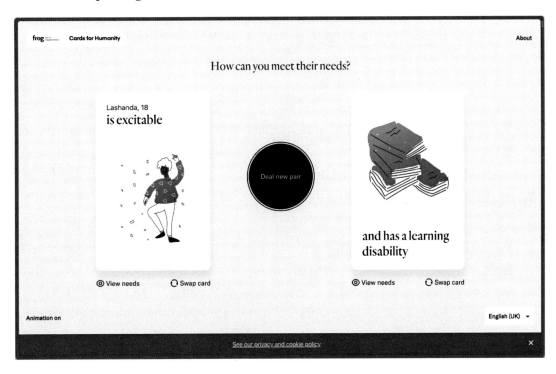

Figure 7-6. *Cards for Humanity, from Frog Design, part of Capgemini Invent*

You don't have to share with your team that you're doing this. In fact, doing so is probably the fastest way to put up barriers between you and your colleagues (being *that person* who is constantly taking notes about other people is *not* a great shtick) and potentially cause some pretty tough "political" situations. My advice here is simple: the impact your work has on the people it is intended to help is more important than some friction and discomfort within your team. The other side to this, of course, is that being taken seriously in the workplace is something that is often afforded disproportionately to the privileged among us, and this kind of assumption-challenging can often grate on the egos of our colleagues. If you are a design manager or if you work with a design manager you trust, this kind of approach is one that's best initiated from a position of leadership.

When we treat personas as a means of challenging assumptions, we start to infuse a form of BS-detection into our early-stage documentation. If you work on a team that already uses standard personas, you might have witnessed the power of a well-placed "but how does this work for Steve the Persona?" when diffusing a situation or settling a debate. If we strive to present a truly challenging and diverse set of personas, we provide ourselves with a safety net should our discussions lead away from compassionate design decisions and veer toward the distracting, the manipulative, or the just plain exploitative.

Consider the following "traditional" persona for an imaginary flight-booking application:

Sandra is a 28-year-old single woman living in Brighton, England. She likes ice cream and taking her dog, Cedric, for walks along the beach. She travels to her company's head office in Seattle on a quarterly basis and rarely travels for leisure. She uses her smartphone to book her flights and is more concerned about getting things done quickly than finding a bargain.

This all sounds pretty solid. We can actually start to imagine what Sandra's preferred relationship with our application might be, understand her motivations, and probably draw out a nice, convenient use case for her time with the app. Sandra is, however, a product of our imagination. She is a work of fiction based on some form of statistical analysis and observation research. We've stripped this prototypical person down into the chunks that are convenient for us to work with. In many cases, Sandra will simply be a byproduct of our assumptions. If we assume that everyone who travels for work doesn't care about bargains and would rarely use our app to book leisure flights, then we've created Sandra to appease these assumptions. Consider the alternative:

Alex is 24 years old and suffers from anxiety. They work from home and enjoy taking hot vacations in the winter. Alex relies on their phone's calendar and schedule to provide an in-depth itinerary of their day. Alex struggles to cope with chaotic or unexpected circumstances. Alex is easily distracted by notifications and ads, and their anxiety is often triggered when their control over the particulars of an event is taken away.

This persona challenges a few assumptions that we might encounter when kicking off such a project: the people using our app will be neurotypical, something as simple as a travel booking app couldn't possibly trigger an anxious episode, and our app will be used in a serene/distraction-free environment. With these assumptions challenged, it forces us to accept the fallibility of the humans we're designing for. We suddenly have to consider how our work might negatively impact someone's life (an anxious episode really is a heavy experience) and how we might take this consideration into the later stages of our project. Let's take a look at a third persona:

Jey is a single parent living below the poverty line. They save enough for a vacation every couple of years and like to let their children choose among a small number of potential options. They often have a limited budget to work with and try to avoid showing the kids the more expensive vacation options. Jey is sight-impaired and struggles to make out smaller forms or words.

In this case, we have a slightly different set of challenged assumptions. From earlier in this book, we understand that there's a cognitive load associated with poverty. We can also infer that, as a single parent, a certain degree of chaos will be the norm in this person's life and start thinking about how to accommodate that. We're also presented with a concept that challenges what we might show this person. If our app makes money through upsells or advertising, we run the risk of showing Jey's children an ad for a trip they simply can't afford. If you're on a limited budget and can only afford to get your children to a place that has a beach and a water park once every couple of years, how would you feel if they suddenly got bombarded with a full-screen takeover ad for an all-inclusive Disney adventure?

For every persona you create, in addition to ensuring they're representative of your research findings, try to also work in these challenges to assumptions. The end result is something that transcends the basic goals of your project and forces you and your team to consider the distinctive environmental and personal circumstances people find themselves in every day. If your personas aren't impaired, frustrated, or cognitively affected in any way, then they aren't real enough to be of any use. And while randomly bestowing our imaginary friends with unfortunate situations or impairments might seem somewhat vulgar at first, it's one step on a path toward imbuing our projects with the empathy and compassion they require.

Finally, and most importantly, only include what might be relevant to your project. So many personas are full of useless information that mostly just acts as noise. Every piece of information you include about a persona should adhere to the following:

- It should be representative of data from your pool of research. Don't just create something that never existed in your observations or other research findings. You may have to fill in some gaps here and there to make believable or challenging personas.

- It should help you make a decision further down the line. Think about what you're building and ask yourself whether knowing this about a persona would impact a decision you might need to make during your design project. Would someone's favorite fashion brand help you decide how you'd lay out information in a submarine dashboard? Probably not. Would knowing about someone's financial anxiety affect the tone of voice you used in a credit scoring application? I'd sincerely hope so.

Get rid of useless data, focus on what's insightful to *your* project, and ensure that there's a precedent for the characteristics of your personas within your research findings. Everything else is noise or design theater.

Empathy Maps

Empathy maps are, in addition to user personas and mental models, the final piece in the rather fuzzy puzzle of *things that distill people down into useful diagrams*. Personas provide us with a brief insight into a fake person's life, interests, and technology preferences; mental models give us an overview of a fake person's thought processes, heuristics, and hypotheses; and, finally, empathy maps let us take our fake people, put them into fake-real situations, and draw some conclusions about what they might say, think, hear, do, and otherwise experience during these situations.

Just like personas, empathy maps are a means of documenting the ever-important ethnographic research we do. My personal rule is to create at least one empathy map for each persona created, making sure that the situations we put them in are as much of an aggregate of our findings as the ethnographic and pseudo-personal information we use. If a bunch of our research participants journaled from busy coworking spaces, for example, then we'd make sure some of our empathy maps "happen" there. If our participants mostly journaled from home, then we'd make sure we set a scene there. See Figure 7-7.

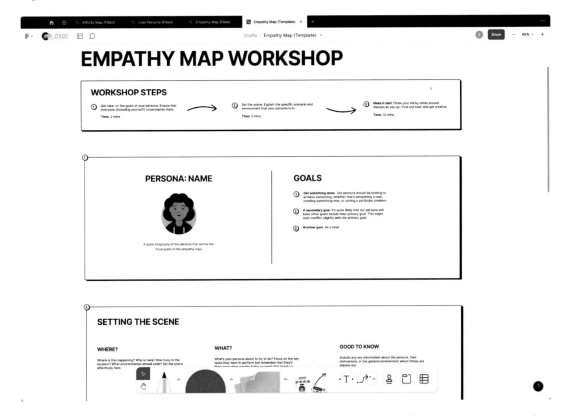

Figure 7-7. *An empathy map template that we will use to fill in our own maps for our own personas*

Traditionally, empathy maps were split into four quadrants: what our persona *says, thinks, does,* and *feels.* Over time, new formats for empathy maps have emerged, with *think and feel* and *say and do* being merged into single categories, and *hear* and *see* being added. The thing here is this categorization almost doesn't matter. The quadrant approach is an extremely useful visualization technique, and the categorization it offers is equally as helpful, but a little pragmatism goes a long way in research documentation. The main goal when preparing for your mapping session is to think of some categories that you feel are most useful to your current project. If you're building a voice-assisted interface, you might well want *say* and *hear* to be discrete sections of your empathy map—think of catching false positives from background voices or idiosyncratic language uses based on location or context.

Personally, I really like splitting my empathy maps as such:

- **Say** represents the internal monologue and any external dialogue of our persona. This includes things they might say about our product—*wow, this is quick!*, if you're feeling optimistic—but also things they might say in other situations, especially distracting ones—*stop biting your sister, this coffee is delicious,* and *biiiiig streeeetch* because if you don't say *biiiiig streeeetch* every time a dog stretches, you're a bad person.

- **Tasks and actions** represent the various things our persona can be expected to do. These tasks and actions aren't just limited to what they do with our product, or even what they do on one specific device; anything from *adding shoes to their shopping cart* to *ordering a second coffee* should live here.

- **See and hear** represents the external and environmental stimuli that our persona will encounter in their situation. Things like the smell of good food, the clatter of coffee, the chatter of humans, and the hustle and bustle of people going about their day around them are all potential inputs to this quadrant. This helps us paint an idea of the attentional distractions we might have to compete with as well as presenting a more believable scene.

- **Feel** represents the emotions, feelings, and thoughts our persona might encounter. We differentiate between *feel* and *say* by trying to keep the *feel* items limited to more immediate or emotional concepts. For example we might include *excited* in our *feel* section, and *I can't wait to get this project signed off* in our *say* section.

I'll also add a few extra sections to an empathy map:

- **Motivators** are there to document the reasons our persona might have to perform a specific action or think a certain way. Motivators are not goals; they're things that prompt us to do the work needed to *achieve* our goals.

- **Distractions** gives us a place to specifically highlight distracting or competing stimuli or concepts. While a lot of what we document in an empathy map is a *potential* distraction, we'll use this area to highlight the most obvious or impactful distractions.

- **Goals** gives us a place to document the high-level goals a persona might have. What are they really trying to achieve by using our product in this particular scenario?

Other empathy map templates will add *pain* and *gain* sections, while others might break out *habit* and *routine* into its own section—especially if the designers are mapping out personas for a product that digitizes a previously analogue process or want to create something that's more of a *companion* app for specific daily routines or habits.

When I look at an empathy map, I want to be able to imagine a story unfolding from it. Regardless of what sections and categories are used, regardless of whether the map is made by one designer or a 16-person, half-day sticky note bonanza, the key factor is that it sets up the parameters for a story: our imaginary person finds themselves in an imaginary place and has an imaginary conversation with our product.

Let's take a look at an empathy map and work backward from there. To start with, we need a persona to work with so, for brevity's sake, let's take Alex from our persona list, plunk them in a busy coffee shop, and draw up an empathy map (Figure 7-8).

Figure 7-8. *An empathy map showing Alex, our intrepid persona, sitting down to do some journaling in a coffee shop*

Empathy mapping can be done by a single designer, but it's just as feasible to turn it into collaborative workshops, assuming that everyone involved already has a good grasp of affinity map and persona work. First and foremost, we want to set the scene. Remind folks (and yourself!) of the persona you're mapping for, introduce them to the specific scenario, and ensure everyone understands the goals that said persona will be bringing into this situation. After that point, this is a pretty free-flowing workshop. Ensure that you converse—even just thinking out loud—while adding sticky notes to the various quadrants and leave time at the end for discussion and wrap-up. For example purposes, we're going with a single empathy map, but you'll likely want to tackle a few during a workshop, ensuring a diverse range of personas, goals, and scenarios. A single empathy map can take as little as ten minutes to run through, so be ambitious, be strict with time-keeping, and you'll be surprised how quickly you can fill up a library of useful empathy maps.

Our main four quadrants give us insight into much of the surrounding events and stimuli that accompany this situation. Actions such as *drink coffee* sit alongside *send link to PO*; feelings like *hunger* or `coffee cravings` are in the same space as their feelings on our product, as well as their intrinsic, self-deterministic thoughts. Empathy maps should paint a wide-reaching picture of the stimuli, mental processes, actions, and reflections that might occur when someone sets out to achieve a goal within our system.

It's especially important here to consider environmental factors alongside internal thought processes and product-specific features. Empathy maps should be as much about what you're competing with—and what expectations you need to live up to—as they are about your product's appeal or the efficacy of its features. Nevertheless, it's totally fine—and encouraged—to be optimistic with some of your sticky notes. If you believe your product is going to make someone say *Wow, this is so fast!*, then by all means, add it in there! An empathy map should present a balanced range of responses, including what we think will excite people.

Distractions, in my opinion, are a must for any empathy map. They show, at a glance, the various factors of an environment that our product is competing against for attention. This lets us, hopefully, see our work as something that exists as part of an extensive and diverse ecosystem of priorities and desires. In terms of a busy coffee shop, an open-plan office, or a busy coworking space, we're going to be faced with myriad distractions. From on-screen notification pop-ups to someone else's phone with the same notification sound as ours to the smell of that one dude who refuses to stop microwaving fish—these all have the potential to drag us away from what we're doing. And I don't care how great you or your boss or your client *thinks* your product is going to be, I guarantee it won't stand up to the momentous occasion of meeting an adorable new office dog. Distractions, perhaps most importantly, also let us get a feel for how much cognitive load we'll *really* have to work with. Going back to Chapter 1, you'll recall that so much of our thought processes and day-to-day interactions are rife with distraction and daydreaming. In ensuring our map's environments account for this day-to-day attentional undulation, we're able to keep our ideas rooted in the chaos and unpredictability of the real world.

Finally, in making room to discuss motivations, we're able to see a more rounded representation of the intrinsic notions people might bring to our product. While goals tend to focus on the utility and final outcome of our product, motivations are self-deterministic. A *goal* of Instagram, for example, might be *upload my latest travel photo*, but motivations speak for the emotions and desires *behind* this goal. Perhaps we upload it to impress our friends with how much we travel or we want to keep it in an easily accessible place for reminiscing. Maybe we're more concerned with the artistic qualities of the photograph and we're uploading it to show off our photography and editing skills. Or perhaps we just think it should exist in the world and we're excited for other people to look at it. Conflating intrinsic motivations with task-centric goals often leads to a limited and insular understanding of an audience, where their supposed motivations read like a salesperson's checklist rather than the complex and diverse desires, motivators, and notions of self we harbor as human beings.

Remember, too, that you're not here to sugarcoat any potentially problematic or toxic attitudes that might be prevalent in your audience. There's no reason why your empathy maps shouldn't include selfishness, neuroticism, or narcissism. If your research shows that certain parts of your demographic are prone to shouting *"I am a design god"* at spontaneous moments during the workday, then throw it in the *say, think, and feel* quadrant. The same goes for displays of self-deprecation, impostor syndrome, workplace anxiety, emotional triggers, and the myriad other negative mental phenomena we navigate on a daily basis.

Putting It All Together

If you've never led a research phase before, then this chapter likely introduced a bunch of new concepts and might have felt a little intense to follow along with. It's important to remember that research phases like this are conducted over days, often weeks, and take a lot longer to conduct than they do to read about in a book. It's okay if this amount of work feels overwhelming while you've been reading through this chapter; there's a lot to consider if you're just reading through linearly. The best advice I can give is to do some dedicated desk research, then get a decent research brief together and then plan and script at least one behavioral interview. Follow along with the sections in this chapter up until then and then take a break while you conduct your interview. That data isn't going anywhere and you can slowly build up a library of behavioral research before moving on to other phases of your research.

Remember that the main goal of this type of research is to help you understand the problem space you're designing around and to help you make decisions in the future. The story you tell around your data, and the empathy and empowerment that come from this, are often undervalued outcomes of this kind of research, and it's key to not lose track of that.

Affinity mapping will help you condense your research into broader findings or problem statements and help build a shared understanding and alignment with your wider team. Involving stakeholders in affinity mapping is highly recommended, too, as not only do you benefit from having them directly work with research data—as opposed to simply consuming a report or presentation—but you also benefit from the different perspectives and domain expertise that they may bring with them.

Personas help you build out archetypes of your target audience and potential users by combining various behaviors and characteristics observed during your interview phase. Personas should challenge assumptions and bias in the team and not simply be a superficial market-level persona. By removing pointless demographic or lifestyle information in favor of more contextualizing and humanizing points such as what makes them anxious or any impairments they might have, you can ensure our personas are well-rounded and realistic.

Finally, empathy maps let you take these archetypical people and place them in an archetypal situation. By including various emotional and environmental factors alongside the goals and behaviors of a persona, empathy maps can present you with a compelling model of a situation. By noting down what your personas say, think, and feel, as well as any tasks or actions they might perform, you can present an idea of how this situation might be navigated. Empathy maps allow you to imagine real people in real situations using your product and can be an exceptionally useful tool for designers.

While there are dozens more workshops or activities you could do as part of design research, the combination of affinity maps, good personas, and realistic empathy maps is, to me, the perfect amount for the vast majority of design tasks. That's not to say that this approach is infallible, or that the three artifacts are an exhaustive coverage of your research needs. Different projects will have different thresholds for information and knowledge when making a decision. Simple lifestyle apps likely carry a wider margin for error than mission-critical infrastructure tooling, for example. It's up to you to know when enough is enough for your projects, but for now, our focus on ethnographic research methodologies, synthesized into these core three formats is just enough for us to move to the next phase. If you liked the focus on diagrams in this chapter, you're going to *love* the next one.

CHAPTER 8

Defining Problems and Solutions

This phase of our project is all about getting from *could* to *should*. Off the back of a well-run and beautifully-synthesized research phase (you did run it well and synthesize it beautifully, right?) we'll start building out definitions for the problems we want to solve and plans for how we might go about solving them. As the last chapter alluded, there's going to be a *lot* of diagramming and workshopping in our immediate futures.

Redefining Diagrams

Most people have a too-narrow definition of what constitutes a diagram. For many, a diagram is limited to some kind of chart or flow—think things like user journey flows and Gantt charts. While these are undoubtedly useful abstractions, pretty much any visual model that represents a system or an idea can be considered a diagram. Wireframes are diagrams; even your final-looking prototypes can be considered as such.

Diagrams are all about simplicity, convergence, and sensemaking (a term coined by Abbey Covert in her incredible work *How to Make Sense of Any Mess*) with a focus on bestowing a messy or divergent pool of inputs with clarity, relevance, and consensus. This is exactly what we used affinity maps, personas, and empathy maps for in the previous chapter; they're all diagrams, and they're all there to help us make sense of the chaos that every ambitious project faces.

The chaos at this point is all our research findings, our teams' ideas, the constraints of our project, the technical capabilities in our team, the market we want to launch to, the preferences of our target audience, the information we don't know we don't know, our process, our goals, and the dozens of other concerns that impact our ability to deliver something great to our audience. It's our job to take all these divergent, often

© Scott Riley 2024
S. Riley, *Mindful Design*, Design Thinking, https://doi.org/10.1007/979-8-8688-0143-3_8

scary inputs, and refine our thinking over time, repeatedly, until we have a shared understanding of just what we're going to build. We start with dozens—even hundreds—of things we believe we *could* do and end with a few things we know we *should* do.

The Importance of Problem Definition

Problem definition directly translates into product and feature requirements. The consensus that comes from a team tacitly agreeing to a problem scope and saying "yes, this is what we will solve for" is the forcing function that takes you from vague ideas to viable product work.

The phrase *problem scope* might have stood out in that sentence and for many folks might be a pretty under-explored concept. We're far more used to witnessing scope at the feature, product, or project level. Freelancers need to know a client's scope to give a good idea of budget, product owners need to define feature scope during a project to avoid feature creep, and engineers need to understand the technical scope of a proposed solution to estimate or break down the work required to code and release it. Problem scope plays the same role but, as you might expect, in the context of our problems.

Problem Scoping

Scoping is the act of deciding what *things* from a pool of potential options should be worked on. When an engineering team scopes features for a sprint, they might be pulling from a backlog of possible work. At this point, they're deciding what's feasible against a number of constraints. By defining a clear feature scope, the team can be efficient and mobilized, knowing exactly what they should be working on. Scope often changes—the phrase "scope creep" exists for a reason—but the act of scoping is, at its core, about manufacturing agreement around where certain resources (time, effort, money) will be directed.

This also lets us infer what *won't* be addressed. Let's say your backlog contains finished design work waiting to be coded up. If your team fills up an upcoming work cycle or sprint with implementing a user management UI, then you likely wouldn't expect your lovely new onboarding designs to be worked on during that time. They're implicitly excluded from the upcoming work, and we'd look a little bit silly if we jumped on Slack and asked the team how they planned on implementing our onboarding work while they were heads-down on user management. Similarly, if you'd planned a design sprint with a clear focus on designing an impactful user dashboard, you wouldn't take kindly to someone interrupting your work to ask you about a completely unrelated file import feature, right?

It's unfortunately and infuriatingly common, though, for teams at the early stages of product definition to forego any kind of problem scoping, leading to design explorations that are far too open-ended or project specs that try to solve far too many problems with a single release. Having a clear problem scope is integral to any early stage project. Not only do you shine a light on the problems you're solving, but you also make a clear statement about the ones you're *not.*

Problem Framing

Defining and framing problems does not need to be an arduous task. The secret here is that you've done the vast majority of the work already through your research and affinity mapping. You'll likely have quite naturally worded your observations—and perhaps even your affinity mapping—in problem-focused language, and while your research affinity map is a broader construct, you can absolutely run a second (or third, fourth, seventeenth) affinity mapping workshop focused around problem statements. And that's exactly what we'll do here.

As much as I'd love to present a genius new workshop or diagram to add to our toolkit, the humble affinity map really is unsurpassed when it comes to converging and consensus-building. We want to take the shared understanding we have from our research and build out a core understanding of the problems that our audience might need to navigate.

It's important during this phase to not veer too far towards problem *scoping.* I like to take something close to an *anything goes* approach with these early affinity maps; if it's present in the research findings and someone on your team thinks it's valid, there's really no reason to veto an idea or a statement right now. Too many people self-censor themselves into stifling their own great ideas or insights because they think their idea is silly or their insights aren't relevant. Encourage folks to let their defenses down a little during these types of workshop: there's no such thing as a bad idea (right now…).

You'll find links to a problem framing workshop in the `8 - Defining Problems and Solutions/[01] Problem Framing.html` file of this book's repository. This workshop is just a spicy affinity map. You're not doing anything different for the first two parts: generating your problem statements and grouping them as you go. There's an extra phase here though, which is all around what I like to call *empowerment statements.*

Empowerment Statements

Now, this might sound all kinds of cringe, and be far too *Design Think-y* for a book that has fired numerous shots at the Design Thinking ethos, but bear with me here—you're allowed one esoteric invention when you write a book, and this is mine.

An empowerment statement is a connecting piece that helps you go from the doom and gloom of observed problems—everything sucks for these people and we have to get them out of this mess—to empowering solutions—these people will have the tools available to them to do great things. While we absolutely must focus on problems people experience, and while design is fundamentally a form of problem solving, more often than not we're *enriching* lives through technology as opposed to *saving* people with it. Now, if—and it's a big if—you're working on a system that is solely focused on eradicating a problem (climate emergency solutions, vaccination rollout programs, etc.), then you probably should stop at the problem statement phase. However, for most of us, we ultimately care about what people can do with the things we make.

Framing everything as a problem that needs solving promotes the kind of savior complex that is far too prevalent in design and design-adjacent fields. It's common to see discourse—especially in the early UX phases of a project—that positions the designer as something of a savant, and users or other system actors as needy, precious beings in need of assistance from The Big Design Team. This ostentatious act of othering plagues many corporate creativity frameworks (hence my reticence to promote Design Thinking as a codified practice) and permeates through think-tanks and celebrity consultants to the point where design becomes a self-perpetuating cult of personality in many circles. I'll be frank: this attitude is self-aggrandizing, insidious, and has no place in a practice supposedly so dependent on the empathy its practitioners can show for their audience. By rephrasing problem statements into empowerment statements (Figure 8-1), we can push back a little on the idea that we're creating some sort of digital savior and remind ourselves we're building something that exists alongside our users' talents, skills, creativity, and willingness to get stuff done. Our work is used in tandem with our users' skills and habits, not in spite of them.

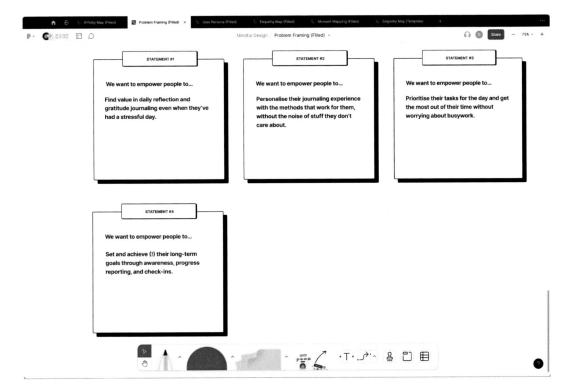

Figure 8-1. *Empowerment statements for our journaling app*

So, for this project, I'm humbly asking that you embrace empowerment statements. Take your problem statement group and reword each of them in a way that can be tied directly to goals, aspirations, or otherwise empowering concepts. Here are a few examples:

- Let's say your problem statement is *people struggle to find time to connect with colleagues in a remote environment.* While you can quite easily take a feature all the way from idea to completion based on this, let's rephrase it to *we want to empower people to make meaningful connections with their colleagues in a remote environment.*

- Or let's take *people struggle to hit their word count for their coursework when they have a tight deadline* and rephrase it to *we want to empower people to track and hit their word goals even when they have a tight deadline.*

239

These are not monumental changes to the original statements, but this is an important step in framing your problems. It's too easy to lose sight of the fact that the people who use our products require utility, competence and seamlessness; they don't essentially require saving from big scary problems.

Solution Defining

At this point, we've made great headway into analyzing a problem space, observing the people that navigate it, extracting insights and problems from our findings, describing observed problems, and scoping and wording the problems we want to solve. That's a *lot* of work! However, this only covers one primary phase of our project, which can ostensibly be summarized as the Discovery phase (more on that later) of a typical design project.

This work simply puts us in a place where we have confidence in our understanding of our audience and thus confidence in the future decisions we must make. With this confidence and a broad consensus on what we've observed and presented about our problem space comes the freedom to finally start exploring potential solutions. After divergence, we converge, so after discovery, we define.

Solution definition is all about exploring the things we could build to achieve our goals. We want to go from a broad range of potential solution ideas to a streamlined and prioritized list of key features or concepts. Our first step is to bring focus back to our empowerment statements. These are our scoped problems, reworded to reflect the fact that we want our work to empower people as opposed to diluting users down to helpless problem-experiencers. We want to use these empowerment statements to explore various ways we could achieve them.

It's important to note that this phase is all about ideation. I'm going to suggest a specific approach to ideation based around the—rightfully somewhat controversial—How Might We method. You can just as easily do your ideation through collaborative brainstorming, mind-mapping, or even just big joint sketching sessions. There are also more specific methods such as Crazy 8s, drafting a fake press release, and much more. This phase more than any is defined more by your culture and your teams' structure and capabilities than by any kind of prescriptive process stage.

How Might We

The How Might We framework is a key component of the Design Thinking movement and has come under some very fair scrutiny during its time in the limelight. How Might We is often positioned as an innovation framework. It actively encourages broad, problem space-level explorations, which can further the savior complex that's already far too prevalent in these "creative problem solving" approaches. We purposefully tried to avoid this kind of self-aggrandizing by turning our problem statements into empowerment statements, so why are we bringing them into a framework that can easily skew towards what we're actively trying to avoid? Well, the main reason for this is that How Might We is actually a much better design framework than it is a lofty system-level innovation framework.

How Might We is fundamentally a structured brainstorming workshop. Traditionally, you bring problem statements to a workshop, and answer How Might We... for every statement. When we bring empowerment statements into this framework, we get a very natural avenue of creative enquiry. If your empowerment statement is *empower people to set up beautiful and useful daily spreads,* then your How Might We question is simply *how might we empower people to set up beautiful and useful daily spreads?*

These questions are prompts for people to start ideating around; all we're doing is framing our existing statements into questions and giving ourselves and our team space to explore them. As such, it's important to remember that at this point, there's really no such thing as a bad idea. I keep mentioning the concept of not stifling others' ideas or creativity during workshopping because it really is key for all of this collaborative workshopping to succeed. When facilitating this kind of workshop, we must strive to not shut folks down, to help the workshop flow without dismissing people, and fundamentally to create and maintain a safe space for people to have ideas and be creative.

You can find a template for a How Might We workshop in `8 - Defining Problems and Solutions/[02] How Might We.html` in this book's repository. There's really not much to it—like I said, this is really just structured brainstorming—but there's still a semblance of structure to the board (Figure 8-2).

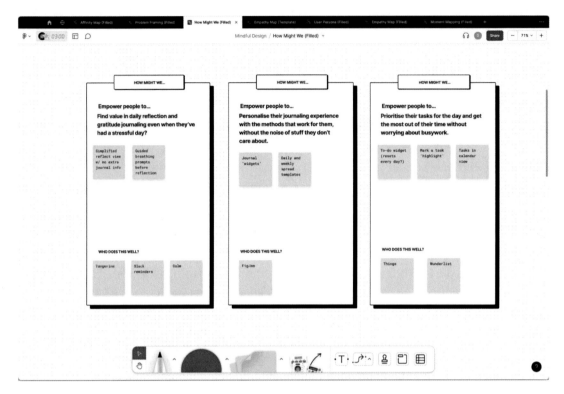

Figure 8-2. *A How Might We workshop, with our empowerment statements laid out as question prompts*

To put your own How Might We workshop together, you really just need to prepare a board with your empowerment statements worded as questions. Get your attendees settled and you can pretty much just dive right in. As always, timekeeping is important, so remember to set out enough time for your specific statements to be explored. Prepare timers for each section and try to be strict with your timings. Most statements will need at least a few minutes of brainstorming, and going over by one to two minutes per statement adds up very quickly when you're exploring several.

You might notice a secondary prompt for each statement worded as Who Does This Well? This allows attendees to give examples of existing products or solutions that do a good job of similar ideas. For example, if you had a live chat idea in your How Might We, then you might list Slack and Discord in the Who Does This Well? section. While not absolutely necessary, many ideas are inspired by existing solutions (everything's a remix, right?) and it's useful to have aspirational examples where relevant.

The goal here is to fill this board up with ideas. That's it. Kick it off, ask the questions, set your timers, and let folks dump their brains. Metaphorically. Once you have a board full of ideas, it's time to refine them into something impactful that we know we can build.

Feature Ranking

If your How Might We—or whatever brainstorming method you chose—session has resulted in a somewhat unhinged amount of ideas then, firstly, great! You've done a good job. Secondly, you and your team are likely feeling somewhat overwhelmed by all the possibilities. Excited, of course. Motivated, for sure. But overwhelmed all the same.

That's where feature ranking—and one of the most important diagram types you can learn as a designer—comes into play. Feature ranking will have you selecting two factors or metrics that mean the most to you and placing the ideas generated in your How Might We session based on where they lie across those two axes. The extremely important diagram we use is ... basically just four rectangles (Figure 8-3).

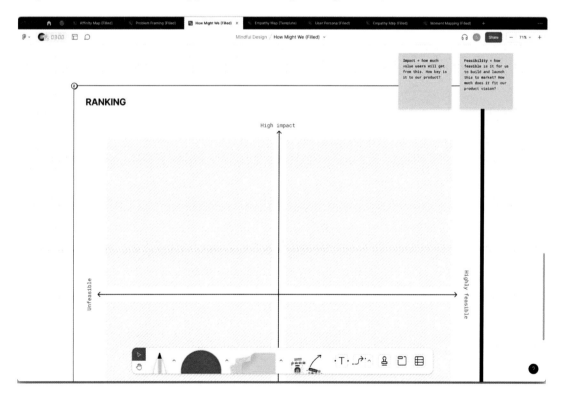

Figure 8-3. *A board prepped to rank features based on their impact and feasibility*

This quadrant diagram might look unassuming but it really is one of the most useful tools to have in your workshopping toolbox. These four rectangles give clarity, spark and resolve debate, give rise to revolutions, and guide evolutions.

Okay, so maybe things got a little dramatic there, but what we have here is two axes that can be used to assess the overall importance of the items we place along them. When it comes to decision-making around features and design ideas, I almost always use *impact* and *feasibility* as my axes. Your organization or team might value different factors in decision making, such as *potential return* and *cost* or *reach* and *confidence*. Whatever your factors are, the goal is the same: find the things in the top right quadrant and build them.

The top right quadrant is your sweet spot. In our case, we have our impact being measured from left (low impact) to right (high impact) and our feasibility being measured from bottom (not feasible) to top (highly feasible). This results in our top right quadrant representing ideas that are both highly impactful *and* highly feasible. We also have an insight into ideas that have limited impact but are highly feasible to build (nice-to-haves), ideas that have a high impact but aren't very feasible (future goals), and ideas that have no impact and would be very difficult to implement (throw them in the bin).

I like to go straight from a How Might We into a feature ranking workshop. It can take some time, and you might want to split it up either side of lunch, but it's absolutely worth following ideation with ranking as quickly as possible. Ideation provides momentum and excitement, and peoples' suggestions are fresh in their head. We can then use that to better elucidate the ideas we want to focus on ranking.

For the ranking side of the workshop itself, treat it similarly to your affinity mapping workshop (you ran an affinity mapping workshop, right?) by bringing ideas in one by one and inviting the suggester to add any context or clear up any confusion; after that, have your team *quickly and roughly* place it across your two axes. You might find it useful to define your axes and remind your team of said definitions throughout the workshop. These will likely be factors specific to how you and your team prioritize work, and not everyone will be as familiar with the language as you. You'll do multiple passes of your board, so don't worry about being perfect first time; just get a quick read on—in our case—what the potential impact of our feature might be on our users and the feasibility of implementing, shipping, and marketing it.

You might find folks are either hesitant to rank things at first or perhaps find themselves hedging a little, resulting in many cards being clustered towards the middle of the board. It's pretty hard to rate things out of context, and every idea that comes in adds a new factor of relativity to our measurements, but moving fast and encouraging folks to be a little more adventurous with their estimates helps get over that initial hurdle. After a few sticky notes, I find workshops like this usually pick up pace and folks need much less prompting.

Once your items are all laid out, do another quick pass. Ask your attendees if they disagree with the placement of any items (try to discourage the loudest person from shouting about how their best idea is bottom-left when it should be top-right, though) or if there are any outliers that might need adjusting. Once you're happy with your placings (Figure 8-4), you have your prime candidates right in front of you!

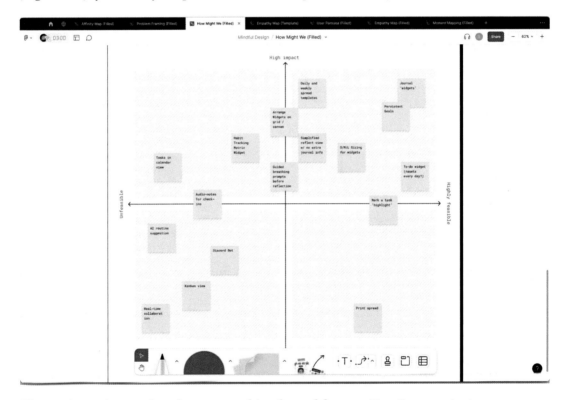

Figure 8-4. *A complete feature ranking board for our Daytime project*

While it's absolutely tempting to just point at the top right quadrant and say "build that," it's quite likely that we have some key things outside of that too. This is also an output of a creative ideation session and likely doesn't include certain *table stakes* items such as user management and permissions. No one sits down to have innovative new ideas and thinks "log-in forms!" Just don't treat the board as a full spec. It's just a culmination of ideas, displayed in a way that makes the highest priority ideas the clearest.

Building an Initiative Canvas

We've being veering a little over into the product lane with a lot of this definition work, but here's where we turn the cruise control off and career unapologetically over the line. I'll say this: if you have a product function in your company, the best thing you can do is learn to collaborate effectively with them. This, invariably, involves getting out of the way when necessary. If you want happy PMs, then this is the part where you do just that.

For the solo designers still reading, let's quickly put a product canvas together so we can cosplay as product people for a little while longer. You can check one out in Figure 8-5.

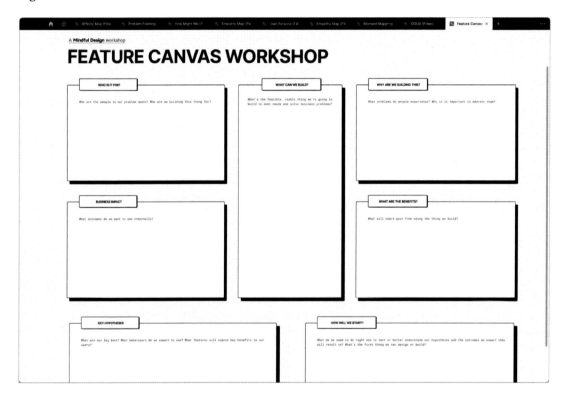

Figure 8-5. *An initiative canvas documenting the features of our product alongside various other factors*

If you've worked on digital products before, this structure will likely look very familiar. The concept of a canvas acting as a form of zoomed-out brief or statement of intent is nothing new, with concepts such as Lean UX Canvas and Business Model Canvas being some of the most widely-used diagrams in modern product and new business model development. The above canvas example is highly derivative of Jeff

Gothelf's Lean UX Canvas (`https://jeffgothelf.com/blog/leanuxcanvas-v2/`) and shares many of the original's goals and purposes, specifically the framing of the *outcomes* of our work.

Why is that required? Well, throughout this entire book I've stressed the importance of understanding the real world outcomes of our work. However, unless the world has drastically changed between the writing and publishing of this book, the vast majority of our digital product design work is carried out under the umbrella of capitalism. The vast majority of that vast majority of our work is carried out under the more specific umbrella of hyper-growth, VC-led capitalism. Designing without a clear understanding of desired or expected business outcomes is almost as irresponsible as designing without a clear understanding of the people our work might impact.

The point here is to provide a cross-team reference and convergence point where *everyone* involved in an initiative can investigate, deliberate, and ultimately provide consensus on the broad *thing* we're going to build, why we're going to build it, and what we expect (or hope!) the business outcomes of our initiative to be. Everything we've done so far has been pretty design heavy. Personas and empathy maps are traditionally banded as UX deliverables, while affinity maps and How Might We sessions are often also design-led activities. Here is where we work with our colleagues in product, engineering, data, and other core business areas to ensure a broad representation of user-, business-, and team-level outcomes.

If you already work in a team that has a clear product process and you don't use this kind of feature or initiative canvas, that's *totally fine*. This could just as easily be an initiative document—also commonly referred to as a pitch, but not the kind of pitch you'd put together if you're an agency trying to win work—or even a backlog of some kind waiting to be prioritized and estimated. Don't dwell too much on the format here, and if you prefer written briefs or other forms of documentation, that's totally fine. Remember that the core goal is to present the expected outcomes of our initiative, contextualized with foundational information about our audience, observations, and solution hypotheses.

Having said that, initiative canvases are useful tools for solo designers or small teams working to a fluid process. If you're a lean startup or a solo builder and don't have a set way of briefing design work, give this a try. You can find both a template and a completed initiative canvas in the 8 - Defining Problems and Solutions/[03] Initiative Canvas.html file or the markdown file of the same name in this book's repository.

Early Exploration

Right, let's check in, shall we? Our research was expertly conducted and beautifully synthesized. We used that synthesis to explore possible solutions, ranked the relative importance of these solutions, and translated this into an actionable, outcome-focused brief. We're finally ready to start exploring our potential solutions.

Everything we've put together so far in our project has been in the name of either understanding what we could build or documenting what we should build. While a *real* design process is rarely this linear—we will absolutely need to revisit and tweak our work to this point as we learn more about our audience and market—the steps we've taken are almost always just enough to get us to this point.

While we could jump straight into pretty much any level of descriptive design or diagraming here—after all, we'll need information architecture, content design, wireframes, prototypes and all sorts of fancy stuff to progress—it's important right now to think about the people who will be using the product we're building. How does our product fit into their life? How might they feel when using it? What situations might they find themselves in?

I covered a bunch of this when you explored empathy maps, but there's another widely-used "map" you haven't yet encountered, the humble user journey map. Let's fix that.

User Journeys

User journey mapping is—surprise, surprise—another design-led workshopping session that benefits greatly from involving other stakeholders from across your organization. I promise we'll be doing some work all by ourselves soon enough, but low-fidelity design work sits in the sweet spot of collaboration in any project, and we're still at the point where our focused expertise is less important than the diverse range of inputs and lived experiences that a good team can bring to our process.

This exercise is often performed prematurely in a design process. I've seen many folks front-load their user journey mapping alongside their persona and empathy map generation as another narrative tool during research synthesis.

When used earlier in the process, user journeys are often extremely broad, with the users' experience with our product listed as one macro step, with very little information about what's happening there. This is fine for journey maps at that stage. They're painting pictures of full scenarios, and it's important to acknowledge that there's a world outside of our product, and that there are steps before and after a user's time with our product where these scenarios play out. This perception of our work as merely one point along a broad timeline of events is incredibly important, and for many projects this alone might justify doing user journeys early in your process.

However, if we're applying user journey mapping later in a process—which is my preferred approach—then we want to have at least a small degree of granularity with the stages we represent. Let's take a look at how user journey maps are structured (Figure 8-6), as it's much better to explain these intricacies with a visual aid.

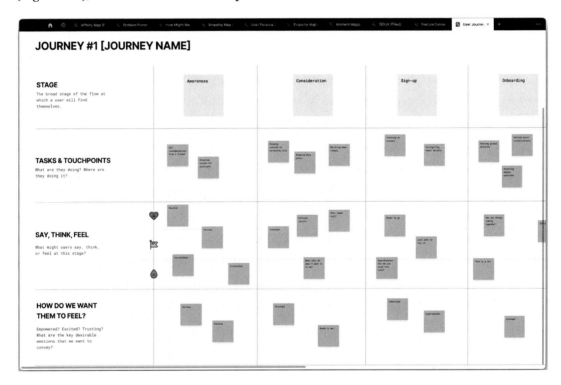

Figure 8-6. *A user story split into specific sections*

User journeys can be seen as a kind of storyboard. They're a linear diagram showing how a person might go from the beginning to the end of a specific scenario. The timing of these scenarios varies greatly, but broadly speaking, these scenarios take place over several minutes or hours, and in many cases even longer still. We'll take a look at more moment-to-moment mapping—think user flows, etc.—very soon, but for now, we can use user journeys to paint the broad strokes of an experience.

It's important to represent the broad phases of a product in these diagrams. While you don't need to scope out specific screens or interfaces, having broad phases such as *sign-up flow*, *onboarding*, and *inviting new members* help us get a little closer to defining a solution. Our goal with user journey maps is to explore what might motivate someone to go from one phase of their journey to another, as well as exploring how users might be feeling alongside how we might *want* them to feel at each discrete stage.

You can find links to both a template and a complete example of user journeys in the `8 - Defining Problems and Solutions/[04] User Journey.html` folder of this book's repository. You'll see that ours is split into broad product areas; however, we start from our marketing site. While it's somewhat common to see marketing sites and other web and marketing assets as part of the product development process, especially when bringing a new product to market, it's more than likely that these assets will be independently worked on. Still, we need to consider its impact on the start of our scenario, especially as it frames the goals and subsequent actions a user might take. This is again simply acknowledging that our product does not exist in microcosm. There will always be steps before that frame and inform plus steps after that show the resolution and reflection of our users' goals along this journey.

For each phase of our journey, we're asking two key questions:

- **How might they feel?** prompts us to consider the full range of emotions a user might be feeling at this point in time. Similar to the "feel" quadrant of our empathy map, it's important to include a diverse range of potential feelings and responses. While optimism is almost prerequisite for innovation, it has its place, and predicting the emotional response of a human being is absolutely not that place.

- **How do we want them to feel?** is much more habitable ground for our optimistic stakeholders. This prompts us to be more aspirational with our thinking. Consider what mindset or emotion might empower someone to move from one phase to another. For example, let's say that during their onboarding a user *might* feel apprehensive and overwhelmed. These are natural responses to trying something new, especially if the thing they're trying is complex or the problems they hope it will solve are causing difficulties in their lives. We can acknowledge the potentiality of this while still thinking in terms of aspirations and motivations. So how *we want them to feel* is likely closer to excited or impressed.

Many other user and customer journey maps will include more data alongside this, including the KPIs or success metrics of each stage, the team responsible, and even the most relevant business objectives. While the simplified version we've used here is great for designers, it's important to adapt to how your team or organization measures business or initiative success. As discussed, product design is almost always done to the backdrop of achieving business goals and financial success. If including desired outcomes or even high-level KPIs along your journey makes sense, by all means do so.

For this project, we'll go with the simple two-question map. Figure 8-7 shows that we've split our map into a few broad phases and illustrated a panel for each one.

The first phase is completely external to our product—and to our company—and serves to set the scene for our persona in our specific example. This is very similar to setting the scene in an empathy map, and you'll often find your earlier empathy maps do the heavy lifting for you here—essentially you're sketching the same scene as a panel, rather than describing it in words.

The next phase is our **marketing site**. This gives us space to acknowledge the fact that people don't tend to just jump straight in to signing up for a product. Even when a product comes highly recommended, we're likely to be framing their expectations and mental model long before a user crosses from the world of "web presence" and into the realm of "product UI." Think about how you might want people to feel at this stage (there's a reason for the questions on the map!) and how they might be feeling. Sometimes we want marketing sites to get folks feeling *hyped* and *excited*, while other times we might prefer them to feel *trusting* and *prepared*.

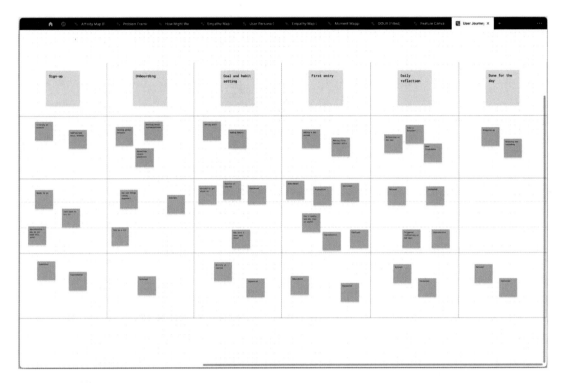

Figure 8-7. *A completed user journey map*

After that is the **sign-up** section, the portal between our marketing world and product realm. This is a pretty straightforward phase of our journey and could quite easily be folded in with our onboarding phase, which comes next. Personally, I like to separate the sign-up and onboarding phases if I know that onboarding is going to be pretty involved and interactive. If you anticipate a much simpler, informational onboarding phase, then you can combine the two.

Speaking of which, our **onboarding** section comes next. This is where we want people to start feeling a little more *empowered* and *informed* about our product. Because we have a pretty complex and highly-interactive solution in mind, it's useful to think of this as separate to our sign-up phase. Sign-up can be pretty linear and leave the user in an empty state; then onboarding can pick up where it left off and start helping them fill things up.

Next is our **goal setting** phase. We know from our observations that many people use journaling to track long-term goals, with yearly and monthly goals being especially common. At this point, we have our first interaction where we can realistically expect a user to be creating important information. This is likely going to include a bunch of conflicting emotions or mindsets as our user takes their first steps with our product, and it's important to document a wide range of potential feelings, as well as using the *how might we want them to feel* section to get optimistic!

We then have our **first entry** phase, where our user is making their first ever journal entry. This is a crucial point in their lifecycle as it represents one of the core behaviors we can expect people to perform in our product. Our goal is to create something that people can use at least daily, if not many times a day, so their first experience with this should be given our utmost attention.

Next up is our **daily reflection** phase, which shows our user returning to their journal at the end of the day to reflect and wrap up. This shows a returning interaction and has us exploring a bit more thought-out, reflective phase of user interaction.

Finally, we wrap things up with a (hopefully) happy little denouement, showing our user enjoying the last few hours of their day, having benefited from some lovely therapeutic journaling. This is pretty optimistic and absolutely represents a success state for our little journaling app. I've found that ending on a high—albeit an artificial one—can help a lot with the storytelling aspect of user journeys, and at this point you've hopefully navigated enough potential blockers to give yourself a happy ending as a treat. If you're working on a high-risks product, you might actually prefer to flip this and show a potential fail state of the product rather than ending on a success. Or do multiple journeys: some that end well and some that end poorly.

However you choose to bring this act to a close, you will likely have a good, broad step-by-step understanding of how a user's time with your product might unfold. What you need next is to get much more granular and start thinking in terms of moments and flows.

Thinking in Moments

Interaction design is all about moments. For our purposes, a moment can be seen as a significant, notable point in time. Opening up a new app for the first time is a moment, creating a new blog post in a writing app is a moment, so is installing a third-party script on a marketing website, setting an alarm the night before a big day, adding an important event to your calendar, or checking off a to-do item that you'd been too anxious to face all week. All of these are potential moments that can and should be designed. While nothing in our interfaces should feel like happenstance, having an understanding of the key moments that can play out within them is critical when it comes to prioritizing our work and deciding where we place our efforts.

Before we progress into documenting and planning these moments, I want to attempt to elucidate what I mean when I refer to a moment of an interface.

If we view our *environment*—the "default" scope of our interface—as an explorable area that communicates many (or all) of the actions that can possibly be performed at any given time, a *moment* is the shift from communicating the possibility of action to the purposeful performing of action. A moment, as a response to implied intent, shifts the focus of our interface from one of communication and exploration to that of task positivity and focus.

Finally, moments can themselves be treated as systematic, essentially being made up of smaller "submoments." In a sense, they're the components of interaction design. Just as in a pattern library, a larger *modal* pattern might be made up of an *overlay*, a *panel*, and a *button* component, so too might an *onboarding* moment be made up of *check username availability* and *avatar upload* moments.

Conducting an inventory of sorts for the moments you expect to appear throughout your interface can be an extremely valuable task, especially as a means of bridging the gap between the more explorative phases of your process and the more practical implementation-focused phases. Your moment list will provide a high-level overview of all the key set pieces in your product and can go on to inform many of your most important design decisions.

Finding Your Moments

Moments are the set pieces of a system. Think of them like the key plot points or action scenes of a story. Forming a list of these moments is, generally, a pretty straightforward task. Think of the places where you feel as though your product will stand out. Your fundamental calls to action, times when a feature solves a particularly widespread or painful problem, and actions that guide people through a tricky path are all candidates for the "moment treatment."

The key moments for our journaling app might look something like this:

- Signing up and creating your account

- Setting up yearly goals

- Setting up monthly goals

- Creating your *first* daily spread

    - Starting a new day based on your daily spread

- Creating your *first* weekly spread

  - Starting a new week based on your weekly spread

- Creating your *first* journal entry

  - Creating any journal entry

- Marking a to-do as done

- Reflecting on your day

You'll notice that performing actions for the first time are listed as separate moments to their repeatable counterparts. It's quite common to see apps hand-hold us through our first forays into key moments—something that you explored in some detail in Chapter 3 when I discussed in-app guidance and onboarding. I recommend doing similarly wherever possible—especially for your complex moments. Treating the first time someone enters a particularly key moment separately from its subsequent occurrence lets us consider how we might want to guide someone through a learning experience, or how we might even want to go a little overboard celebrating the success of the action. While subsequent journal entries might become straightforward, maybe even habitual, for many folks, their *first* entry is likely going to be framed very differently. Noting down key *firsts* is one of the most important aspects of moment mapping.

You can list your moments however you want. It'll likely come as no surprise to learn that I prefer a FigJam sticky-note canvas, but they could just as easily be a bullet list in a document or even a nicely designed poster if you want to be super extra. Figure 8-8 shows a moment list for our journaling app, and you can find links to both a template and a filled example of a moment mapping workshop in the `8 - Defining Problems and Solutions/[05] Moment Mapping.html` file in this book's repository.

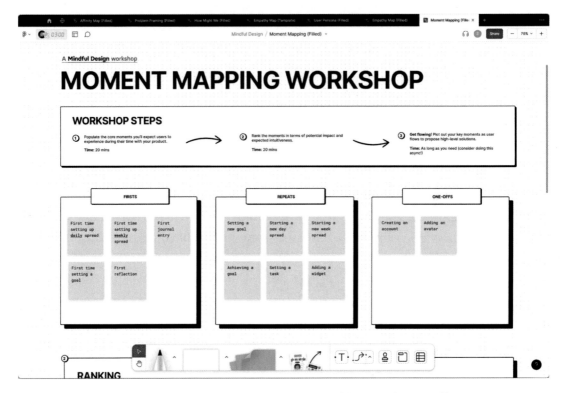

Figure 8-8. *A moment list split into firsts, repeatables, and one-offs*

This is an incredibly simple canvas: three boxes, one each for *first-time*, *repeatable*, and *one-off* moments. First-time moments are exactly as mentioned: moments that we might want to treat or frame differently when they're done for the first time. Repeatable moments will paint a broad picture of the common, day-to-day use cases of our product and will represent moments we expect someone to perform multiple times throughout their time with our product. Finally, one-off moments represent important moments that we reasonably expect to happen just once, or at least very rarely—think things like signing up or uploading an avatar.

Moment Ranking

Remember when we did feature ranking and I mentioned that four simple rectangles might just be the most important diagram type you encounter in design? Well, here we are again. This time, we want to take our moments and explore their impact against the potential intuitiveness of the moment. Figure 8-9 shows our moments ranked in this format.

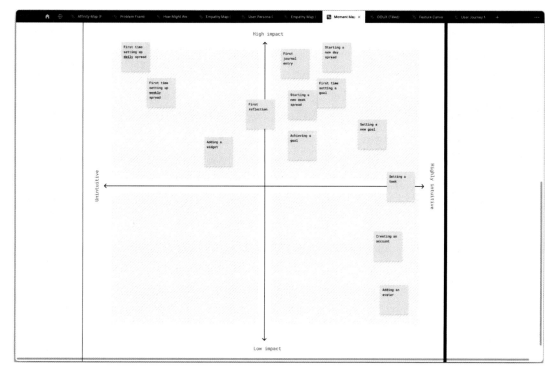

Figure 8-9. *Moments ranked in terms of impact (top to bottom) and intuitiveness (left to right)*

This gives us a perspective on what our key moments are and also how our users might perceive them. I prefer using *intuitiveness* as a second axis for moment ranking because it's a huge factor in how we might present our moments. A moment that's high impact but somewhat unintuitive might require more care, more progressive disclosure, or even a different tack entirely than a moment that's high impact but highly intuitive. The goal of our moment ranking is to contextualize the flows we produce in the next phase. How intuitive we expect a certain moment to be will heavily inform this.

The listing and ranking of moments can be done collaboratively as a workshop, and I highly recommend doing so. However, these are simply inputs, contextualizing the flows we need to create from the back of them. This is where we get heads-down and stuck into some deeper design work. Wrap your workshops up, thank your attendees, and dive right into the first stage of solution exploration.

Moment Flows

If you've used user flows in the past, then you'll be right at home with moment flows—mostly because they're basically the exact same thing.

The primary difference, and really the only reason that we call them moment flows (aside from it sounding more exciting) is that we want to focus on moments being discrete, standalone things that *can happen*. The majority of user flows are too prescriptive and too linear, representing ostensibly divergent interactions as part of a linear flow. Thinking in systems and moments instead of flows requires us to shift our process a little, too.

Most user flows will actually contain multiple moments stitched together in the name of convenience and optimism. Now, many products will be super linear, and many still will actually consist solely of a single moment. Inherent linearity itself isn't the issue here, more the forcing of nonlinear moments into overly-linear flows. Single moments often represent our system contracting to become linear, an act of designed placemaking based on user intent shifting our UI from explorative to task-focused. However, on completion, we're always thinking about this expansion into the "open world" of our nonlinear system. While certain interactions will enable or simplify future interactions, they don't necessarily always preclude them.

Moments exist as discrete, end-to-end combinations of interactions. You could quite easily take a standard user flow approach and document a moment with it, and, in many instances I would encourage doing so. A moment is a concept—it's a way of saying "this particular combination of interactions represents an important point in the lifecycle of our product's use." User flows are documentation, and they represent just one way we can document our moments.

Moment flows follow the same principles as user flows, with the goal of creating high-level, step-by-step diagrams representing the path a user might take through a specific moment or scenario in our interface. Think of the progress through a moment flow as a walking path or cycling trail; each step along the way is a signpost that tells our user what is possible at this stage. Just like real-world paths, moment flows can branch off in different directions depending on the decisions or preferences of our user, and just like real-world paths, progress through moment flows can be impacted by wrong turns, dead ends, and shiny objects.

Just as we did with our journeys and empathy maps, it's important to not lose sight of the goals and motivations that might frame or impact someone's path through each moment, as well as what the completion state might be.

It's also important to remember here that we're proposing a solution, and that this is likely the first level of granularity where we start to think in terms of interface specificity. While our empathy maps and journeys represented scenarios and broad phases of an interaction lifecycle, the moment flows will be much more granular, and we'll find ourselves suggesting broad interaction stages and discrete product screens. However, the temptation to go deeper is as prevalent as ever, and we should be well aware of the risks present in diving too deep too soon.

As mentioned, treat each step of a flow as a signpost, a screen, interaction, or prompt within our UI that explains what's possible and where our user can go next. You'll see in our flow that we've broken the onboarding phase down into some discrete moments, including setting up a daily spread. In that specific moment (Figure 8-10), we have stages such as *empty spread state, adding a notes widget, adding a task list widget, reordering widgets,* and *saving daily spread template.*

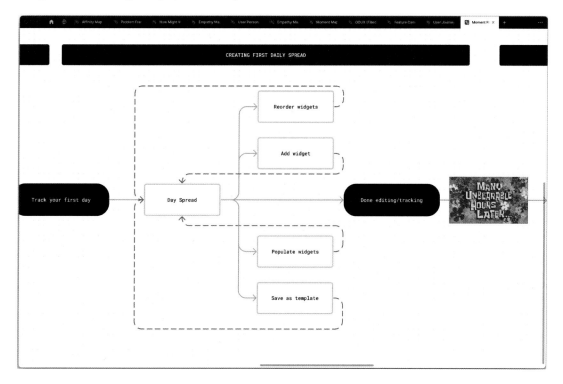

Figure 8-10. *A broad, step-by-step moment flow*

The moment-to-moment flow and possibilities in our interface will ultimately define any experience that happens within. Let's wrap this section up by having a look at what any moment should consist of.

A Goal or Motivation to Start

Every moment stems from a need or desire to achieve or perform something. Beware of goals that sound like features. Goals guide people to impactful changes and desired outcomes, and there are often myriad intrinsic motivators that contextualize someone's goal. Documenting this is key and something we should be well-practiced in at this stage of our process, but now is not the time for complacency. Always set the scene.

Possibility Framing

Moments don't happen if people aren't aware they can. You'll explore the concept of action possibility in the next chapter when we start dissecting the anatomy of interactions, but a teaser: showing that something is possible is more difficult than it sounds. Folks' mental models, industry- and technology-level conventions, and even the environment in which they're using our stuff all have an impact on how well-framed a moment might be.

Discrete Action Steps

Users progress through a moment by making various decisions at various times. The more confidently a user can make a decision, the more seamless a moment will feel to them. This is where we use concepts such as progressive disclosure (and in general just good information architecture) to present enough information with enough clarity to empower decision-making.

A Denouement

Just like good stories, moments don't generally end abruptly. Upon completion, moments generally bring respite, relief, and reflection. Robbing someone of this by professedly telling them to piss off as soon as their task is done can be jarring, and taking the time to mark success appropriately is key to realistic moment design. Remember too that moments result in *real-world* impacts. Your in-app success state isn't the real ending; that's for your users to experience intrinsically.

   Put this all together and you'll see that moments are ostensibly stories. Storytelling is at the core of what we do in design, and part of the purpose of moment mapping is to continue—perhaps even retell—the narrative built during our research and synthesis stages. The foundational goal of moment mapping is not to tell stories; it's to define the discrete macro-interactions that we need to build, but if your moments read like storyboards, you're probably doing something right.

This is also the first point where it'll likely start to feel like you have a real idea for a real interface down on paper (or more likely, down on screen.) With these discrete phases mapped out, you'll likely be brimming with design ideas. Take a look at what we've got with our moment maps: a list of the highest-value interactions we expect people to perform, a broad idea of the journey they might take to get there, and a moment-by-moment play of how things might unfold. It's going to be hard *not* to be thinking in screens and buttons right now! However, we're missing one pretty key thing: how do all of these discrete concepts fit together? We have zoomed-out journeys and zoomed-in moments, but that's either too vague to elicit action or too granular to describe a complete product. Here's where we get to piece things together, with the bonus of being able to practice our much-vaunted optimism to boot.

Happy Paths

While we eschew user flows in favor of moment flows, we can still afford ourselves a little optimism and idealism. A *happy path* is an idealized imagining of someone's path through our product or service. Think of it as a combination of discrete moments and positive decisions that take a user from an initial goal to a warm and fuzzy achievement state.

To build out a happy path, we can arrange our moment flows into key phases or stages and place them in a theoretically ideal order of completion. In a left turn from many of the approaches and workshops we've explored throughout this book, we want to remove obstacles and distractions here, with the goal of imagining an ideal scenario. This can help highlight key phases and moments and also present a broad idea of the *hook* of our product.

You can see in our happy path example (Figure 8-11) that our onboarding phase is split between multiple discrete moments, such as *creating first goals, building first daily spread*, and *making first journal entry*. We then have a general usage section where we have users creating journal entries, checking off to-do items, and finally reflecting on their day, each split into a combination of discrete moments.

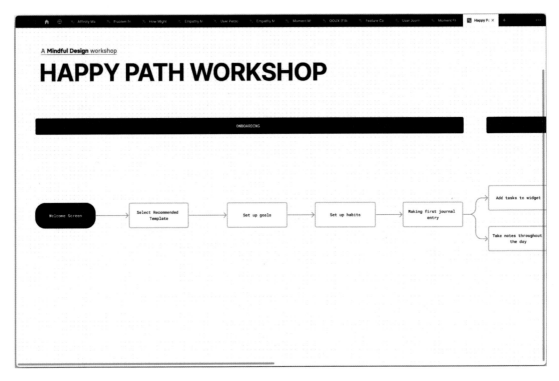

Figure 8-11. *A happy path for a user's first day or so with our product*

Our goals with happy paths are to lay out a potential end-to-end experience with our product. In terms of granularity, they sit somewhere between journey maps and moment flows, and they closely resemble a user journey map, especially with the splitting of stages into broad phases. The only real difference is that we want to piece this path together with the moments we've defined, whereas a user journey is often the *input* to our moment mapping. We're essentially zooming in to define our moments and then zooming out again to lay them out in sequence.

Putting It All Together

Over the last two chapters we've gone pretty hard on the diagrams and super low-fidelity work. This work, especially the exploration phase, is going to be highly iterative, and you should expect—heck, even demand—tight feedback loops and lots of reworking of ideas and flows. Keep things loose, disposable, and open-ended right now, and work with your team where appropriate to build confidence and rework ideas.

There's no right or wrong answers at this point, and there's no real magic way to predict when you're ready to move on. You and your team could fall in love with your first happy path, or it could take several revisions and revisits to arrive at something that feels right. Expect to be back here again soon, too, as these explorative steps get repeated for new hypotheses, product pivots, or different approaches.

Looking back to the very beginning of this chapter, I mentioned this phase is all about going from *could* to *should*, and that's precisely where we want to find ourselves right now. It should feel as though we have a good solid direction and definition of what we want to design and potentially ship to our users and we should be able to imagine how things might start taking shape.

How Long Should All This Take?

Design and product delivery processes are more complex to write about than they are to actually get up and do. While the past few chapters have been full of workshops, diagrams, documentation, and process, you can feasibly get to this point in a couple of weeks if you're well-practiced in facilitating the workshops and delivering on the work you're accountable for. If you're just learning, or if your organization is a clusterf#@k, or if you're working in an industry that requires the utmost rigor or bureaucracy, then of course this can take longer. But in small, efficient teams, progressing to design after two weeks of research and ideation is more than doable.

I'm a big proponent of a six-week MVP for most product projects. It's a timeframe that I've found to be somewhat palatable to both contributors and stakeholders, and if everyone involved in an initiative is available, efficient, and competent, really great ideas can form in six weeks. I want to stress, though, that this is somewhat aspirational. People take time off, research reveals completely unexpected outcomes, new opportunities arise midway through exploration, and dozens of other factors impact the duration of our projects.

The main thing here is to not get overwhelmed with the amount of stuff there is to do. Reading about processes and taking time to digest *why* certain things work can be equal parts exciting and terrifying. If you're an experienced designer, most of this might be tweaks or iterations to stuff you're already doing, if you're a new designer, most of it will likely be something you've studied or read about before. These are proven phases, intended to give you the confidence you need to progress deeper into any project, but they don't take an age to conduct. On the contrary, we want to heavily optimize these phases with a focus on getting the maximum gains from a low time investment. As mentioned, we'll be repeating these phases more often than not, and complex, ostentatious process theater just won't cut it here. Keep things cheap, keep things fluid, and use only the most appropriate tools from your toolkit to arrive at a decision.

Carve Your Own Path

If you're following along with the journaling app we're building throughout this process, I strongly encourage you to go down a different direction than the one presented here and in the project's files. We're about to go into solution design, touching on things like system mapping, wireframing, prototyping, and final design work—and I think it'd be pretty dull all round if you just took the ideas presented here and mimicked the solutions. There are dozens of ways a journaling tool can solve the problems identified, and going off in your own direction now means you'll be working on your own ideas throughout the rest of this book. How would you do things differently? What features do you think folks would respond best to? Every product is powered by a different vision, and what problems are and are not solved by this product is a function of that vision. Think about what your vision might be for a journaling tool and how it might differ to the one presented here. Would you focus more on note-taking? Perhaps on affirmations and reflections? Would you allow for huge amounts of customization or would you want to build an opinionated product that promoted best practices? How would your key moments and features be prioritized based on this?

If you've been working on your own project from the get-go, then revisit your core vision before you work through your ideation phase and remind yourself *why* you wanted to build it in the first place. Sometimes a great idea just doesn't fit with a vision—shared or otherwise—for your product. Being opinionated during problem scoping and moment ranking is important; otherwise you end up with passive teams who are scared to pick a focal point or build opinionated products.

Finally, it's important that this book—while intended as a useful learning tool—can't magically make you creative or give you the tools to unlock collaborative divergence within your team. A lot of the work we're doing here requires divergent thought and creative work. While the workshops presented are designed to encourage and promote these mindsets, it's on you and your team to do the work and have the ideas that actually allow you to move forward with your project.

Having said that, our workshopping days are over. We know what we want to build, we have big ideas, and we're ready to get stuck in to exploring how all of our key moments might play out on a screen. The final practical chapter of this book is upon us, and it's a doozy. We might even design something in a design book. What a life.

CHAPTER 9

Execution and Evaluation

We now have a solid, multi-faceted plan for what we want to build, backed by research, and put through the scrutiny of problem definition and solution exploration. Our empowerment statements give us our key product hooks, our moment flows provide the discrete moment-by-moment experience on which we want our users to embark, our initiative canvas lays out our intentions and desired outcomes in a team-agnostic model, and our user flows and happy path help us envision how all of this links together. Our next steps are to define, describe, and *finally* design both the system and the interface that will deliver on this plan.

We'll explore a nifty framework for mapping out a system without focusing too much on structure or hierarchy, look at how information architecture is foundational to good design work, learn about placemaking, visit a magical museum, draw some interface ideas, and finally get a prototype in front of real humans. This is the core of a design process and where all of our ideas, planning, and graft manifest as a valuable, shippable digital environment. Let's do this.

Object-Oriented UX

Object-Oriented UX (OOUX from now on) is an approach to early stage design and information architecture proposed by Sophia V. Prater (ooux.com) and conceived during their work on CNN during the design of a results-tracking website for the 2012 U.S. presidential election. Since its inception, Prater has refined this methodology to an art, producing an unsurpassed approach to making sense of early stage design chaos. I was first introduced to this while working for a large financial services company, and I'm not exaggerating when I say it completely changed how I think about early stage design work.

© Scott Riley 2024
S. Riley, *Mindful Design*, Design Thinking, https://doi.org/10.1007/979-8-8688-0143-3_9

Fundamentally, OOUX revolves around describing a system based on its constituent objects, the data that describe them, the actions that can be performed against them, and the potential relationships between them—all without implying hierarchy or linearity.

OOUX is more than just system documentation, though, and is unto itself a form of ideation and creative brainstorming. Mapping out objects and data can feel dry, and an OOUX board can start out feeling like nothing more than a fancy schema. However, the focus on relationships after the initial mapping is one of the most powerful creative prompts I've encountered.

When you break it down, this makes total sense. Creativity is all about divergent thought—connecting concepts and ideas in ways that perhaps aren't immediately obvious. By taking the core objects within a system, documenting them without hierarchy or implicit structure, and then asking *how might X relate to Y?* over and over again, we're making space for creativity without the dreaded "blank canvas" that can feel like the death knell of creativity for many of us.

Figure 9-1 shows an example of the Objects portion of an OOUX board, and Figure 9-2 shows the Relationships section.

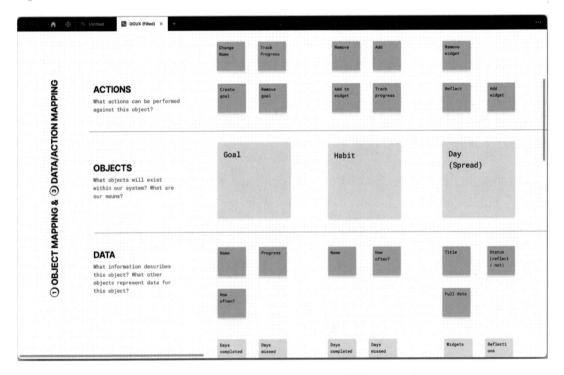

Figure 9-1. *The object map portion of a sample OOUX board*

When conducting an OOUX workshop, you have two goals: firstly, you want to build out a high-level map of the objects in your system. For new products and new ideas, this might be a little tricky because it's not always obvious what your key objects will be. Secondly, you want to brainstorm possible connections and relationships between your objects.

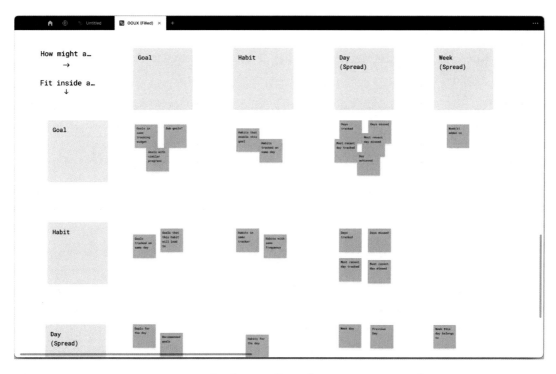

Figure 9-2. *Mapping potential relationships between system objects*

Objects

Objects are the nouns of our system, and they represent the *things* that users and other system objects will encounter. If you're designing a trip-booking product, then your objects might include *hotels*, *apartments*, *rooms*, *bookings*, *hosts*, and *guests*. If your trip-booking product also lets you arrange transport, then your object list will also likely include *taxi services*, *booked rides*, and potentially even *drivers*.

Let's document some of the objects for our journaling app—or your own project if you're following along. You can find an empty OOUX workshop, as well as a link to a filled example, in the `9 - Executing and Evaluating/[1] OOUX.html` file in this book's repository.

Our first goal is to explore the *nouns* of our system. What *things* have we been referring to during our ideation and definition phases? Make sure you have your project brief, affinity maps, and initiative canvas up for reference, and start throwing some sticky notes around! Here's our final object list, with a quick definition of each object:

- **Users** are people who have signed up to our app. Simple, really.

- **Goals** are trackable goals that users have created.

- **Spreads** are predefined layouts that can be associated with a month, day, or year.

- **Months** are the individual months of the year, and each month has its own spread.

- **Weeks** are the individual weeks of the year/month, and each week has its own spread.

- **Days** are the individual days of a week, and each day has its own spread.

- **Task-lists** are widgets designed to contain tasks.

  - **Tasks** are individual tasks that can be added to task-lists

- **Trackers** are widgets designed to track progress towards stated goals, habits, or predefined trackable items.

  - **Trackable items** are individual items within a tracker widget that can have progress, rating, or completion values associated with them.

- **Free-writing blocks** are widgets that allow users to free-journal or take notes.

- **Calendars** are widgets that show a user's calendar scoped to a specific month, week, or day.

- **Stickers** are decorative graphics that can be placed anywhere on a canvas without impacting the semantic content of its blocks.

- **Reflections** are notes taken during the reflection phase of a day.

Note that we've documented lower-order widgets individually (e.g., to-do list, habit tracker) as opposed to having a global widget object with a type attribute. This is a conscious decision. Given how we expect widgets to work, and how integral we expect them to be in our product, we're able to describe each individual widget much more clearly with this kind of separation. Depending on your product or your direction, you might want to have more "prototypical" objects that are separated by type (e.g., a taxonomy object with a type of "tag" or "category" in a blogging platform), or do what we've done here and have individual objects for each type. The difference is nuanced but can imply a lot about how you and your team envision your object structure in terms of prototypes and composition.

Relationships

We're now moving on from the dryer, documentarian approach to system mapping and towards the more divergent, creative realms of brainstorming and ideation.

How objects fit together is a vital property of a system. Some systems have shallow (or no) nesting and linear navigation pathways. These systems read like flowcharts. Others have deep nesting and nonlinear navigation pathways. These systems read like spirals. Most systems find themselves somewhere in the middle: a few layers of nesting and a manageable degree of intra-object relatedness.

We'll use a matrix approach for mapping our object relationships. Once you're done cataloging your system objects, bring them over to the relationship mapping section and arrange them vertically down the left of the chart. These will be the "parent" objects. Next, duplicate them and lay them out into a horizontal row at the top of the chart. These will be the "child" objects. With that done, we want to use a *how might X fit inside Y* prompt to populate potential relationships.

This is the area of OOUX that tends to need the most explaining, as it can be quite esoteric. You'll notice that we've labeled the row of stickies across the top as "How might a…" and the column of stickies down the left hand side with "Fit inside a… ." This is to help us form a sentence as we work our way through each object.

For us, that means asking things like *how might a day fit inside a week?, how might a goal fit inside a month?, how might a week fit inside a goal?,* and so on. For a travel-booking product that also allows users to arrange day trips and other excursions, you might ask something like *how might a* **property** *fit inside an* **excursion**?, which generates ideas such as *properties near this excursion.* For a pet-sitting product, you might ask *how might a* **pet** *fit inside a* **pet** (okay, so that's some weird syntax, but work with me) and come up with the idea of *pets with the same breed* or *pets with the same owner*. You might also ask *how might a* **sitter** *fit inside a* **pet**?—sitters who've sat this pet before, sitters who might be a good fit—and *how might a* **pet** *fit inside a* **sitter**?—pets near this sitter, pets this sitter has sat before.

Many of these connections will feel obvious, especially if your system has some kind of inherent hierarchy or ownership. Think of our journaling app: of course days are going to live inside weeks, which will live inside months. And of course to-do items are going to live inside task widgets. However, there's still room for creativity—if we ask *how might a day fit inside a goal?,* we might propose showing days where we made progress towards a goal or days where we fell short of our expectations.

This approach to divergent relationship-making outside of a typical hierarchical architecture can be an incredibly valuable part of any design process, especially when our underlying systems are complex.

Data and Attributes

All objects are described by data and metadata. It's how you differentiate between one instance of an object and another. If we're building an app for booking dog sitters, then we're going to have an object of *dog*. However, what our users encounter will more specifically be an *instance* of *dog*. To identify this instance, we'll have a name, a breed, an owner (which is also an object instance!) and perhaps even their favorite treat.

As such, an object's data is what helps us identify a specific instance of that object and distinguish between all instances in a list or collection. Let's take a quick pass through our objects and start adding some data to them (Figure 9-3).

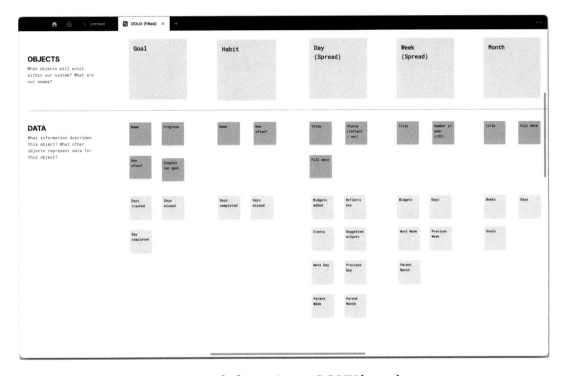

Figure 9-3. *Data mapping and objects in an OOUX board*

When associating data with an object, we're essentially documenting what information we should store against any discrete instance of that object, with the goals of clearly defining each instance, allowing instances to be easily differentiated, and highlighting the key information users might find important. Let's take our **Trackable Item** object as an example, and build out a data set:

- **Title** refers to the text used to name or describe the item, such as Guitar Practice or Daily Yoga.

- **Rating Type** refers to the type of rating used when reflecting on the item and can be one of

  - Binary (was the item done/not done)

  - Ranking (a ranking between 1 and 5)

  - Balance (a balance between one value and another, such as Work/Life)

273

- **Rating Value** refers to the tracked value of the item and is contextual to the rating type (0/1 for done/not done, a numerical value for ranking, and a percentage split for balance).

- **Position** refers to the individual items position within a list of trackable items.

- **Parent** widget refers to the widget that this trackable item lives in. This is a nested object.

- **Day** represents the individual day on which this item was tracked. This is a nested object.

Note that we also want to catalog any nested objects here too. For example, we're going to have a lot of widgets that have a Day attribute, indicating which day it's associated with. Inversely, we're going to have days that have a list of widgets, and months and weeks will both have a list of days. Your relationship map should give you everything you need in that regard.

Action Possibility

Just like in the physical world, objects in our digital environments often present action possibility. Objects, almost by definition, are interactive, malleable things. It's incredibly rare to see an object (at least insofar as we've defined "object" for this exercise) that doesn't have an interactivity layer. During my years conducting these workshops I've never encountered one, and I genuinely doubt such a thing exists. Objects without interactivity are just data or decoration.

Our job, later in our process, will be to take these action possibilities and determine how our objects should be styled and presented to communicate such possibilities. Right now, though, we're mostly concerned with documenting them.

The process of documenting possible actions is pretty straightforward. Go through every object and brainstorm the things you might need to do to it. Use the object's attributes that you've already documented as a guide here because if the data is manipulable, you're guaranteed to need to design the interaction that allows for this manipulation. Figure 9-4 shows potential actions documented against a subset of our objects.

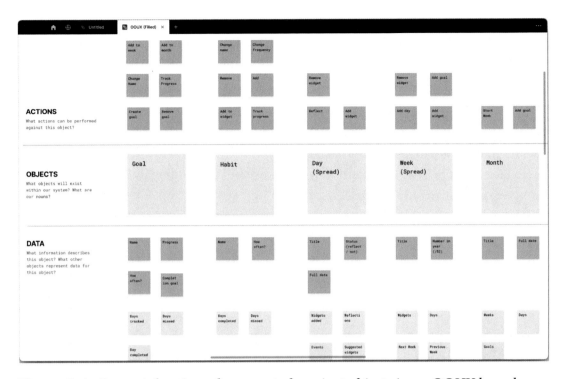

Figure 9-4. *Potential actions documented against objects in an OOUX board*

Once you've documented your potential actions against your objects, you have a complete map. Let's take a step back and look at what we've created. It's essentially an inventory of everything we might need to design, at a component level. We have our entire system of objects, the data that describes them, the relationships that connect them, and the interactions they must present. Yet, there's no implicit hierarchy or structure—aside from knowing how other objects might nest inside another—so have we just made a glorified spec? Well, *kind of.* But that doesn't tell the whole story.

Objects as Conceptual Components

While UI-level components are nowadays ubiquitous, integral to almost any interface, and the core of any design system, objects give us components at the conceptual level. Knowing that we have to design a *dog* component for a dog-sitting app is likely not going to surprise us, but OOUX—through the "objects as data for other objects" relationship paradigm—shows us the many different contexts in which we'll need to describe a *dog*.

This can dramatically change not only how we think about our tasks at a conceptual level, but the entire makeup of our interface in an overt, literal manner. OOUX shows us that we need to design. Running with the dog-sitting example: A view for "dog" in the following formats: a dog profile view, a dog item in a list of dog search results, a dog item in a list of previously-sat dogs for a sitter, a dog in the context of a booking, and so on and so forth. This contextual underpinning is what separates OOUX from other documentation and ideation approaches.

In fact, if you're in a particularly workshop-averse environment and—for whatever strange reason—can only do *one* early stage design workshop, then make it an OOUX workshop. You'll find you have a great balance between system-level documentation, conceptual and object-level understanding of a system, contextual information to guide your designs, a schema-like structure to ease collaboration with your engineers, a set of actions and calls-to-action that can easily be interpreted as a moment map, and the creative brainstorming that comes from mapping relationships between objects.

Diving Deeper

It's important to point out here that popular approaches to OOUX have evolved over time, especially with its application within enterprise products or highly complex systems. Our humble object map fits nice and neatly into a single FigJam board and acts as a self-documenting workshop canvas, and this only works because of our project's scale and scope. Larger projects (think enterprise product lines with lots of integration or incredibly complex medical systems) tend to need a more documentarian approach with more in-depth object lists and even—whisper it quietly now—*spreadsheets* finding their way into our lovely world of design and sticky notes.

I've made a point in this book of presenting a process that I believe in, that's free of the typical design theater you see in many corporate innovation frameworks, and that is as well-documented as such an involved approach can be. However, this must be balanced against crediting folks properly and not misrepresenting their work. As such, it would be remiss of me to not point out that, at the time of writing this book, Sophia V. Prater has a whole host of paid and free resources on OOUX. If you've enjoyed this high-level intro and want to go really (really!) deep: take her course, subscribe to the OOUX newsletter, and dive into the excellent content over at `ooux.com`.

While I've tailored my approach to OOUX based on feedback I've had from countless client sessions, and the manifestation of it in this book is somewhat modified, if it's as revolutionary to your process as it was to mine, then absolutely dive deeper into the subject. As with many areas of this book, I hope this can be a spark to further, deeper enquiry.

Placemaking

Placemaking is the art of turning a space into a place. Places are designed spaces: environments wherein the contents dictate—or at least heavily suggest—possibility. It's easy to think of interface design purely as a product of interlinked screens, each designed specifically for its purpose—moving a user from A to B to C until eventually their path is complete. This linear approach to design is not without merit, especially for informational/marketing websites and constrained flows within products. It is important, though, to use linearity sparingly when we design; linearity is a function of user intent, or more specifically, it is a function of our *confidence* in divining user intent. The more confident we can be in our prediction of such intent, the more we can get away with limiting options and presenting folks with linearity. However, as we build more complex environments, and as expectations for product capabilities grow, we can't rely solely on cobbled-together, linear flows.

That doesn't mean, though, that the alternative lies solely in pure ambiguity. Presenting users with vague, unopinionated environments in the name of autonomy and discovery is just as reckless as constraining a flow to banal linearity in the name of efficiency and predictability. Linearity is a scale, a gamut that we too often polarize and rarely explore to its full extent, and the most well-designed interfaces seamlessly transition between modes of linearity without creating undue dissonance. Placemaking is the core skill that makes all of this possible.

Making Places Out of Spaces

Imagine a large, open field somewhere. This field—while maintained, cleared, and monitored—is just a very large, very nice patch of grass. This is a *space*. Now imagine what folks might do in this field. Walk their dogs? Play football? Ride horses? Roll around and frolic like whimsical lovers in a Jane Austen novel? There are really no rules and no limitations, but there's also nothing here that affords any specific interaction, thus no predictability and nothing we can do to encourage or afford certain behaviors and interactions.

Now, imagine the same field but paint a few lines on the grass and put up some goal posts. While it's just as possible to frolic, ride, and dog walk, we're now clearly communicating an optimal purpose for our field: we want folks to play football. Conversely, let's say we take our field and dig out a grid of planting patches: we've now made an allotment. Add a swing set, slides, and climbing frames and you've got a kids' park. Let's say our field is large enough to allow for all of these options; we just need to split it up and add paths, signs, and other embellishments and affordances and we have a large public park with football fields, dog-walking areas, communal planters, and play areas, all of which are navigable and practical.

This is placemaking. The extent to which we "make" a place depends mostly on how predictable or controllable we want our environment to be. If we want our field to be used exclusively for football, then we might fence off separate pitches and let folks operate on a first-come, first-served basis. If we wanted to encourage dog walkers, we might put up dog waste bins and even add in some canine agility implements or build closed-off areas for responsible off-leash dog roaming.

Now, you can still walk a dog on a football pitch and you can still play football in a dog park. Placemaking is not about hard limits or overt control. It's about creating opinionated environments optimized for certain activities and filled with elements that imply and communicate specific action possibilities.

Digital Spaces and Places

Transforming a football pitch into a dog park and a dog park into an allotment and an allotment into a green field perfect for some good old-fashioned frolicking and … you get the idea … takes a lot of time and effort in the real world. In the digital realm, however, we can transition between places or place modalities in pretty much an instant. While it's certainly not advised in a single product, it's completely possible to go from an online store context to an audio recording context in the click of a button. In the context of an operating system, this is everyday behavior. We're constantly switching between different apps, all with their own approaches to placemaking. Our real-world, physical places require travel to get between—or time to rearrange—whereas our digital places give us the power of teleportation.

This isn't inherently positive or negative, but it does present many opportunities and many pitfalls. On the negative side, it can be disquieting to be thrust into different environments without adequate framing or cognitive preparation. And when those environments are poorly designed, this disjointedness increases by orders of magnitude. On the more positive side, we can have a degree of fluidity with our places that just isn't possible in the real world.

To illustrate this, imagine a futuristic museum that shifts its exhibits based on the goals, preferences, or even whims of a visitor. You enter through reception straight into the Ancient Egypt room. Next, the Space exhibit intrigues you; space is cool, right? Let's check it out. One breath later, you're learning about black holes and supernovas and thinking about how dull Mars will be once all the rich people move there. Speaking of which, let's have a gander at the French Revolution exhibit—suddenly the planetarium is disbanded and you're surrounded by guillotines and Phrygian caps.

This would be bordering on impossible in the real world. Not only would it be expensive and intricate and full of risk, but museums are also communal places, and little Timmy's day would be ruined if, right in the middle of going absolutely bonkers over a triceratops, everything shifted at random and he had to learn about the economic structures of the Ottoman Empire. However, in the digital realm, this is our norm. Our places shift and fluctuate in both subtle and overt ways. We can go from the *Ancient Egyptians* to the *French Revolution* to *100 Amazing Shrek Facts* in a relative instant. Our experiences are (or should I say *can be*) personal, tailored, and informed by our previous actions.

Home Comforts

Placemaking isn't a stage of a project or a phase of a design process; it's a philosophy that guides decision making throughout. Everything from how we name our contexts and objects through to how a button responds when it's hovered has an impact on how our *place* is perceived. Fundamentally, placemaking is based around the knowledge that what people *will do* is framed by the information an environment presents them with. Our settings dictate our possibilities.

Our journaling app requires a lot of placemaking as we're looking to present a fluid, nonlinear digital environment that borrows from the more constrained and, frankly, ancient page-based approach to journaling. The act of recording our thoughts onto external media is literal millennia in the making, and we can't propose something radical without bringing in familiar elements and metaphors for common practices. Give people what they're used to. Then, when your inevitable need to go against the grain arises, you're able to do so in a familiar, predictable, comforting place.

Evaluative Research

If a section on evaluating design work falling slap in the middle—rather than at the end—of a chapter discussing said design work feels out of place, then you might suffer from the all-too-common brain worm that tells many a designer they need only user test their stuff when it feels done. It's okay. We've all been there. We're here for you. You'll get through this. We'll brave it together.

In reality, delaying your evaluation is one of the easiest ways to tank a project, and there's a reason I'm talking about user testing before we even have a wireframe. Firstly, you should be prepared to test your wires from your very first sketch onwards, and secondly, you should be testing *before* you even start on your wireframes.

Each subsequent section of this book will wrap up with a note on what questions we're looking to answer when we take our work through evaluative research, but let's have a quick primer on the approach we'll take.

Test Early, Test Often

I am not, by any stretch of the imagination, a manic shaker. I've been described as many things in my life, but manic shaker is not one of them. However, if I was to ever become one, I would manically shake every designer I've met and worked with while shouting *please just user test your f#$*ing wireframes.*

User testing is cheap and straightforward to conduct. It's proven. It's enlightening. If you're waiting until you have a polished, approved prototype that you're blissfully in love with before you put it in front of actual humans who might want to do actual things with it, you are going to be sad. Very sad. Curl-into-a-ball-and-cry-about-button-copy levels of sad.

Evaluative research is not a one-and-done thing. It's something that every phase, every pivot, every iteration, and every concept should go through. If you're proposing something that impacts usability, you really, *really* should explore whether it's doing so in a positive way. User testing wireframes—or even your wording and information architecture—doesn't have to be involved or arduous. In fact, 90% of the time you're essentially asking some version of *what does this concept mean to you?, what do you think would happen when you click on this?*, or *what do you think you'll see behind this tab?* If people can answer mostly correctly to these questions for the various contexts you're looking to test, you're almost always good to move on.

Information Architecture

OOUX helped us build a model of our system by describing all the *things* that can live in it, what information those *things* might be described by, and what actions might be possible to perform against those *things*. As wonderful as it is, it does not give us any inkling as to where these things should live, how they should be grouped or structured, and what kind of hierarchy they should fit into.

This is where Information Architecture (IA from now on) comes into play. Put simply, IA is the practice of structuring and organizing content in a way that is conducive to our users achieving their goals. You explored how to perceptually group items in a designed environment when you looked at Gestalt way back in Chapter 2 and IA is the precursor to this; while we can use Gestalt to *show* grouping and relatedness, we still need to know just what those groups and their constituent parts actually are.

IA As Mental Model Resolution

One of the key roles IA will play in our project is translating what is usually an amorphous, vague blob of conceptual objects into a structure that adheres to—or purposefully subverts—the mental models of our users. Knowing how an audience thinks about information allows us to structure and present content appropriately, especially in the context of helping people achieve their goals.

Let's look at our journaling app. The ubiquitous mental model we've encountered is that of a daily journal—with almost all of our research participants following some kind of "bullet journal" methodology. This gives us a very clear indicator of a prevalent mental model, and our first step should be to document the qualities or properties of this, paying particular attention to how information is structured and how concepts are grouped.

As a starter, we know that bullet journals are often split into months, weeks, and days, with each broad time unit having its own spread. We've observed participants talking about monthly, daily, and weekly spreads. This also gives us a semblance of expected hierarchy, with monthly spreads usually containing broader information and higher-level goals or commitments and weekly or daily spreads containing more granular items.

We can also observe that a physical journal has particular properties. It's a page-based concept, with most participants using their journals as a kind of linear timeline. Each monthly spread acts as an introduction to the weekly spreads and each weekly spread either *contains* all the days of the week or acts as a similar introduction to the individual daily spreads of the week. This is also where we notice our first clear point of divergence in mental models. Some people prefer to have every day of the week laid out on a single two-page spread, while others prefer entire pages per-day. This doesn't change our overall hierarchy (days still "live inside" weeks) but it does present us with two, seemingly equally viable models for splitting up journal weeks into days.

Finally, we also observe how *time* can have an impact on our audiences' mental models. Many folks start their day by either writing their tasks down or performing their "daily pages" ritual—a pattern we noticed where people free-write at the start of their day to get their thoughts out of their head. During the day, we've observed people using journals more fluidly, taking notes, checking off to-do items, and generally jotting down their thoughts. Towards the end of the day, we observed people writing their daily reflections, practicing gratitude, and tracking their habits, mood, work/life balance, or progress towards goals.

Let's Architect

IA for a digital environment is very different to IA for a website or a brochure. While traditional, content-focused IA practices like sitemaps and indexing are still useful and applicable to product design, our approach to nonlinear product design means we're going to be thinking a lot more about groups or chunks of information and objects than we are about linear, linked pages or screens.

OOUX gives us the perfect jumping off point for our IA work; after all, we've just documented all of our objects and every potential piece of information we might want to show about them. Here we can focus more on *context*. In what contexts should we show what information?

Many objects will have at least two contexts—a detail context and a list context. Think of a typical online store: browsing categories or searching for items will give you a list of results, and you can interact with an individual result to view a more detailed page for the item. Trying to cram every attribute of an object into the limited space of a list item is a fool's errand, and progressive disclosure, as we've explored, is imperative when it comes to navigating more complex conceptual spaces.

This is true too for our potential actions. Objects can be manipulated in certain ways, and we don't always want to show every possible action in every possible context of an object. This could be because an action doesn't fit within the context of the current flow, is too complex or overwhelming to surface in a space- or attention-limited context, or too destructive or impactful to include as part of the more "common" interactions exposed on an object.

With all that in mind, our first step is coming up with our broad contexts. Think of a *context* here as a broad replacement for *screen* (for the product designers amongst us) or *page* (for the web or print designers). Remember that we're designing digital environments and will be dealing more with shifting contexts than we will with well-scoped, well-divided screen or page structures.

Refer back to your moment maps or happy path from your early stage work and keep your OOUX open (in fact, keep your OOUX open indefinitely; it'll be your best friend for a while) as you brainstorm your contexts. Think about mental models and existing content structuring paradigms, too. The whole *files live inside folders, which can live inside higher-level folders* paradigm is a tried and tested structure, and there's a reason we can't escape the metaphor.

Our Key Contexts

As well as understanding our granular object contexts, we also need to present core, system-level contexts to our users.

You can find an IA board, as well as a link to an already-filled example, in the `9 - Execution and Evaluation/[2] Information Architecture.html` file in this book's repository.

The goal with an IA board is to decide on a broad map for your environment's structure and contexts. Fundamentally, we're taking all of our objects and asking *where should it live?* and *what other objects should it live there with?* This, though, sounds deceptively simple. The decisions we need to make at this stage are integral to the success of our product, and conceptual grouping is a difficult, nuanced task. Grouping and categorizing content is also rife with potential bias—just like any phase of our design process—and we must be careful to not introduce idiosyncratic structures because it makes sense to us or our stakeholders. Treat IA with the same respect you plan on treating your wireframes and prototypes: eliminate bias through reference to research and test your assumptions with real humans.

We start by brainstorming our broad contexts (Figure 9-5). For our journaling app, we have the following core contexts:

- **Month** is the broad overview of the selected month.

- **Week** is the weekly spread context for a selected week.

- **Day** is the daily spread context for a selected day.

- **Goals** is the goal-setting and management context.

- **Habits** is the where the habits our users want to track are set up and managed.

- **Reflection** is the daily wrap-up context.

And we also have a couple of standalone contexts:

- **Onboarding** is the context for a brand new user's first experience with our product.

- **Search** is the context for displaying search results.

- **Account** is the context for managing a user's account, including log-in information and billing.

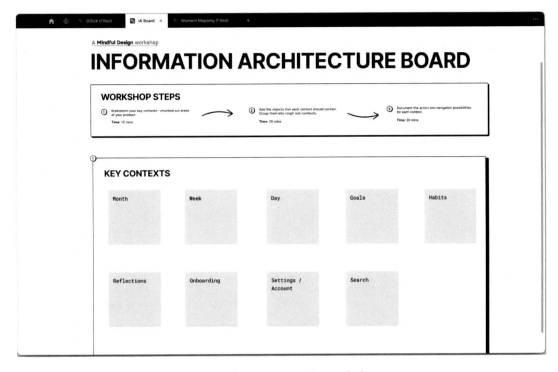

Figure 9-5. *Key concepts mapped out in an IA workshop*

With these mapped out, we can start filling them up with our objects. Work through each context and add the objects you think you might want to show. Don't worry too much at first about hierarchy or information density; just have a quick pass. Work through each context until you're broadly happy with the content you expect to include and then move on to the next. After your first pass, it's time to break out the scalpel and get a little more surgical with things.

Subcontexts and Hierarchy

Each of your broad contexts will likely contain multiple subcontexts and will definitely need to present a hierarchy of sorts. But what are subcontexts exactly?

If we think about a web page—let's say a Home page—as a broad context, then the subcontexts within might be things like Welcome Section, Feature List, Blog Links, Customer Testimonials, and so on. For digital products, our contexts are usually a little more ambiguous, and our subcontexts are often more interactive and nested. If we think about a Permissions Management context in a product, then subcontexts might be User Lists, Roles, Invite Links, and SSO settings. Our User List might also be contextual, with search, filtering, and list/grid view. See Figure 9-6.

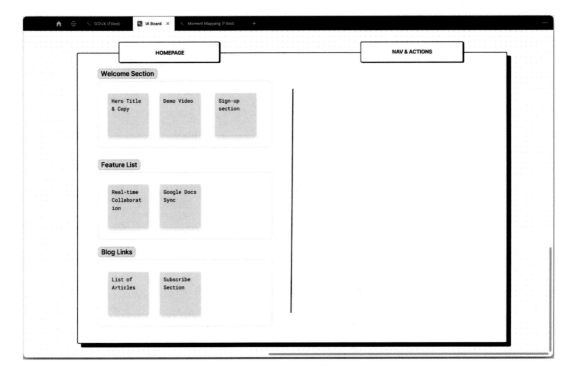

Figure 9-6. *An organized IA board with subcontexts and hierarchy documented*

Again, let's work context-by-context in our IA board. Do you have any objects that make sense to be grouped together? If so, into which broad subcontext should they be placed? Visually group your objects into subcontexts and give those subcontexts a name as you go. You might group objects (or object lists) such as *Page Views List, User Segment Breakdown,* and *Key Funnels* into an *Analytics* subcontext inside *Dashboard* context, for example.

Once you have your subcontexts, order them vertically, with the most important items at the top. Yes, *most important* will be subjective and often imbued with a notable degree of bias. Remember to keep your audience's mental models in mind, and as always, lean on your research findings. What's important to your organization isn't always what's important to your users—don't make the mistake of assuming such.

Navigating Between Contexts

Having a clear idea of what contexts we require, and what objects and content should exist in those contexts, is only one half of the equation when it comes to effective information architecture. The other half is deciding how people will navigate to, from, and between these contexts.

In the IA workshop, every context has a separate section to document this navigation approach, and the thought process here is really just going through each of your contexts and asking two questions. Firstly, *should we be able to get from Context A to Context B?* And secondly, *how might we get to Context A from Context B?* See Figure 9-7.

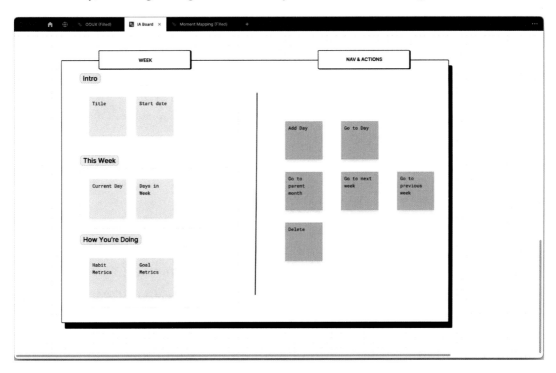

Figure 9-7. *An IA workshop showing navigation possibilities*

In this example, we're working on the navigation for our *Day* context. Let's go through our other core contexts one by one and ask our two big questions:

- **Month**: We should be able to get to a month context from a day context. We could do this by having breadcrumbs to get to the parent month.

- **Week**: Again, yes! And also again, good old breadcrumbs.

- **Day**: We should be able to get to one day context from another day context. We could do this by having next/previous navigation (bonus points here for adhering to the page-by-page mental model of physical journaling!).

- **Goals**: We should be able to get to a goals context from a day context, but only if the **goals** widget is added to the spread. We could do this by having a "go to goals" link in the widget itself.

- **Habits**: Similarly to goals, we should be able to access our habits context from a day context, but only if the user has indicated they want to track habits during their day.

- **Reflection**: We should be able to get to a reflections context from a day context—it's one of the main actions for a day! We could do this by having a persistent "reflect on your day" prompt somewhere within the daily spread.

Global Navigation

At this point, we should be able to make a decision as to how we want our global navigation to be structured. It might surprise some to see such an important concept appear so late in a process, but in my experience it's much more straightforward to plot out global navigation when you know the constituent parts and key contexts to which you need to provide access.

Many times, your global navigation is simply a list of your most important contexts. Many simpler websites will take this approach (how many times do we see Home, About, Features, Pricing, and Contact in a marketing site's top nav?) Other times, your global navigation will be a filtered view of a key object—such as Overdue and Due Today in a task management product.

For our journaling app, we're able to cheat a little, as we already have an intuitive navigation structure implicit in our mental models. Days live inside weeks, weeks live inside months, and months live inside years. Our global navigation then is pretty straightforward: list all the months of a year, list all the weeks in that month, list all the days within that week. Sorted.

Okay, so maybe it's not *that* simple. We need to account for goals and habits, which are global, as well as account management and application settings. So we'll need a combination of deeper-nested year/month/week containers as well as some flat, top-level containers for settings, goals, and habits.

In my experience, documenting your global navigation as a separate context—exactly as we've just done with our key contexts—is the best approach. Create a new context called Global Nav and work from there. Yes, this will feel repetitive, yes, you'll likely spend 90% of your time copy/pasting, and yes, that 10% of the time you spend brainstorming a viable navigation pattern will be worth the repetition. See Figure 9-8.

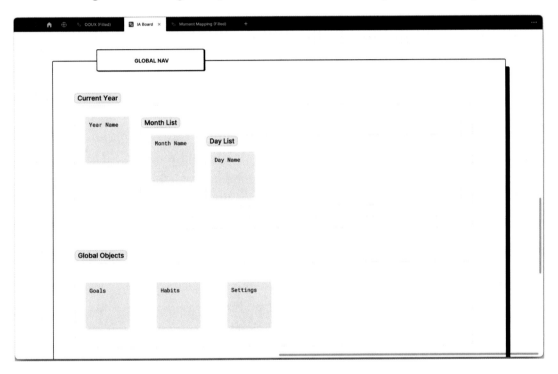

Figure 9-8. *A Global Nav context in an IA board*

This presents us with a bunch of global, navigation-focused actions we need to design. Firstly, we need to have a mechanism for switching or expanding the selected year, month, and week, and we need to design what the resulting state of our navigation looks like at each point of filtration.

With that, we're done. Put the kettle on. While it's boiling, zoom out and think about what you've just built: this is the contextual layer of our system and one of the last abstractions we need in place before we start making "real" interfaces. Kettle still going? Good, because we've got to talk about words.

It's All in the Name

Names and labels are integral to good IA. And to almost everyone's continued dismay, naming things is *really f$#*ing hard*. Good naming is all about being specific without being obtuse or niche. Being too technical with your wording can constrain your user base from the get-go, and being too vague with your wording creates an ambiguous, amorphous lexical mess.

Take Slack, for example. In it, a "place where messages and files can be sent" is called a *channel*. A "group of replies associated with a single message" is called a *thread*. These words didn't come from thin air; someone chose them (very well, I might add), and they're now ubiquitous. Now, these aren't new words for new concepts. RFC used channels to describe the same concept decades before Slack was a thing, and threads have existed for longer still, perhaps most notably in the halcyon days of internet forums. Slack uses appropriate, familiar, and simple-enough (although this will always be relative) terms to describe these key concepts. How different would Slack feel if channels were called folders? Or doo-dahs? Or water-coolers? Or Super Cool Message Containers?

Naming our contexts is just as important as naming our objects and our containers, too. Home *feels* different to Dashboard, which feels different to Feed, which feels different to Hub, but all *could* be applicable and interchangeable within a specific context. Similarly, Activity, Notification Center, and Inbox could all be used for the same context. What we're looking for here is wording that's *most appropriate*. It has to describe our concept well (a page full of charts and summaries isn't well-described by "home" but *is* well-described by "dashboard") and fit the mental models of our audience.

Let's look at some of the broad terminology we're using and how it might relate back to our audience's mental models.

- **Spreads** represent day-, week-, and month-level canvases that can be filled with content over time. We're pretty confident with this terminology as it appeared countless times in our research!

- **Widgets** represent individual items that can be placed on a canvas to build out a spread. We're not super confident with this terminology as it's not really represented in the physical journaling space. While it's a pretty common phrase among technical folks, we can't be sure that our audience will understand or gravitate towards it.

- **Reflections** represent individual reflection moments that can be instigated at any point during a date. Again, the idea of reflection journaling is evident in much of our research findings and we can be pretty confident in it translating.

We need to ensure that the words we're using resonate with our audience and communicate the concepts they represent effectively. The right balance between specificity, character, and utility will always depend on the type of product you're building, the uniqueness of your key concepts, and your audience's tolerance for esoterica.

Information As Designed Content

One of the main tenets of information architecture is that *information is a mental construct*. We give people content and cues, and they turn that into codified, useful information through their experience perceiving and processing it. This might sound esoteric, but you already encountered this at work much earlier in this book. Just as vision and perception are two parts of a multiplayer process, so too are content and information.

If information is content made conducive to a goal, then our IA and early content design are the first rungs on the ladder towards a designed environment. Words are our most prototypical abstractions of ideas. If people don't understand the language we're using, we're failing at the first hurdle.

It's easy to fall into an assumption loop when it comes to information architecture. It's human nature to categorize, and you'll be doing so subconsciously whether you like it or not, long before you actually start laying out and grouping objects. Our brains have a remarkable habit of convincing us that what makes sense to us is correct at a more objective level, as opposed to our perception being one of myriad potential lenses through which to view a system or environment. After all, we know that we prefer immutable schemas and that our approach to categorization greatly informs our lived experiences.

Make a conscious effort to remove bias from your IA decision-making. Resist the urge to go into auto-pilot and keep in mind just how foundational and impactful these early decisions will be on the remainder of your project. Unchecked bias at the structural level will manifest throughout your designed model in much more insidious, unpredictable ways.

Evaluating IA Work

When evaluating your information architecture and early content work, focus on the following key questions:

- **Do people understand our terminology?** If our home screen is called a *dashboard*, what does that imply? Can people intuit the content or purpose of it? Ask this about all main contexts. Make sure to use clear, predictable, and appropriate language.

- **Are we proposing a good broad structure?** We should be confident that we're arranging information into chunks that make sense to real humans.

One of the main things we need to test for in our information architecture is the concept of "widgets." As highlighted, the wording here isn't really represented in the journaling world and might be too rooted in more technical language.

Similarly, we want to make sure that the broad structure we're proposing makes sense. Do people actually think about goals outside of the context of their days and weeks? Do they really think in terms of days, weeks, and months? Is a spread for each of these time divisions appropriate or desired?

If we're confident in our information architecture, then we can bring that into the next phase. Let's draw some rectangles!

Wireframing

We now have all the key ingredients we need for effective placemaking. We've got a system map of sorts from our OOUX board, with a focus on objects, relationships, and action possibility. We also have the broad contexts we must expect to design around, as well as which objects we expect will exist within—and how important they are—said context. Finally, we have a good idea of how each context might be navigated.

Given these conceptual, contextual, informational, and structural components, our next job is to piece them together into a bonafide digital environment. While it's tempting to feel like we've got the bulk of our product figured out, and while the momentum generated from piecing together the discrete components of our idea into something that's finally resembling a *whole* is intoxicating, it's important to acknowledge that we *still* have a bunch of unanswered questions. Wireframing is all about getting answers to those questions as quickly and effectively as we can.

When thinking in terms of environments, moments, and mental models, we'll be doing a lot of metaphorical zooming in and out in terms of our processes. This is just as true for our wireframing as it is for our visual and interaction design phases. As you progress with your wireframes, make sure that you're questioning your solutions against existing mental models that you've (hopefully) managed to garner from your customer and competitor research.

Thumbnail Sketching

We can bridge the gap between our IA and our wireframes through thumbnail sketching—the subtle art of drawing small rectangles inside big rectangles.

Thumbnail sketching is all about getting ideas out quickly. We're concerned about broad strokes, not discrete elements, and we're still in the very metaphorical, low-fidelity stage of our work. We'll be creating thumbnail sketches for each of the contexts we identified in our IA work. If you're strapped for time and want to limit your contexts, pick your most important, your most unique, and your most complex contexts and thumbnail each of those.

To start thumbnailing, you just need a few rectangles. Feel free to grab a thumbnailing template from the `Chapter 9 - Execution and Evaluation/[03] Thumbnailing.html` file in this book's repository, which also includes links to completed thumbnails for each of the contexts in our journaling app, or just get your notebook, sketchbook, or stone tablet out and draw yourself some container rectangles. See Figure 9-9.

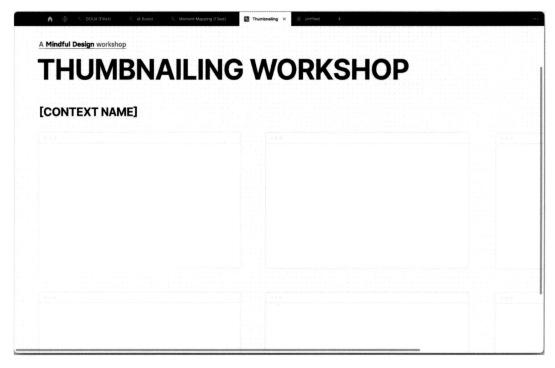

Figure 9-9. *A blank thumbnailing template ready for good old rectangles*

The goal here is to take our broad information architecture and explore different ways we can lay our elements out. Do we need a sidebar? Or a top nav? Why not both? Should our main content area be a grid view? Or a more traditional vertical section flow? By thinking in very broad blocks, we can rapidly produce dozens of potential layouts. Some will be viable, some will be fanciful, some will be terrible. Use this as a chance to loosen up and try new things.

Move fast and set yourself a goal of filling 6-12 thumbnails in one sitting. You'll notice that the first few thumbnails come readily and easily—namely because you'll almost always have an idea in your head of your interface before you even start sketching and because you'll have seen examples in your competitor research. Things get harder and harder as you exhaust your initial, most obvious ideas. Don't stop until you hit your thumbnail goal and don't worry if your ideas are outrageous or silly at this stage. Figure 9-10 shows the results of a thumbnailing session I did for our hypothetical animation app.

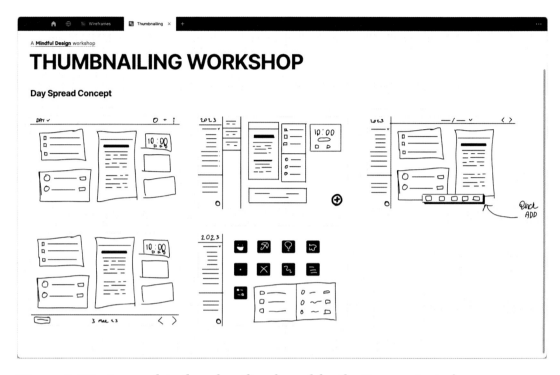

Figure 9-10. *A complete thumbnailing board for the Day context of our journaling app*

The point of thumbnailing is to explore solutions for visually arranging your broadest application areas. Think in a suitably broad mindset when doing this exercise. Even at this point, however, consider convention and mental models. There's a reason that apps in the same problem space are often structurally similar, and it rarely comes down to a lack of creativity on their design teams' part. Even at this early stage of wireframing, we need to be thinking about how we balance what we believe to be an elegant or innovative solution with the mental models and convention that we *know* our customers will expect. Now, we don't have to think this critically *while* we thumbnail; this is our unconstrained and expressive flow of creativity, after all. However, when it comes to *analyzing* them, our most creative solutions are often our least practical.

Layout Sketching

Once you have two or three potentially workable thumbnails of whatever fidelity makes you happy and confident, you can start putting together some basic interface sketches. Think of an interface sketch as an iteration on your thumbnails. Here, we'll start introducing actual words, at least for our main actions and headings. We'll also start separating our interface elements more granularly, through shading, highlights, and hairline borders, as we break away from simple rectangles and lines. This is a notably fluid part of the design process and so much of it depends on your confidence in your previous work. If you're comfortable with your thumbnailing results and have a strong candidate to take into prototyping, you might want to pay a cursory nod to layout sketches and expedite your path to prototyping.

If you're not super confident with your thumbnails and you have several options you think might work, try upping the fidelity a little and working at a larger size. Still, stick to mostly rectangles and lines, but don't be scared to add a little shading or highlighting here and there. Alternatively, perform even more rounds of thumbnailing. The beauty of these stages of our process is that everything is so disposable and so quick to create.

You can do your layout sketching on paper, in your digital drawing tool of choice, or in a design and prototyping app (Figure 9-11). Some masochists even use Keynote for this. Don't ask.

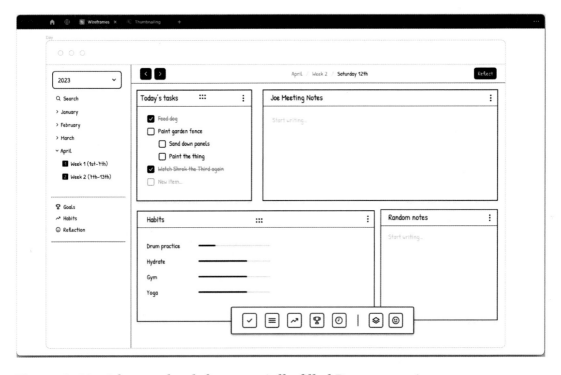

Figure 9-11. *A layout sketch for a partially-filled Day context in our journaling app*

Think carefully and deeply about the actions you're presenting to people in these layouts. Make liberal use of both your IA board and your object-by-object level

Don't rush through this, though, as there's one key aspect to layout sketching that we've yet to consider during our wireframing: content. This is likely the first phase of our project where we'll be placing content into its proposed context. Moving with too much haste from thumbnails to interactive prototypes can leave content under-baked and leave your content designers playing catch-up. Our information architecture will have done a bunch of heavy lifting in terms of how we name things, as well as what our broad contexts and objects might contain, but that doesn't always translate neatly when laid out in context. Work with your words people—or learn to become a great words person—to get a head start on content design. Use this as a chance to test it.

We also want to make sure we take care of the basics. Things like correct titles, pagination where required, and well-structured content all help with wayfinding and grounding a user in a moment.

Low-Fidelity Prototypes

Static wireframes are an artifact of design best left in the past. If you're designing an interface, your wireframes should be interactive, and it's imperative for modern designers to get comfortable with designing for interactivity by default.

Just as layout sketches give us a blueprint for our final static UI, low-fi prototyping should give us a blueprint for our final interaction design. Many of the key tenets of interaction design are laid out a little later in this chapter, but there are some notable differences between low-fidelity prototyping and the more in-depth, higher-fidelity interaction design that might first spring to mind when you first think of prototypes.

Fundamentally, when we build out low-fi prototypes, we're building out the *paths* through our *place*. In our magical, mythical museum from earlier in this chapter, if everything instantly transitioned from Ancient Egypt to Space to the French Revolution, then we'd likely leave people suffering with some kind of migraine, motion sickness, or fear of ankhs. Seamlessly transitioning between contexts is integral, but before we design that, we should really make sure that the context switches themselves make sense.

If you created your *final-ish* layout sketches in a design tool that also has prototyping features, you've got a head start. If you didn't do that, then now's the time to switch from scribbles to screens. This isn't a how-to-prototype book. Most tools will let you program navigations from one frame, screen, or artboard to another based on user interaction. Don't think about fancy transitions or animations right now, just get the basics down: *when I tap this button, take me to this screen.*

Remember, the goal of low-fi is to be disposable. If this is the first time you've crossed the line into *real* design tooling, the temptation will likely always be there to make things look prettier than they need to at this phase. Making stuff look nice is time consuming and really not important right now. It will become so—very soon—but at this stage we need rough and ready, and we need it fast.

Keep It Cheap!

Low-fidelity land is a wonderful place. While transient and ephemeral, we're also creating some incredibly approachable artifacts that can build momentum and answer some of our biggest unknowns. The iterative cycle of ideate → test → iterate → repeat should be extremely tight, especially during the early stages of wireframing. Everything is gloriously disposable and *hopefully* comes with limited attachment from us or our team.

Given all of this, it's important to stay on track when wireframing. Know what questions you need to answer and tailor your evaluation to exploring this. Know your threshold for moving on to the next phase. Test radically different ideas and see what sticks. All of this is possible provided you're working in a way that is conducive to iteration and have the space to fail.

Remember that wireframes are diagrams; they're not shippable, they're not final, and they're not there to simply be colored in by a visual designer once you're happy with them. Wireframes facilitate conversation and help us make better design decisions when we eventually do go deep into a potential solution. Don't over-produce (or over-value) your wireframes. Black and white, crappy fonts, and non-animated interactions that take hours to throw together are exponentially more valuable to us than well-styled, fully-animated prototypes that take days.

Evaluating Wireframes

Wireframing is multifaceted and multiphased, and we should be evaluating each phase before moving on to the next. Let's take a look at a happy path of testing our various wireframe stages and when we might move on to the next.

During our **layout sketching** phase, we want to know:

- **Is our content working well in context?** We have an approach to wording our objects, contexts, and actions that we can and should test. This is a good time to do it. Ask things like *what do you think this means?*

- **Are we matching people's mental models?** People need to spot potential and possibility even when presented with very broad structural concepts. Ask things like *what would you expect to see behind the Goals tab?* and *what do you think you can do on this screen?*

And during our **low-fi prototyping** phase, we need to ascertain:

- **Are we creating intuitive paths?** Navigation in context has a habit of throwing up pitfalls we didn't initially anticipate. We need to ensure that the shifts between our contexts are intuitive, expected, or predictable. Ask things like *where would you expect this link to take you?* and *where do you think you can go on this screen?*

- **Are we progressively disclosing correctly?** Progressive disclosure is key to any interactive environment, and low-fi prototyping is a perfect place to ensure that you're undulating between information densities correctly. Ask things like *do you have the information you need to make a decision?* and *what would you need to know here to help your decision-making?*

Again, we'll almost definitely want to revisit different phases of our wireframing process, especially as we have a few key concepts to sketch around. This will make for a fluid and iterative approach that many folks can find disorienting. We could easily find ourselves testing multiple sketches for our Month context, deep in the weeds producing a low-fi prototype for our Onboarding context, and wrapping up a successful prototype for our Reflection context.

Trying to wireframe an entire product in this fashion is absolutely a challenge, and you might benefit from taking a few contexts at a time, treating your list of contexts as a backlog. Conversely, you might be like me and love a bit of chaos, in which case, do it all at once and enjoy the ride.

Interaction Design

With some well-tested and well-received wireframes under our belt, we can move on to high-fidelity prototypes. This phase is all about getting seamless. We've made order out of chaos, we know how we want to structure our system, we know what conceptual components we need to design around, we know where things will live and how things will behave, and we know how all of this fits together into a navigable, experiential whole.

Fourth-Dimensional Design

At risk of sounding overly prosaic, *time* is an all-too-forgotten medium of our design work. Our discipline's roots in graphic and visual design, and the relative incapabilities of our target technologies during the vast majority of UX and product design's existence, has left us far too entrenched in static thinking. Throughout this book, you've been encouraged to think more in terms of digital environments, to embrace nonlinearity, and to leverage progressive disclosure

Linear and Non-Linear Design Timeframes

Here's a fun one. Our "design time" is rarely linear. An animation will last 400ms (more or less) if it's programmed to do so, and a countdown timer will tick down accurately where needed, but more often than not, our "design time" is non-linear—mostly as a sequence of causes and effects. Our units are *whens* and *thens* as opposed to seconds, minutes, and hours. This might sound esoteric, but it's an important distinction.

Other media that are experienced over time, such as music or movies, occur mostly across linear timelines. Sound or images are emitted from a device, travel to us, get picked up by our senses, get translated into signals our brain can grok, are cognitively perceived, and we feel some feels. This happens linearly and predictably for the duration of the experience. We might pause a movie, skip a dud track on an album, or otherwise manually interrupt the linearity of our chosen media, but *by default* they take place over linear timelines.

Interactive media, on the other hand, while still taking place over time, are experienced as sequences of inputs and outputs, causes and effects, and decisions and responses. Fans of old school *choose your own adventure* novels will be familiar with this concept, which has also found its way into more modern formats such as Netflix's *Black*

Mirror: Bandersnatch. Framed as an "interactive film," *Bandersnatch* presents the viewer with various options at key points of the movie, with branched logic dictating what subsequent scenes the viewer will (and will not) be shown.

Video games work this way too. While many games will include cutscenes—in-game "movies" that help advance the story, usually allowing no or limited player control—they're predominantly experienced as a series of causes and effects.

Interactions As Moments

One of the many benefits of taking a moment-based approach to design is that the framework scales. Whether that's scaling upward to think about how the discrete, broad components of a wide-reaching system interact or scaling downward to the finer details of micro-interactions, describing, drawing, and annotating the stories that accompany interactions is—in my experience at least—an extraordinarily valuable habit to introduce to a design process.

Interaction design is increasingly becoming more and more important. As technology advances and operating systems and browsers become more capable of supporting rich interactions and myriad input and output modalities, the central role that interaction design plays in any product is unavoidable.

Good interactions make use of a wide array of design disciplines. Visually, they need to be on-brand and consistent, and they should adequately signify possibility. From a motion-design standpoint, easing harmoniously between interaction states is integral to ensuring a smooth interactive flow. Everything from copy and microcopy to managing cognitive load to the easing curve or spring physics used when animating an element needs to be constantly balanced throughout our interactions.

But what *is* an interaction? It's not the element itself—a button, of course, is not an interaction. It's not *quite* the words in or around the element, although describing an action is important to causality and communicating possibility. Nor is an interaction the specific animation or string of animations that occur after an action is attempting. Interactions are abstract, undulating entities. They simultaneously exist as a communication of action possibility, as state manipulators, and state communicators. Such eulogizing, though, essentially leaves us with *Schrodinger's Interaction*—something that can only be defined based on its current observable state, which is just a little too pretentious. Yes, even for me.

Instead, interactions can be seen as micro-moments. They're *things* that play out progressively dependent on human action and our system's state. Interactions push our stories along, one by one—with every button click, every swipe, hover, or scroll helping us further toward our goal. If we see our moments as the stories of our work, then interactions act simultaneously as plot points and segues, providing the key action points for progression as well as controlling the transitions between different states as this progression occurs.

So, what makes a good interaction? Given that we know interactions are somewhat abstract concepts, liquid in their definition, we can be sure that context will play a deciding factor in the efficacy of any interaction we design. If something is supposed to be extraordinarily intuitive, then an interaction that has us stopping to think is likely a poor choice. Likewise, if an interaction is supposed to slow things down and have us purposefully interact with a feature at a deeper level (as discussed in Chapter 3, this is an essential characteristic of learnable interfaces), then speed must take a back seat to understanding or learning.

Let's look at a riff on the moment framework from the previous chapter and apply it to the more granular, minute-by-minute moments that our interactions represent.

Framing Action Possibility

As discussed throughout this book, a moment, plot point, interaction, or *any* narrative or conversational tool is nothing without effective framing. Framing allows someone to preemptively envision what a certain interaction might do. The obvious example here is button text—with one of the key (albeit most-ignored) tenets of interaction design being that button text *should describe the action that will be performed*. Poor framing is, in my experience, one of the most avoidable yet predictable errors in interaction design.

Framing is placemaking manifest. We craft the items in an environment—elements, content, copy, and system state to name a few—to imply action possibility. Our goal is to convey, using all the tools we have at our disposal as designers, what is possible—even what is encouraged—within a given context or environment.

Gestalt rears its wonderfully practical head again here—perceptual grouping and consistency between elements is incredibly important to communicating action possibility and causality. Signifiers and conventions also play hugely important roles in interaction framing. Buttons that are obviously tappable, drag handles on draggable objects, clearly highlighted drop zones, obvious states for check boxes or toggle switches, loading indicators, progress bars, and myriad other considerations all have a potential impact on how well-framed an action is.

The key phrase here is *action possibility*. While entire interface states can often be devoted to convincing, pushing, or nudging (or whatever over manipulative verb we're controversially comfortable using this week) people into performing an action, seeing an interface primarily as an open venue and a communicator of action possibilities offers respite from constant persuasion and illusions of control.

Acknowledgment

During a conversation, when someone provides their input, they usually expect it to be recognized. Even if we have nothing to offer to a particular conversation point or we need to pause and think, we'll generally at least *acknowledge* that something has been said. Interaction design is no different. When we do something—whether that's clicking a Submit button at the end of a long form or performing a simple swipe to change an image's filter—we want to be told that our message has been received.

Now, in my experience, it's extremely rare to find someone who expects digital interactions to be instant. Most of us are all too familiar with loading spinners, progress bars, and general janky latency. Even as network speeds and average device capabilities continue to improve year after year, the very nature of internet communication means there will almost always be *some* kind of delay to interactions that rely on network communication. However, fast acknowledgement does not have to depend on fast server response times (although that invariably helps) or instant app loading.

What many of us *do* expect to be close to instant, however, is some form of *acknowledgement*. Think about a conversation where you've been asked something that's required you to think a little. Maybe you've been asked a tough question or you're trying to remember something that's relevant to the conversation. In such a situation, we can find ourselves doing all kinds of strange gestures and facial expressions to signify we've acknowledged someone's input. The old trope of people looking "off and to the right" when trying to remember something is a classic example, but everyone is different. Some people will nod along to show (or feign—you know who you are) interest and presence, while others will verbally "mm-hmmm." When we need a moment to think, some of us might pull that strange scrunched-up pouty face or stare up at the sky. The fancy among us might even prod our chin or press a finger to pursed lips to really hammer home our consternation.

Interactions should work no differently. If our system has to speak to another (our front end to an API, for example), one of the worst things we can do while that time passes is *nothing*. Simple loading spinners are ubiquitous in modern applications for this very reason. Performing the digital equivalent of a typical "I'm thinking ..." gesture lets someone know, pretty much instantly, that their input has at least been acknowledged.

How you acknowledge an action is going to depend heavily on context, constraints, and the personality you're trying to convey. A ubiquitous example of acknowledgement is turning button text into a loading spinner—which works extremely well if you know your wait time will be relatively short (Figure 9-12).

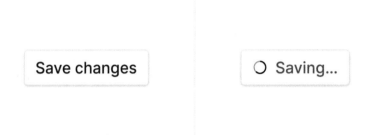

Figure 9-12. *The before (left) and during (right) states of a button that acknowledges input*

This approach is effective for a number of reasons. First, a loading spinner is an extremely common convention, found in the vast majority of mainstream apps, and it communicates a clear message. Second, by replacing the button text, we're acknowledging an action in the same context that it occurred—yet another point for perceptual grouping. Finally, by replacing the action's text, we subtly and temporarily remove the action possibility from our interface.

Respond

Once our exhaustive-yet-exceptionally-well-designed waiting period is over, our interfaces must respond to the action that's just been performed.

There's not much to this section that hasn't already been covered in the earlier exploration of moment endings. An interaction's response is how we let someone know whether their intended action worked or failed—which is an abstraction of telling them whether or not (or to what degree) their goal was achieved.

Responses, like acknowledgments, can take many forms depending on context and relevance. Success and error flash messages are extremely common (Figure 9-13).

✓ **All good!** Your content has been imported and is ready for editing.

⇳ **Oops!** Looks liked we couldn't sync your content. **Retry**

Figure 9-13. *Examples of different messages that we might display in response to an attempted action*

Other, more subtle, forms of response can be beneficial too, especially when space is limited or when the interactions we're designing are themselves small and subtle. The spinner-inside-the-button from Figure 9-14 could, for example, present a brief success message in the button itself, before returning back to its default state if appropriate— essentially making for a single-element micro-interaction.

Figure 9-14. *A sequential flow that could quite easily portray an entire micro-interaction contained within a single element*

Just as a moment's ending should offer some form of reflection, so too should an interaction's response. If the interaction has fundamentally changed the system state in any way, then finding a way to reflect this will be a major factor in our response. In Chapter 2, you explored how animation can assist greatly in indicating state changes as the result of an interaction, but sometimes the best response to an interaction is to simply reveal more information or show new forms of action possibility. An image upload interaction might result in a new UI state that gives you the option to post the image or to add a description and tags before saving.

Always Forgive Mistakes

Throughout this book, I've tried to be as open as possible to different approaches to design, workflow, process, and implementation. As a field, digital design is, comparatively, in its infancy, and I truly believe there is no place for dogma or bullheaded absolution in such a fast-growing industry backed by an ever-changing landscape. *However*, this is where I break my own rule and espouse an absolute: *Always let people undo their major actions.*

No matter how well-framed, how wonderfully acknowledged, and how extensively optimized our interactions are, nothing can truly prevent mistakes. For too long, digital interfaces laid mistakes squarely at the feet of humans (or, to be less passive, designers of these interfaces deferred blame to the people they're supposed to be making things for) and forced us into constrained and intimidating "Are you absolutely positively sure?" moments to mitigate the accidental performing of destructive or highly volatile actions.

"Are you sure …" is a framing device. It, in a roundabout way, lets people know that a specific action is not to be taken lightly and that *bad things* can happen if someone performs it. I'm not suggesting that this approach to framing needs to disappear, but I feel it's imperative to acknowledge how much of a roadblock this truly can be to creativity, self-expression, or just simply avoiding a state of sheer panic over a button press.

My personal rule is to treat a modal as a lazy design decision unless I know I've explored all over avenues, and to me, "are-you-sure?" modals are the culmination of this. No matter how much we convince ourselves that enough defensive measures will stop someone clicking the "Yes-I-want-to-delete-my-entire-digital-history-let's-go" button accidentally, someone is going to do it, and they're going to be very, very sad. Preemptive modals are a poor and lazy safety net for *us*—designers and developers. *Undo* is an empowering safety net for the people we design for.

As discussed in Chapter 3, an undo feature implies that mistakes are fine and expected. In an interface that allows for—or attempts to foster—creativity, autonomy, and self-expression, this is absolutely integral, but even in our general, everyday-use applications, it can save us.

Since Google Inbox (and later Gmail; RIP Inbox, we miss you) implemented "undo" for message sending, I've been saved from probably a dozen truly embarrassing email moments—ranging from calling someone by the complete wrong name to pasting in a link that was absolutely, assuredly *not* the link I was supposed to be sending to a client. While these situations might not have resulted in total catastrophe, written communication on the web is *hard work*, and often even just knowing you've sent an email with a pretty major typo in it can weigh heavily on your mind post-sending.

By implementing undo functionality, we're baking in a subtle degree of peace of mind. We're offering a statement that, even when you really do mess up, you can always escape back to the previous state like nothing ever happened. It might be technically difficult at times, it might seem pointless in your project, but trust me: implement undo and redo by default. Make it a principle that finds its way into the breadth of your work.

Putting It All Together

The irony of exploring progressive media, design as a function of non-linear timelines, and moment-to-moment interaction design in the static context of a book's pages is absolutely not lost on me. So, let's dive into a prototype for our journaling app. You can find a link to a Figma prototype in the `9 - Executing and Evaluating/[04] Prototype Links.html` file in this book's repository.

Here's where everything comes together and we have our first, testable prototype to take into user testing and beyond.

At this point, there's not much to say that hasn't already been covered in the preceding sections. You can create an account; set up some goals; create your first monthly, weekly, and daily spreads; add and complete tasks; and reflect on your day. See Figure 9-15.

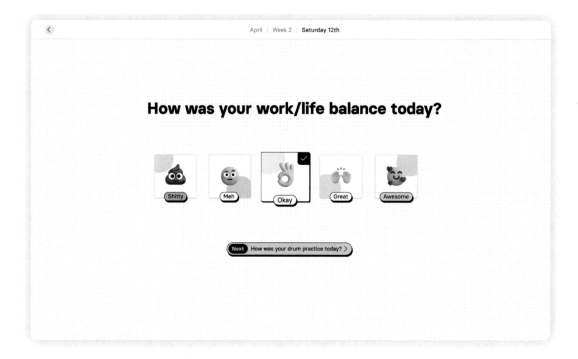

Figure 9-15. *A final screen from our designed prototype*

Everything you see in this prototype is a result of some or all of the phases presented in this book. Our sidebar approach with easy access to goals can be tracked backwards from final design to wireframe to information architecture and eventually all the way back to those early research observations showing us that folks who journal tend to keep track of goals at a high level, usually for the entire year.

Similarly, our "spread" approach is straight out of the bullet journal mental model, as is the structuring of our key contexts into months, weeks, and days. We also have some adorable extras like stickers and other decorative elements. Because we like fun things, yes, but also because we know that people who journal tend to enjoy the creative side of the process. This ability to decorate and customize on top of the more utilitarian components of their environment is a deliberate act of placemaking.

There are many other touches in our prototype that relate directly back through all the key topics and activities we've discussed in this book. There's very little in there that's incidental or accidental, and almost every design decision can be traced back to a more global decision or observation made earlier in our process. In fact, this method of decision-tracing is a fine way to spot assumptions in your own work.

As an extra challenge, if you've been working on your own project throughout this part of the book, take a look at the elements or design decisions in your prototype and have a think as to *why* they're there. Is there a clear, articulable reason for a certain element? You don't always need this, but if your work is full of decisions that can't stand up to a few *whys*, then you might be operating a little too much on assumptions.

This is where the project diary mentioned all the way back in Chapter 6 again shows its value. If you've kept a log of key decisions throughout your project, you should never really find yourself on the back foot or scrambling for answers. Sometimes you'll have taken a certain approach due to pure instinct or for a reason that's not obvious until you sit down and reflect again—and that's *totally fine*. Not everything we do is rational, nor does it always fit nicely into process or record-keeping, but there should be far more examples of rational, considered decisions in your work than there are intuitive hopeful plays. Taking the time to record, reflect, and introspect your decisions is a valuable habit to build.

You might have noticed that we've not really touched on visual design throughout this chapter. We'll fix that shortly, as we wrap up our project. Coming up, we'll finalize our work, put principles together that feed into future iterations, and look at how we can implement the concepts and process points presented throughout this book in responsible, ethical, and outcome-focused manners. We're almost there!

CHAPTER 10

Responsible Implementation

Everything you've explored throughout this book has, I hope, presented a counterpoint to the often insidious and exploitative methods of modern digital products. Beyond this, however, I hope the studies, concepts, and suggestions within have—even in the tiniest of ways—contributed to a positive shift in your mindset or approach to designing and building digital products. I truly believe that by embracing openness and exploration, by creating products that can be used in many different ways, and by treating the workings of the mind as insightful allies rather than obstacles that we must hurdle or manipulate to achieve success, we can lay the foundations for a more sustainable, compassionate approach to design and, ultimately, technology as a whole.

As designers, we must accept a certain implicit responsibility to leave the world a little better off than we found it—and not just for people who look and think like us. The ability of technology to augment human existence is an undoubtedly exciting concept and the impact of digital products on the world stands to be monumental. Yet we still operate in an industry that's rife with naivety, bias, and systemic oppression. As designers, this means that we're often presented with ideas and problem definitions that are rarely harmonious with humans outside of the affluent world of tech entrepreneurship.

To achieve these goals, especially in an industry that seems to operate by its own rules, eschewing ethics in the name of profit under the cover of the mystique of programming and technological innovation, we must ensure that our process serves to elevate those who are far too often underrepresented in our work.

In closing out this book, I'd like to present a few final thoughts on these responsibilities, as well as some considerations that didn't quite make sense to include elsewhere. Indeed, this chapter will read quite differently to others in this book, as I career between various talking points. I'll cover how craft pays an integral role in

© Scott Riley 2024
S. Riley, *Mindful Design*, Design Thinking, https://doi.org/10.1007/979-8-8688-0143-3_10

placemaking; how ideas can be challenged through an important workshop and brainstorming technique; how homogeneity is unavoidably limiting opportunity; and, finally, tech's role in the advent of a difficult, tumultuous sociopolitical climate (spoiler: it's got a lot to answer for).

Finishing Touches

It's important not to lose sight of where you are in a project. As important a moment as reaching a final, validated prototype is—and you should be incredibly proud of making it this far—it's not a finished product. It's tempting to rush to ship an interface. You've spent enough time in the realms of low-fi abstraction; surely now that you have something high fidelity, you're just building what's in front of you, right? Well, not exactly.

As you've been prototyping and exploring, you've likely focused on your core contexts, moments, and hooks. Having a viable, validated approach to exposing these to your users is invaluable and absolutely core to manifesting your ideas as useful, successful products—but you're not done yet. The implementation stage is where you can get truly granular and transform a solid, functional design idea into a perfectly-made *place*.

Slow Down and Make Things

While this book's focus lies somewhere between early stage UX and broad interaction design, I can't stress enough how important the finer design details of a project are. Too many early stage practitioners undervalue the transformative beauty of incredible UI and motion design, and I want to make it abundantly clear that the primary reasons for much larger swaths of this book not being devoted to these areas of design are two-fold. Firstly—and frankly—I'm not an amazing visual designer. I can hold my own, but it's not my forté, and I think digital design peaked in 1996 with the Space Jam website (Figure 10-1).

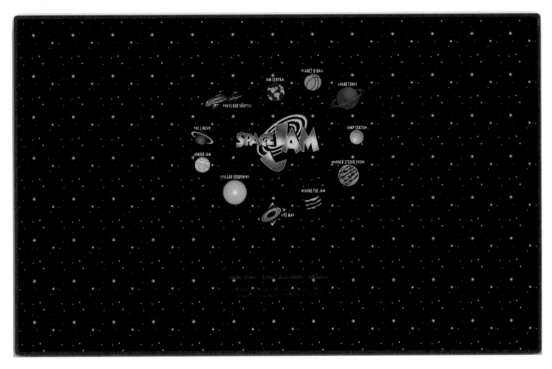

Figure 10-1. *The Space Jam website. A true masterpiece*

Secondly, while absolutely possible to learn, craft like this is something that develops over time, with constant practice, and is extraordinarily difficult to lay out in a couple of chapters of a book. There are no formulas to finding the right colors (as much as there are shortcuts to finding good ones) and there's no substitute for a well-trained human eye when it comes to the minutiae of animation timing, easing, and staggering.

One thing I do know is that well-crafted digital environments don't get rushed out.

The 80-20 principle or Pareto principle—the notion that 80% of outcomes come from 20% of causes—is often bastardized and bandied about in product design to suggest something like 80% of our outcomes will come from 20% of our efforts, and the "move fast and break things" mindset alongside the much-vaunted notion of Minimum Viable Products often lead to work being shipped prematurely. Unless buggy interfaces that look like glorified wireframes is just the latest trend.

These products are not destined to fail—far from it, the bulk of the problem-solving has been done—but they're also not destined to be incredible, at least not until the important, time-consuming craft work is done. A sense of craft is what's going to get you through those thousand tiny decisions about styling, spacing, placement, typographic touches, animation parameters, flourishes, and interactive embellishments. It's the willingness to spend 80% of the time on that final 20% puzzle piece because you know that great work is unlocked there.

Craft Pays Off

Yet again I'm drawn back to FigJam, and the whimsical, grounding touches that present a layer of fun and approachability on top of a robust and trustworthy underlying system. Workshops and diagramming can often be *boring*—you've just read three chapters about them for f$#* sake, so I expect I'm preaching to the choir right now—but these subtle touches break up the monotony and sheer inevitability that we face when we pull up a brainstorming board or kick off an OOUX session. We workshop because the outcomes are valuable, the synthesis we perform is productive, and a shared visual language makes collaboration more seamless. Even I don't find workshopping autotelic, and I've written a bloody book about it, but the levity and consideration baked into the FigJam interface makes what could easily be a functional, grin-and-bear-it moment into something quite delightful.

FigJam is better than Miro because of the craft and character that has gone into it. Not because it has better features, but because the features it does have are better made. And that's not me throwing shade at Miro—it's a fabulous product built by a lovely team. Nor is it me baselessly fawning over FigJam or Figma—Figma is a monolith in the design world and I have no emotional attachment to the organization whatsoever. This level of craft constitutes what makes Linear better than Trello or Jira, what makes Slack better than Microsoft Teams, what makes macOS better than Windows, iA Writer better than Google Docs, and Arc better than Edge. This feels controversial to say in the realm of digital products, but no one would bat an eye if you posited that a handcrafted, intricately-finished bookcase was better than a cheap IKEA disasterpiece held together with dowels and regret.

Doubling down on craft is part of a long game bet on quality. All other things being equal, it *will* pay off. Competing on features is a fool's errand—anyone can ape a feature from a competitor, and millions of us can build requested functionality to a shippable standard. Competing on quality scales. People like nice things. People appreciate well-built things. People gravitate towards beautiful things.

You can't add "make it lovely" to a backlog, though. Yet again Agile stops us from having nice things.

Make It Fast, Make It Seamless

Add keyboard shortcuts to everything. Build your apps offline first where appropriate. Make performance, perceived wait, and time-to-seeing-some-actual-relevant-information a joint endeavor between design and engineers. One of the worst things you can do is hand over a fantasy-land mockup and tell an engineer to "make it snappy." Performance matters and speed should be a core metric for any modern product, but performance doesn't purely manifest in latencies and bytes transferred. Speed is as much perceived as it is experienced, and a confusing, information-dense page that loads in an instant is still a bad page; you just get to bad faster.

Put common actions a few keystrokes away. Command bars and launchers like Raycast (Figure 10-2) provide a completely different navigation paradigm, where context is less important than clarity and intent. Put certain actions behind simple keypresses, like Linear does with their chainable, contextual shortcuts (Figure 10-3)

Figure 10-2. *Raycast presents navigation and action possibilities in an auto-complete command bar that can be launched regardless of context*

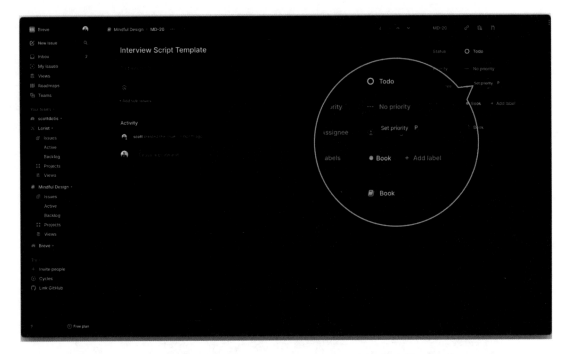

Figure 10-3. *Linear allows certain actions or navigation to be performed via single keypresses, allowing advanced users to breeze through the interface*

Sidenote: Learn about code, not *to* code. Understanding the constraints of the medium you're designing for is non-negotiable but you don't have to build stuff if you don't want to.

Get comfortable defining what *good* means in the context of your project and its goals. Be accountable for quality, and don't shirk the responsibility that comes with this.

Process Is a Guide

Process is not a panacea. As much as the second half of this book has been structured into something that resembles a linear process, I want to stress how important it is to not get hung up on process dogma. Every documented process you've encountered is an idealized abstraction of how this kind of work plays out in the real world, and whether you're following Design Thinking methodologies, Double Diamond, Agile, or whatever other esoterica is being bandied around to help late-career professionals sell books and workshops (hey, shush), you will absolutely benefit from being pragmatic, not dogmatic.

Our job as designers is to make sense of mess, bring order to chaos, and empower decision-making. We must do this for our users, of course, but we also need to do it for our colleagues and stakeholders. Early stage startups are their own brand of chaos that don't even touch, never mind overlap with, most of the machinations of enterprise organizations. Agencies will work differently to SaaS organizations, single-product teams will work differently to those managing a product suite, and no one organization within these categories is prototypical.

Yes, we need a process, but that process can and should be malleable based on constraints. Blindly pushing for your favorite framework without first ensuring it's even compatible with these constraints will only lead to pain, tears, and someone at the back of the room meekly asking if we should try Kanban again.

Sometimes you'll need to do things in a weird order to get the answers you need. If you're wondering if something is technically feasible and have no clear answer, you're really gonna need to code that up sooner rather than later. If you're worried about an idiosyncratic wording choice that only makes sense in the context of an interaction, testing the wording by itself is futile—someone's going to need to prototype that interaction.

Sometimes you even need to take risks, bite the bullet, and skip stages or phases of a process entirely. Building without researching is a huge risk, but if for some reason you've got eleven seconds to get a feature live, asking to stop for a week-long diary study isn't going to fly. Your team structure will dictate this, too. Design-minded engineers can work with incomplete prototypes whereas engineers who don't care about design might need more guidance. Design systems let you prototype with realistic components much sooner in your process—but beware the dangers of trying to evaluate structural broad strokes in the context of a real-looking UI.

Being versatile and resilient is more important than being incredibly effective in the confines of a rigid process, especially if you turn into mush when it eventually gets derailed. Lean on process, work methodically, with rigor and accountability, but don't be scared to get fluid and try new things.

Process Is Cyclical

If you're already aware of the *Double Diamond* abstraction of the design process, then you might have clocked to the previous chapters roughly adhering to the discrete phases presented by it. If you're not familiar, the Double Diamond diagram represents an approach to design where you work through four key phases: Discover, Define, Develop, and Deliver. Arranged into sequential diamonds, you're able to plot where your phases diverge—that is, have you thinking broadly, generating ideas, and working fluidly—and where they converge—wherein you constrain your thinking, focus on evaluation, and ultimately make a decision (Figure 10-4).

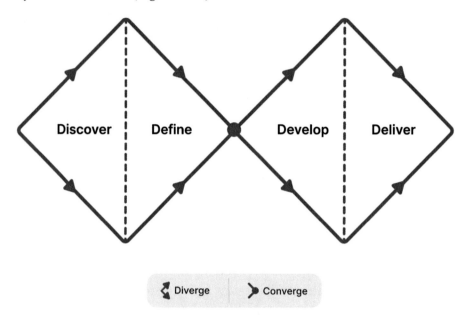

Figure 10-4. *A typical Double Diamond process*

This is useful at an extreme level of abstraction, but under even a modicum of scrutiny you can start to see cracks. You diverge and converge dozens of times throughout each core project phase. Discovery, for example, is not purely divergent—there will always be convergence, as you ensure that you're asking the right questions, reflecting on research sessions, and recruiting properly. That doesn't make it a *bad* diagram (arguably, trying to convey nuance in an abstract diagram is far worse!) but it does limit its usefulness to the broader side of the abstraction spectrum.

Books are linear media and, as such, imply linearity by default. Don't let that lead you to believe that the phases laid out here are so linear. More realistically, these processes are sequential cycles, seeing you ship your way incrementally toward your goals, as opposed to months of closed-off, divergent work resulting in either shipping a "big reveal" product that's barely been seen until it's deemed "ready" or an expensive monolith that's fundamentally broken. Cycles like this are designed to get ideas, concepts and—indeed—prototypes in front of the right people, at just the right time (Figure 10-5).

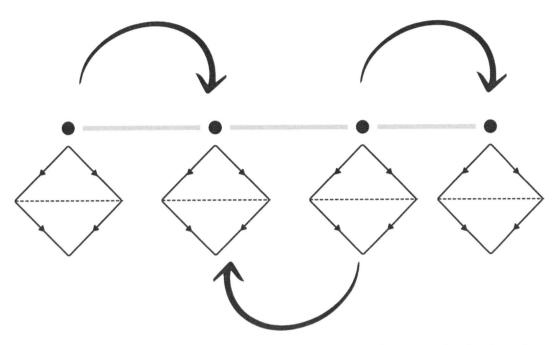

Figure 10-5. *A more cyclical double-diamond process where you skip back and forward between multiple points of divergence and convergence*

Not only does this get you to a shippable product much faster—you're able to shift focus and try new things far more often. It also opens you up to entire new evaluative approaches, such as closed beta rounds and feature-flagging for controlling which cohorts you expose new features to, and A/B testing and persistent user testing for cyclical evaluation of your work. You also get live data, bug reports, and feedback from people who are actually using your stuff.

This, however, shouldn't lead you to rush head-first to shipping at every available opportunity. Think of it as a dozen opportunities to do an amazing job.

Get Your Principles in Order

Become principle-led and you can imbue your process with the qualities you need to exhibit throughout your work—provided you have good principles in the first place. Too many people treat principles like a top-down diktat rather than a bottom-up framing mechanism.

Principles Power Decision-Making

Principles don't just describe what your ideal qualities are. "Make it fast" is an awful principle because it's isolated, unqualified, and painfully obvious. It's like a client or your boss telling you to "make a good design"—useless filler in lieu of actual words. "Speed over decoration" is a better principle in that it shows what you might need to sacrifice in order to achieve a desired result. It states that you're inherently okay with a spartan visual style if it results in notable gains in speed.

When documented, your principles should be clarified with one or two sentences, so you don't need to make these principles highly prescriptive or overly wordy, but words matter. Milquetoast, utopian quips like "make it snappy" or "it's gotta look great" do more harm than good.

Principles Aren't Assumed

You don't just pluck principles out of thin air. Like any other decision-making tool, principles should relate back to your observations and describe things your audience actually *wants*.

If you know that your product is going to be used by people who need to do a straightforward but important task as quickly as possible, the "speed over decoration" principle makes a ton of sense. Conversely, if people might use your product to reflect after a hard day, you might choose "calmness over delight."

Principles Are Hierarchical

You shouldn't treat all principles equally. Have an *above all else* principle that communicates the most important characteristic you must portray in your work. If speed to the nanosecond is critical for you, then "speed above all else" is your guiding principle. Your journaling app might have a guiding principle of "autonomy above all else." Your favorite social media platform probably has a principle of "engagement above all else." Look where that one got us.

Principles are opinions. If they're not raising eyebrows, then they're too banal or diluted to be useful. Designing and building a product will always be a series of balancing acts, and without good, solid principles that actually empower you to move in certain directions, you can find yourself rooted.

Let's take a look at the principles of the journaling app we've been building.

Autonomy Above All Else

Journaling is a personal and often emotional process. Allow for autonomy by presenting options and unconstrained action possibilities. Never nudge.

Calmness Over Energy

This is a calm product. Avoid high-energy animations and overly characterful interactions. Lean into reflective moments and make them set pieces.

Malleability Over Structure

Spreads are infinitely configurable and every widget should feel interactive. Make movement satisfying with snaps and settling animations. Focus on physical malleable properties of elements. Squishiness is underrated.

Just-in-Time Over Stickiness

Journals should be there when you need them, not designed around continued, regular, or predictable usage. Don't prompt people to use the product.

Whimsy Over Austerity

Journaling can be self-expressive. Be fun, whimsical, and laid-back. Use a spartan visual language, but don't be cold or distant with the interactions and tone of voice.

Note that these principles are in order of importance: we rarely sacrifice calmness for whimsy, and if we had to choose, autonomy will always win out against the other principles. Avoid treating principles as a place to just brain-dump what you think good design is or should be; it's not the purpose and it's a surefire way to alienate your team.

Principles Unblock Decisions

All of the above points and examples lead to one key factor when it comes to evaluating your principles: they are—like much of the workshops and artifacts you've encountered thus far—decision-making tools.

If you can read one of your principles and understand how it might help someone choose between a notable decision during the design and development of your product—let's say an engineer with limited time needing to choose between implementing a high-fidelity animation or reducing loading times—then it's probably a good principle.

Involve Others

Were you surprised by just how many of the activities in this book were collaborative? I'd hope not, but the uncomfortable reality is that cross-organizational teams rarely have collaboration figured out, and so many phases of your approach can suffer due to a lack of collaboration.

The trope of the *lone wolf* designer is one that belongs firmly in the past. Too much credence has been paid to wunderkind designers who just need coffee and the latest Tiesto in their headphones to create masterpieces. Designers who can't involve stakeholders and colleagues from around an organization or who can't talk to customers are hamstrung from day one.

The trope of *everyone being a designer* is also just as garbage a concept that still inexplicably gets rolled out during cross-organization process discussions. Everyone *impacts* design, but you're doing the work and you bring your expertise, and you *must* guide folks through your process—it's part of the job. Lumping every potential impactor under an umbrella term just conflates the very real responsibilities and accountabilities you have as a designer with the abstract, tangential causality of input and influence.

Part of learning how to design is learning how to think in certain ways. We're always encouraged to find problems, analyze discrete interactions, and are cursed to spot details like bad kerning, mismatched radii, and unrealistic drop shadows forevermore. A trip to the grocery store with us is a waking nightmare as we point out how the own-brand coffee packaging would look much nicer with an *ff* ligature, or how the self-checkout interface can be streamlined by placing the scanner closer to the basket shelf, or how shoplifting is our civic duty and provides a meager but knowing relief from the struggles of living every day under capitalism. Okay, maybe that last one's best saved for a different book.

The point is, constantly looking at the world through a designer's eye builds up a kind of subtle, irrefutable myopia, the antidote to which is other people's voices. Design with your colleagues in engineering, workshop with your salespeople, even invite users to brainstorming sessions. Use every chance you get to gather unique perspectives from a diverse group of humans.

Practice Your Craft

As much as capitalism (and product owners) might want you to believe it, not everything you make has to be for profit or to move KPIs in the right direction. If you find it fun, design for fun. Bake practice and learning time into your daily routine if you can. Do it during company hours. Leaders: Promote a culture of learning and off-board experimentation within your team.

Take well-designed products and reverse engineer them. Recreate a screen from your favorite interface and you'll learn more about design tools in a few hours than any long-winded video tutorial can teach you. Take a great product and map out its IA, or take your most-used app and draw up an OOUX board for it.

Craft is all about delivering closely to your current personal ceiling. Learning and improvement is all about raising that ceiling over time. Sometimes you need to knuckle down and deliver to the best of your current abilities, and other times you're better served getting out of your comfort zone and learning something new to actively raise your ceiling—even if you're a little further from maximizing your output or quality.

Purposeful Pessimism

Involving a wide range of people in your process inevitably brings biases and clashing mental models. Let's explore the idea of using purposeful pessimism and cynicism as a design tool, not a personality trait.

The concept of a "black hat"—a term I find weird and uncomfortable and will refer to as "purposeful pessimism" from now on—comes from *Six Thinking Hats* by Edward DeBono. In DeBono's framework, group participants wear "a specific hat and are requested to respond according to their hat." Yellow is the "optimistic" hat, for example. The black hat is the hat of the pessimist. Its wearer's goal is to provide some much-needed cynicism to a brainstorming session or workshop.

While I personally believe DeBono's framework doesn't translate well to design, the concept of purposeful pessimism is an intriguing and important notion for modern design work. Firstly, purposeful pessimism is a point where everyone on a team is given permission to be a little bit negative. In the sunshine and lollipops world of tech startups where being unhappy is a cardinal sin, this can be extremely cathartic.

Secondly, it's an antidote to hubris.

Most people think their ideas are good. It's just part of who we are. We're more attached to things of our own creation (like the IKEA effect, discussed back in Chapter 1, where we prefer something we've made ourselves, even if it's objectively horrible compared to a premade version). This can often lead to some really tricky degrees of bias in a project. By having an agreed-upon session or an agreed-upon part of every session for purposeful pessimism, we can go some way to removing this stigma that negativity is unproductive. It's even better when the person who has the debated idea is able to think objectively as a result of pessimistic discourse.

Most importantly, however, it forces us to consider vulnerable, divergent, and underrepresented members of our audience—something that technology companies are notoriously bad at doing.

Purposeful pessimism is a simple but nuanced method to brainstorming. My advice is to work it into every important brainstorm you have—especially anything that involves new feature discussion. The rules are simple: you find ways that a proposed implementation can fail. Failure in this sense is not "missing a KPI." It's a fundamental failure at serving a person, achieving a goal, or solving a problem. This also includes allowing means of exploitation or using a feature to cause others harm.

When performing this kind of work, it's important to make sure that all participants understand that just as brainstorming is a loose and fast-paced exercise, so too is this pessimistic analysis. Not every suggestion for how something might fail will be valid, and any proposed reasons for potential failure don't diminish an idea—they just provide important context that would otherwise be missed.

As an action example, take Twitter's "report" functionality. Reporting allows someone to report another person's account, stating a reason for their report, and optionally including a number of posts that support a claim. Approaching this pessimistically, a potential misuse of the feature could be in the mass reporting of a group of people another person simply dislikes. This potential problem would then feed into the finer implementation details. If we were considering automatically putting a reported account on hold, for some strange reason, this would present a glaring potential abuse of our proposed functionality. Anyone could misreport someone and get them instantly suspended.

Thinking of ways in which your ideas could encourage negative attitude or behavior is a slightly trickier approach. A common example is be platforms that include "up-voting"—a feature where people can up- (and sometimes down-) vote a particular story, comment, or post. Let's say we were working on a product that allowed people to ask a community a question, where members of that community could up-vote suggested answers to help deem the most applicable. The optimist in us might suggest that rewarding question-answering can create a friendly, helpful attitude. However, it can also create one of snobbery, holier-than-thou, and one-true-method mindsets. In this case, we'd want to greatly consider how to foster the right kind of attitude, both when asking and answering questions—a difficult concept, for sure, but one that could make the difference between an empowering and collaborative knowledge base and a toxic cave of *"well, actually..."* meninists.

Purposeful pessimism shouldn't discourage you or your team from going ahead with a feature that you feel is integral to your product, but it should at least *contextualize* both the feature and your overall problem space. Often, too, it's the seemingly most innocuous features that can go horribly wrong—just ask Meta.

Facebook's Celebration of Death

Meta's Facebook has seen its fair share of oblivious features—some, in particular, that would have benefited from *any* form of foresight that wasn't blind optimism such as "On This Day" feature and, more infamously, the "Share a Memory" and "Year in Review" features.

These features involved Facebook algorithmically selecting one or more photographs, videos, or posts from a profile and turning them into an often cute, often quirky, shareable image or video. Most of the posts generated were what many would deem as "fun"—cute selfies, pictures of dogs, all to the tune of typical stock, inoffensive, upbeat music loops. Except, when they failed, they failed *hard*.

One person had a supposedly fun, dancing illustration superimposed on their mother's grave. Another was shown a slideshow of their house burning down. Dozens of people have been prompted to "share" glamorized or decorated photographs of dead relatives, dead pets, and abusive ex-partners. These are clear features where emotional harm was caused through a poorly thought-out feature. They represent prime examples of things a healthy dose of cynicism could have preempted.

These issues might seem ignorable to many people. They're *just algorithms* at the end of the day. They can't be mean, or racist, or misogynistic, or transphobic. They're just 0s and 1s, right? Wrong. In these kinds of cases, no one but the team who designed and built the feature into the product is to blame. Whether a feature messed up due to human error or a poorly optimized algorithm, that feature went through multiple people's mental spaces before it was launched. Either no one saw how it could fail, or the people who did neglected to speak up.

Normalizing structured and purposeful pessimism in the name of providing yourself, your colleagues, and your team with a deeper understanding of the problems you expect to face—as well as the platform to speak out—is a core responsibility of a designer.

I'm sure that when Twitter was founded, its creators didn't expect it would one day become the virtual stomping ground of modern-day neo-Nazis. However, there's a fuzzy chain of events, starting with a failure to clearly define the parameters of acceptable use for their platform, passing quickly by a categorical failure to deal with bot accounts in the build-up to the 2016 U.S. presidential election, and ending somewhere right about now, where CEO Elon Musk—after purchasing the company for an astoundingly overvalued sum and renaming it to X to seemingly show the world how well he could handle a divorce—is forced to reckon daily with how a gross misrepresentation of the notion of freedom of speech has turned the platform into a hive of alt-right sock puppets, dangerous *incels*, and misinformation peddlers.

Hindsight, as they say, is 20/20, but a small part of me wonders how different Twitter/X would be as a social space today if just a little more foresight went into dissecting how the platform could be exploited—something that the team should be no stranger to, given the platform's historical role as a hub of exploitation through underhand trolling tactics and long-standing, targeted harassment campaigns.

High morale and momentum are great tools for a project, but there comes a point when blue-sky thinking needs to meet down-to-earth reality, and the reality is that anything that can empower and encourage an individual or a group can almost always be used to denigrate and oppress another. When you think about this, you start to explore your problem space in a specific way. When you examine issues of cultural sensitivity, you start seeing ways your ideas can be used for nefarious measures, and if you give a damn, you add these problems to your understanding of your underlying system.

This can be hard to swallow for many people, especially founders who believe that their ideas will fundamentally benefit the world, but every major tech company and product has its issues. Facebook has launched tone-deaf features on many occasions. Airbnb hosts have been shown rejecting the patronage of people of color while accepting white visitors for the exact same vacation conditions. Twitter is full of actual Nazis. Almost every major tech product out there, *especially* those that involve elements of social interaction, has failed its vulnerable customers to varying degrees. Our job is to, wherever possible, provide the tools to at least attempt to discuss these potential failings.

We won't make any friends while we do it, but if we, our colleagues, our bosses, or our investors want to claim social consciousness, we have a duty to explore the murkier side of our products.

The Role of Choice

Ultimately, design's role in providing platforms for self-expression and creative problem-solving gives us another variable that we must consider: choice.

The discipline of design is that of balance. We're constantly, throughout our process, trying to find the right combination of qualities to suit our goals. Whether that's through something as simple as settling for a darker text color to meet contrast guidelines, or whether it's through something as complex as limiting the moving elements in a virtual-reality experience to combat motion sickness—we're faced with dozens, often hundreds, of decisions every day that all boil down to finding moments of balance.

The very presence of a need to strike balance shows that ours is a practice of compromise. Choice, then, is yet another component of design that needs balancing. On one end of the choice spectrum you have limited, single-purpose products—those that require nothing but a single interaction to serve their purpose, such as the ill-fated Amazon Dash Buttons (Figure 10-6), where a single button press to order a specific product was the solitary available use-case. Yes, these were real, actual products. No, they don't sell them anymore. No, none of us are surprised.

Figure 10-6. *The simply astonishing Amazon Dash buttons that I constantly have to remind myself weren't an April Fool's joke. (Alexander Kirk, via Wikipedia Commons, CC BY 4.0)*

I call these kinds of products "spiralizers" after the wonderfully single-purpose kitchen utensil of the same name. The glamorous world of the utensil industry has, in recent years, become rather enamored with products that Alton Brown—the famous chef, author, and television host—has taken to rather disparagingly labeling as "unitaskers." Unitaskers, as the name suggests, exist to perform one task. Whether the marvel of innovation is the pizza scissors, the wonderfully esoteric avocado slicer, or the bedrock of any good kitchen, the spiralizer, the influx of gadgets that sell themselves on the basis of doing one task really, really well has left us with an abundance of cheap, tacky tools in our kitchens.

Now, there's likely plenty of reasons why these utensils sell well. They're foolproof, they're often cheap, and they're almost always exceptionally well-advertised. However, they don't do anything that we couldn't do with a simple, well-made chef's knife. If we spend a little time learning some basic knife skills, we suddenly have one tool that can confidently relegate an entire suite of unitasker utensils to that one junk drawer that everyone has in their kitchen. While I'm loath to present myself as a culinary snob (I lost the tip of my thumb grating a beetroot, so who am I to talk?), there's something about having a small set of tools that you're comfortable and confident in using for a vast array of tasks.

I believe that while single-purpose apps are still going to be made in droves—and that the constant bombardment of distractions and information we're exposed to might make these types of product more needed—one of the true joys of design lies in creating a product that can be used in unexpected ways. There's something special in seeing our work used in ways that we never even envisioned or applied to problems we never thought it could solve.

Part of this comes from a much-needed rescinding of control. This apparent desire to persuade and nudge people down linear paths that I've spent a large part of this book attempting to assuage is something that we, collectively as an industry, need to look to move away from. Too often, we sacrifice choice and openness in the name of perceived surety through constraint. If our goal is to create an environment of possibility and exploration, we need to get comfortable with randomness and idiosyncrasy.

Once we've broken free of the constraints of linearity—and checked our ego at the door in the process—we can start to look at choice as a variable in our work.

Choice Abundance

Choice abundance represents the opposite end of the spectrum to the aforementioned unitaskers. At this boundary, the most empowering example I can offer is musical instruments, or to get more abstract, music as a system unto itself. Musical instruments offer us an almost infinite palette of actions with which to express ourselves. The emotional landscape of music is an immense, somniferous blanket that enshrouds us all. From upbeat dance tracks to solemn hymns to exhilarating orchestral movements to angsty emo to visceral hip-hop to whatever the heck dub step is, music's role as an encapsulation of human emotion lies in the abundance of possibility—as a system of the loose rules and undulating schemas it provides and manifests.

Musical instruments are still built to specifications. They're still *designed* to meet certain goals. A standard piano, at the surface level, is a tool for performance and composition that allows 88 different notes to be sounded by the pressing of their corresponding keys. However, some 300-plus years into its existence, people are still finding millions upon millions of unique ways to create art with a piano. When we sit down to play, we're not limited by the tool in front of us, but by our mastery of it and our imagination. We strive to improve because we *know* that there's more we can achieve. Playing an instrument or creating music in any way is a journey. We embark on this journey for myriad reasons, but we stick with it because we know that there's still more to come. We're able to look at 88 keys, or six strings and some frets, or a computer program full of soundscapes and intuitively know that we'll never exhaust the possibilities that these things present.

Closer to home, we see variations of this every time we do our job. Design tools let us express our ideas—some of which can, and do, change the world—through rectangles, lines, and shadows. While we might have our processes, cheat sheets, and shortcuts, every design we create is something that never existed before we laid it down on a digital canvas. We're living proof that a blank canvas and some rudimentary tools can lead to creations and moments that transcend the apparent constraints of the tool or medium we operate in.

Why, then, when we're staring at these tools for hours upon hours every day, do we seem to favor selling people products that sit far from the realms of divergent thought and far closer to whimsical unitaskers? Why do we witness, every day, humanity's willingness to improve often abstruse skills in the name of self-expression and problem-solving yet deem it suitable to leave them time and again with the digital equivalent of an avocado slicer?

The Path to Unitasking

First and foremost, we leave folks with these digital avocado slicers because it's *easy*. Single-purpose applications are easy to scope, easy to define, easy to explain, easy to sell, easy to measure, and easy to iterate on. That all adds up to an inherently marketable— albeit somewhat unambitious—product. Considering the still-far-too-homogenous makeup of the technology industry, the fact it exists as a self-serving economy, and the fact that venture capital is, at the time of writing, still the de facto means of valuing a company, we find the perfect recipe for an echo chamber.

To flip the discussion on its head, products that limit choice usually arise from under-researched approaches to shaping narrow problem definitions. Narrow problem definitions arise from a shallow pool of lived experiences. Shallow pools of lived experience arise from homogeneity—a lack of diversity that means innovation and potential impact is stifled almost by default. When an industry decides that plucky upstart founders who "solve problems" and "get shit done" belong on a pedestal, when the distribution of venture capital is based on an almost instinctive appraisal of the usefulness of a product, when a gross misinterpretation of the satire that is meritocracy becomes the prevalent religion to its core demographic of white 20-something Californians, then the problems that get deemed worthy of solving tend to have a very noticeable, very white, *very* upper-middle-class feel to them.

Presenting choice in abundance is indicative of a willing abdication of power. Any time we present someone with more choices—more ways of interacting with a system, more opportunities to experiment, more problems with which to aim our product at—we're potentially empowering them. While we should strive to reduce noise, limit pointless features, and be ever cognizant of the attentional impact of our work, we must still acknowledge that choice, openness, and diverse action possibilities are also integral pieces of the puzzle.

That's not to say that every possibility should be presented outwardly as a decision to be made—decision overload is just as problematic as information overload, after all. There's a huge difference between offering a useful means of customization or self-expression and passing the buck. Moreover, the message here is simple: design products that can be used in multiple ways to achieve multiple outcomes. Stop being precious about solving one, clear problem and start thinking about the diverse range of problems and people that exist within your problem space.

It's easy to claim, "This product fixes your problem," with the caveats that, first, someone needs to be experiencing the exact same problem its creators claim to have solved and, second, the product is used in one set, pre-agreed way. All this does is perpetuate the current climate of narrowly defined products that work for a narrow audience, impacted by the narrow-minded decisions of a homogenous power structure. Diversifying action possibility—adding more choice—maximizes not only the range of problems that your work could be applied to, but also the chance that your work can be used in new, inspired, and unintentional ways.

This diversity of problem definitions doesn't just pop up by accident, nor does it come as a result of learning or knowledge. It comes from including a broad range of experiences, sexualities, ethnicities, gender identities, and cultures throughout our process. The manifold dangers of homogeneity are still all too rarely discussed in technology spheres, yet nothing limits a product faster than a too-narrow notion of the problems it's supposedly solving and the people who supposedly experience them. This, again, is why diverse recruitment and compassionate, empathetic interview methods are so, so important.

If we buy into the idea that, in fact, we humans are a creative and social species with wide-ranging intrinsic motivators—as opposed to closed-off, behaviorism doers fueled by dopamine and waiting to be nudged—then we know that supporting self-deterministic activities—creativity, autonomy, mastery, and social belonging—all but *requires* us to present a diverse range of possible actions and applications.

Above All Else, Give a Shit

At the time of writing this book, we're in an age of political turmoil and incessant toxicity, where the founder of the world's most-used social network has to dodge questions about his company's role in the viral spreading of false news and propaganda; where the CEO of another company has yet to find a solution to an open rise of neo-Fascism on the platform he spent dozens of billions of dollars on during the world's most expensive mid-life crisis; where companies that would otherwise be regulated, unionized entities were it not for their ability to ghost through entire markets under the umbrella of "technology" companies get carte blanche to dodge regulation and taxation. I'm reminded of our assumed role as designers. We're, supposedly, "the voice of the user." How are we even close to achieving that given the state of our industry? Concepts such as delight, experience, seamlessness, and innovation are losing meaning, banded around by privileged, coddled, corporate shills as a justification for their self-aggrandization and impractical intellectualism—spouting hallucinatory nonsense about empathy from ivory towers while the world boils. Sooner or later, design, like technology, will have to answer for its role in this tumultuous period.

Somewhere in the pursuit for unfettered growth and profit, design's perceived role has shifted from democratization and empowerment through technology to invasive and manipulative vehicles of pop science at the behest of founders and investors. At a point in time when democracy is failing its most vulnerable, where racism and jingoism permeate every crack in the facade of social media, where the voices of those calling for a white ethnostate are amplified exponentially on a platform that is grossly incapable of suppressing hate speech, where online tools are used in months-long targeted hate campaigns, I feel it's an important time to revisit our ethical responsibilities.

While it would be absurd to lay the blame of such sociopolitical malaise squarely at the feet of design and technology, somehow our industry has dehumanized people at a time where we need most to see the vulnerabilities we supposedly design for. By breaking away from the common trend of self-serving, narrowly defined problem spaces, by seeing people—all types of people—for who they are, we can look to bring humanity and compassion back into our process.

Homogeneity's grip on the technology industry is something that needs to be tackled from multiple angles—and design is but one of them. Many of the tech darlings we elevate to the point of hero worship boil down, in essence, into a category of "things white dudes' parents used to do for them until they moved to Silicon Valley" (a functional category, if you think all the way back to Chapter 1; isn't learning fun?!) These products make it easy and cheap to get rides to work—while capitalizing on systemic oppression and non-unionized labor. They make it simple to get dinner on the table—while heaping more pressure on an already overworked and underpaid industry of service and delivery workers. They make it easier to get your laundry done, easier to find a place for your fourth vacation of the year. Some of them even make that grueling last half mile of your trip to work slightly more bearable by polluting the streets with god-forsaken electric scooters. Our industry darlings are standing on the shoulders of a crumbling gig economy and economic depravity.

There are many trade-offs to this incessant pursuit of lukewarm innovation, though. An astonishing number of products that we hold up as trailblazing innovators exist because they've found technological solutions to exploiting loopholes. Whether that's "technology" companies that are able to drive down prices due to dodging government regulations, CEOs with the charismatic depth of an STD claiming anti-union rhetoric as the key to success, the tone-deaf social media platform that refuses to do anything about its Nazi infestation lest it damage vanity metrics, or just your average everyday monolithic company paying 1% of the tax it's supposed to—the apparent need for tech to subvert humanity and democracy to succeed is a vile byproduct of untempered attempts at innovation, using nothing but a framework of rhetoric, blame deflection, and a tone-deaf agreement that certain, arbitrary metrics are somehow directly translatable into fiscal value.

Modern-day tech capitalism relies on an onion-skin model of subversion. Everything from where the money comes from to pay salaries, to the Rosetta-Stone-needed levels of legalese in terms and conditions, to the general public's willingness to gloss over the systemic oppression that is as integral to the bedrock of tech innovations as the server stacks and app stores they exist on feeds into this implicit permission society gives 20-something tech dudes to "go off and innovate."

All of this leads us to a landscape where social media platforms suddenly become arbiters of perceived truth and conduits of political clout. Where the companies that make the devices, operating systems, and browsers on which we live incrementally more of our lives are responsible for everything from waking us up in the morning to helping us maintain our mental health. The more this perpetuates, the more of a responsibility design becomes, and the harder we must work to serve the needs of real, fallible people.

People Are Not Edge Cases

People are messed up. They do weird things to themselves that fly in the face of survival instinct. Some of us harm ourselves because of chemical imbalances in our brains. Some of us have eating disorders. Some of us have drug addictions. Some of us can't answer the phone or hold a conversation with a stranger due to anxiety and panic. Some of us spend our life savings gambling. We're human beings and we grieve and we screw up and we get excited about silly things and we're sometimes just as likely to sabotage ourselves as we are to celebrate or reflect positively on our life.

Until we factor this into our work by showing compassion, researching properly, educating ourselves on our privileges and biases, and until we earn our ridiculous salaries, day rates, egregious company perks, and the pedestals our industry so adores by actively designing and building for vulnerable, oppressed, and divergent human beings—how can we possibly say we're making this world a better place? By releasing yet another product that is only usable by those who meet our ridiculously narrow defaults, who are capable of expending the cognitive cost of "normal" attentional faculty—whether through not experiencing poverty, anxiety, sociological impact, or neurodivergence—or who simply fit nicely into our abstracted assumption of what makes for a *normal* human being, what are we really contributing?

Fundamentally we need to ask ourselves a difficult question: are we conduits or gatekeepers? The deepest craft in design exists in simplifying complex systems, abstracting them in ways that the general population can understand, and creating a designed model that allows for observation, impact, and change. This is what we're taught to do. It's what we practice every day. It's what we *all* should be good at—and I'm willing to be that you're more than capable of such transformative craft. However, the same skills and processes that harbor such potential to democratize also provide us with all the tools we need to exclude and even oppress. The positioning of design as problem-solving and the positioning of practitioners as some form of saviors is an abhorrent spandrel of the cult of personality we attach to our industry figures.

As the interface between an underlying system and the model of that system in someone's head, we can either introspect our system through the lens of humanity, or we can attempt to contort and convince and persuade humanity to interact with our system in ways we desire. The former is, simply, our job; but it's hard, and we'll face battles and make enemies and likely get pushed back from many sides. The latter perpetuates the rather dystopian notion that humanity—including our cognitive faculty and even our very concept of self—is subservient to technology. That being *hooked* on apps, feeling the *dopamine squirt* of notifications, and generally being *the good user* is simply the price of admission into a world of possibilities. At least, a world of possibilities if you're a well-off white person in or around a major metropolis and own a $1,000 phone.

The capabilities of our technology are truly astounding. We must harness these capabilities in ways that enhance the human experience. Currently, how many of us can honestly say that we're achieving this with our work? More often than not, technology with the power to be truly transformative is placed in the hands of a fortunate, privileged few. Our vision for technology is constrained by perverse, hegemonic machinations that proliferate throughout an industry that treats neoliberalism as a religion and meritocracy as scripture, as opposed to the satire it originated as.

Design should exist to serve humanity. Real humanity. Not some essence or abstraction of humanity, not the privileged, amalgamated assumptions of four white people sitting down to solve the next mundane problem in their lives. But real, fallible, vulnerable human beings. Humans whose daily struggles and sacrifices in the face of a world and an industry that shows them nothing but apathy and disdain deserve more than being relegated to a casual footnote on a persona or a box-checking exercise in our research.

Above all else, this is the essence of this book. Not to make our jobs easier, not to present yet another design framework that gets replaced after a six-month trial, but to offer an antidote—however small—to the incessant push for interaction design to be persuasive. Or convincing. Or manipulative in any way. If this book has whipped you into a stupor and made you want to run out, all guns blazing, to try and fix the very fabric of digital design, then awesome! Thanks for the passion. However, if it's taught you even one single concept that you can bring into your next project to make your work a little more mindful, that's just as good. The monolithic problem of design as a force for profit above all else is one to be chipped away at, from many angles, for a long, long time.

This stuff also takes time and energy, and not everyone has a large enough surplus of both to implement a whole host of changes in one fell swoop. I totally get that. Just as much as I face a task beyond the scope of this book to attempt to let these ideas reverberate through and beyond my little corner of the design world, so do you, dear reader, have a similar task to affect change in yours. The people we work with will be just as fallible and disoriented by new schemas and concepts as the people we design for, and this kind of change will take time. While I've tried to make the ideas within this book as transferrable to current design processes as possible, there's no avoiding that with lofty goals come uncomfortable changes.

I hope you're on board with that, and if you are, from the bottom of my heart: *Thank you. You've got this. Go be lovely.*

Index

Printed in the United States
by Baker & Taylor Publisher Services